THE COMPLETE HISTORY OF
NORTH AMERICAN
RAILWAYS

THE COMPLETE HISTORY OF
NORTH AMERICAN RAILWAYS

Edited by Derek Avery

THE WELLFLEET PRESS

Printed in Italy

First published in the United States by
The Wellfleet Press
110 Enterprise Avenue,
Secaucus, New Jersey 07094

ISBN 1 55521 375 8

Produced by
Brian Trodd Publishing House Limited
27 Swinton Street
London WC1X 9NW, England.

CONTENTS

1	First rails and false starts	11
2	New horizons	19
3	War and the westward tide	25
4	The Pacific Railroad	33
5	The western railroads	45
6	Regulating the railroads	59
7	Private enterprise and public service	71
8	Canadian railways	95
9	Building the railroads	155
10	Steam locomotives	175
11	Diesel and electric power	191
12	Passenger services	211
13	Freight transport	238
14	The great steam locomotives	258
15	The major railroads	286
16	The new age of US railroading	314
	Index	348

WHEEL NOTATION:
STEAM LOCOMOTIVES

Steam locomotives are described by a three-figure combination which refers to the number of wheels, usually made up of driving wheels (shown here as black open circles) and bogie or trailing wheels (shown in blue). The first figure denotes the number of bogie wheels at the front, the second gives the number of driving wheels and the third figure the number of trailing wheels. If the locomotive is a tank engine, a 'T' is added after the third figure.

0-4-0

2-2-2

0-6-0

4-4-0

2-4-0

4-6-0

0-6-2

4-6-2

4-4-2

2-10-0

2-8-4

WHEEL NOTATION: DIESEL AND ELECTRIC LOCOMOTIVES

Diesel and electric locomotives are denoted by the number of axles. Letters are given to the driving axles (A=1, B=2, C=3, D=4) and numbers given to the carrying axles. Independently-powered axles are denoted by an 'o' following the letter. A plus sign accompanying bogie locomotives indicates that traction stresses are transmitted through an articulated member which connects the bogies, rather than via the frame. Power transmission is shown here by black open circles and the carrying axles are in blue.

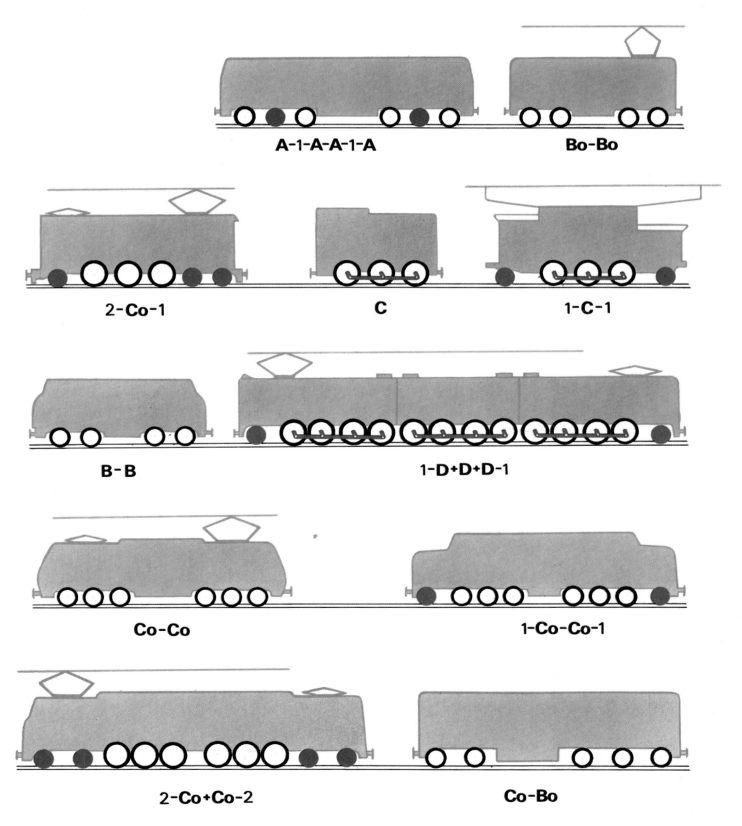

A-1-A-A-1-A

Bo-Bo

2-Co-1

C

1-C-1

B-B

1-D+D+D-1

Co-Co

1-Co-Co-1

2-Co+Co-2

Co-Bo

FIRST RAILS AND FALSE STARTS

By the beginning of the nineteenth century, with independence won and the Indians largely subdued, the great tide of western movement across the North American continent was gaining momentum. High taxes, rising land prices and a rigid social order along the Atlantic coast, compounded in the southern states by soil exhaustion and the spread of plantation agriculture, provided the motivation for hundreds of thousands of Americans to head for the interior.

The routes they followed were the new roads – at that stage little more than tracks hacked through the undergrowth – that led west from Boston and New England along the Mohawk valley to Lake Erie, from Philadelphia and Baltimore across the Appalachians to the Ohio River valley, and from Virginia and North Carolina to Nashville and Louisville. Thereafter the rivers provided the main communications, and in the first quarter of the century new routes appeared. The paved National Road was completed to Wheeling, on the Ohio River, by 1818, and in 1825

the Erie Canal was opened between the Hudson River and Lake Erie across northern New York. From the south the fertile plains of Ohio, Indiana and Illinois were being penetrated by the first paddle steamers.

The result of this movement was the cultivation of vast new areas of land and the creation of huge surpluses of grain and other produce, just as the first factories were introducing industrialization to the northeastern states and the south was turning increasingly to cotton production. The merchants of the east coast cities could see their future in the exchange of food from the interior for their manufactured goods: the only problem was transport. The roads across the mountains were too slow for large-scale transportation of grain, while the river routes south to New Orleans, and the subsequent sea journey from the Gulf of Mexico to the eastern ports were not only slow and tortuous but also encountered climatic conditions which were potentially damaging to the merchandise.

The Erie Canal proved to be the first

The ceremony held to mark the official start of building the Baltimore and Ohio, on July 4, 1828.

breakthrough, making possible dramatic reductions in both the cost of transport and the time taken. A direct consequence of its success was the establishment of New York as the leading center for trade, and this in turn provoked the other northeastern ports to seek their own connections with the interior.

The immediate clamor was for canals, but the formidable difficulties of driving canals through the intervening mountains proved all but overwhelming. Philadelphia devised, and persuaded the state of Pennsylvania to build, a system of canals which by 1834 reached as far as Pittsburgh; but in order to cross the mountain ridge goods had to be hauled ten miles up a series of inclined planes and coasted down the other side before continuing their journey.

Another canal, the Chesapeake and Ohio, was begun in 1827 under the joint sponsorship of Baltimore and Washington, D.C., but the same year saw the

The B and O locomotive *Atlantic* in a symbolic scene showing the rivalry with the canals.

foundation of an entirely new enterprise that was to overshadow the canal and revolutionize transport. This was the Baltimore and Ohio Railroad, chartered by the state of Maryland on February 28, 1827, and inspired by reports of steam engines in England that traveled at speeds three and four times the 4 mph that was the best the canals could offer. From Baltimore to the Ohio River, where the rails would link up with the river network that carried most of the trade in the interior, was 380 miles across an imposing mountain range, well over ten times the length of any railroad previously attempted; but despite a general lack of railroad-building experience the scheme was pursued with a vigor to match its ambition.

Army engineers called in to conduct a survey chose a route that started off along the Patapsco River, before cutting across country to follow the Potomac through the Caboctin mountains. Work

was begun on July 4, 1828, and within three years profits from horse-drawn traffic on the first few miles of track encouraged the B. & O.'s directors to take a bold new step. In 1831 prizes of $4000 and $3500 were offered for the best steam locomotives delivered by June 1 that year: the engines were not to weigh more than three and a half tons, and must be capable of pulling a 15 ton train at 15 mph.

By this stage a number of steam locomotives had appeared in the United States. The first was a little engine built by an early American advocate of railroads, Colonel John Stevens, and demonstrated on a small track in his garden. The first commercial models, however, were imported from England, ordered by Horatio Allen on behalf of the Delaware and Hudson Canal company. The D & H was building a canal from Rondout, New York, to the Carbondale mines in northwestern Pennsylvania, when the difficulties of building through the last 16 miles from Honesdale led company engineer John B. Jervis to investigate the possibility of

substituting a railroad. Allen was sent to England to buy iron rails and any locomotives he considered suitable; the first of them, *America*, built by Robert Stephenson, arrived in New York in January, 1829.

Another three locomotives were ordered from the Stourbridge firm of Foster, Rastrick, and although two of these, *Hudson* and *Delaware*, were destroyed by fire in the shed where they were stored after their arrival at Rondout, the *Stourbridge Lion*, having been tested at the West Point Foundry in New York City following its arrival in May 1829, was shipped to Honesdale. On August 8 the *Lion* was prepared for its first trip, and in view of the warped wooden rails and twisting course of the track, Allen took the footplate alone. Setting off boldly, Allen and his new engine rattled along the 500-ft straight that preceded a sharp curve leading onto a trestle bridge. Defying predictions of disaster, the *Lion* negotiated the curve, crossed the bridge, and after a three-mile spin through the woods returned safely to its starting point to

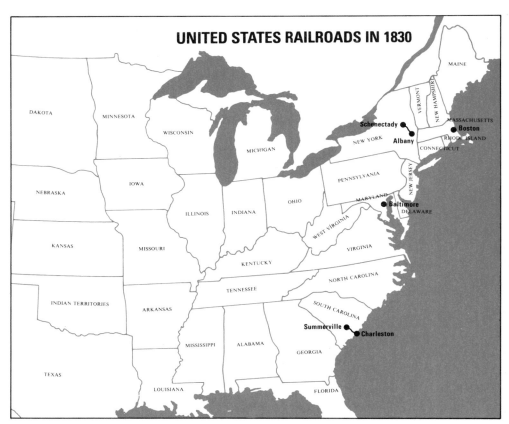

UNITED STATES RAILROADS IN 1830

By 1830 railroads were being built westward from Boston, Albany, Baltimore and Charleston. Early operation was by horse traction, as recreated (below) outside the Baltimore and Ohio's original station and old engine shed, now a museum, at Mount Clare, with a reconstruction of Peter Cooper's experimental locomotive *Tom Thumb*. The illustration opposite shows *Tom Thumb* overshadowed by the ghostly outlines of one of the 80-mph President class locomotives built for the B&O's new through service between Washington and Jersey City in 1927. First locomotive run in America was made by the Delaware and Hudson Canal's *Stourbridge Lion*.

complete the first locomotive journey in America.

Allen may have been lucky. The subsequent career of the *Lion* was marked by frequent derailments, and it was relegated to service as a stationary boiler in a Carbondale foundry, though rebuilt for the Chicago Railway Exposition of 1884 and ultimately preserved by the Smithsonian Institution.

The Baltimore and Ohio, meanwhile, had begun operations, and in 1830 one of its shareholders, Peter Cooper, built his own locomotive. Designed merely as a demonstration model, Cooper's *Tom Thumb* weighed only one ton, used gun barrels for boiler tubes and incorporated a fan driven by one of the axles to provide draft for the fire. Nevertheless, on August 28, 1830, *Tom Thumb* pulled a coach carrying 36 passengers along the 15 miles of track from Baltimore to Ellicott's Mills at speeds up to 18 mph. On the return journey a horse-drawn railcar on the parallel track challenged Cooper to a race, and was convincingly outpaced before the belt to the blower fan slipped, the fire died, and the horse car was left to come home alone.

Cooper, however, had made his point. The winner of the resulting competition, and the only entry to meet the conditions, was the *York*, designed by Phineas Davis, a Philadelphia watchmaker. The B & O ordered 20 improved models, and these 'grasshopper'

engines, with vertical boilers driving the wheels through rocking beams, proved capable of pulling 50-ton trains on the railroad's winding track. Many remained at work for up to 50 years, and the last was not retired until 1893.

Already other firms were experimenting with locomotives. In 1830 the *Best Friend of Charleston* was built by the West Point Foundry for the Charleston and Hamburg Railroad, then under construction by Horatio Allen's new employers, the South Carolina Canal and Railway company. After breaking a wheel on its first run, the *Best Friend*

performed rather better on its second attempt, reaching 20 mph with a train carrying 40 of the company's employees.

Before being destroyed by a boiler explosion a few months later, the *Best Friend* was joined by a second locomotive from the same firm, the appropriately named *West Point*, which had a horizontal boiler rather than the vertical type used on the earlier engine. A third West Point product of that year, the *South Carolina*, had two boilers carried on separate four-wheel bogies and each driving one center-line cylinder. On December 25 the *Best Friend*

inaugurated the first regular steam-hauled service in America on the Charleston and Hamburg's first six miles of track.

The West Point Foundry was soon busy with locomotives for other railroads. In 1831 it supplied the *De Witt Clinton*, named after the governor of New York and designed by John B. Jervis, to the Mohawk and Hudson Railroad, which had been financed by Albany and Schenectady businessmen to connect Albany with the eastern end of the Erie Canal. The following year another Jervis design for the Mohawk

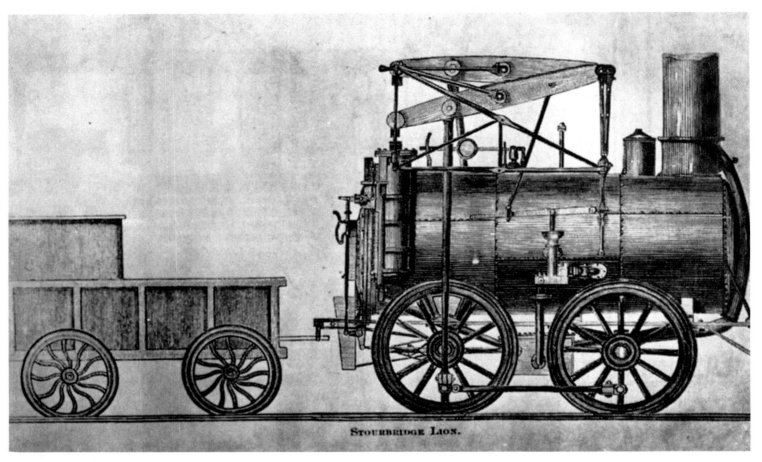

STOURBRIDGE LION.

and Hudson, the 4–2–0 *Experiment*, for the first time succeeded in overcoming the instability which had bedeviled the earlier locomotives. This instability was a result of the twisting and uneven tracks on which they were required to run, and to which the rigid-framed four-wheelers were poorly suited; it was overcome by the use of a three-point suspension. The axle for the main driving wheels was mounted in a bearing at each end in the usual way, but the front of the engine was carried by a four-wheel bogie to which it was attached by a single central pivot. This arrangement left the front wheels free to adapt to variations in the track, and the 4–2–0 formula was soon being adopted by other builders.

One of these was Matthias Baldwin, of Philadelphia, who began by studying a Stephenson *Planet*-type engine, the *John Bull*, which was imported in 1831 by Robert L. Stevens for the Camden and Amboy Railroad of New Jersey. Baldwin built a similar machine, the 2–2–0 *Old Ironsides*, for the Philadelphia, Germanstown and Norristown Railroad. Baldwin's next design, *E. L. Miller*, for the Charleston and Ham-

burg, was a 4–2–0 with a 'haystack' type firebox, and a similar arrangement was used by another Philadelphia builder, William Norris, in his *George Washington* of 1836.

The idea was taken a step further by Henry Campbell in a 4–4–0 built for the P G & N in 1836, but it was in 1838 that the real breakthrough was made, when Joseph Harrison patented his system of equalizing beams to support the

DEWITT CLINTON

coupled driving wheels. This suspension, in combination with the pivoted leading bogie, enabled all the wheels to remain in contact with the track, whatever its variations.

All this locomotive building was a reflection of the spread of enthusiasm for railroads, an enthusiasm which had different motivations in different parts of the country. The success of the Erie Canal had inspired the Baltimore and Ohio and the other northeastern railroads, while the old southeastern ports of Richmond, Charleston and Savannah were anxious to extend their trading areas west in the wake of expanding cotton cultivation. The South Carolina Railroad was built to Hamburg on the Savannah River in an attempt to divert river trade away from Savannah, and after its completion the Charleston merchants financed the Georgia Railroad to extend the line to Athens and Atlanta. Savannah responded with the state-backed Central Railroad of Georgia, which was begun toward Macon, and the Monroe Railroad from Macon to Atlanta; and Richmond aimed to capitalize on its canal to Lynchburg by building the Lynchburg and New River Railroad, the ultimate objective of which was the Ohio.

Meanwhile, the western states, whose mounting surpluses of grain and other produce had inspired the earliest railroads in the northeast, began to improve their own internal communications. Again, the Erie Canal provided the initial stimulus for much of the activity, and Ohio, Indiana, Illinois and Michigan all embarked on ambitious

schemes for canals designed to connect the existing waterways and the Great Lakes. This would free them of their dependence on the New Orleans markets and would, in theory, be paid for by the increased profits that could be expected from the easier flow of produce.

In the 1830s railroads were added to the canal schemes, but the rate of construction failed to live up to the ambition of the plans or the abandon with which the various state administrators borrowed money to finance them: the financial crisis of 1837 and the economic depression that followed left the states with huge debts and little to show for them.

In Ohio the Little Miami and the Mad River and Lake Erie railroads were planned to link Springfield with Cincinnati and the Ohio River to the south and with Sandusky on the lake to the north. But an 1837 law, by which the state agreed to buy one-third of the stock of any railroad which had raised the other two-thirds, saw $3,000,000 appropriated by 40 spurious builders before it was repealed in 1840. Millions more dollars spent by Indiana resulted in a few miles of preparatory grading on the Madison-Lafayette and New Albany-Crawfordsville roads before they were sold. Illinois, in 1837, decided to build the Illinois Central from Cairo in the south to Galena in the northwest, plus the east-west Northern Cross and Southern Cross roads; but by 1842 only half the Northern Cross, from Quincy to Springfield, had been built.

To the north, the Erie and Kalamazoo Railroad, the first in the west, had

reached from Toledo to Adrian by 1836, and when statehood in 1837 gave Michigan a freer hand, northern, central and southern railroads were planned to cross the state: again, millions of dollars were raised and spent, but the banks that had guaranteed the loans collapsed, and in 1842 construction ground to a halt.

Other railroads were planned by citizens of the river cities to the south, who were keen on the idea of having a choice of outlets. The Louisville, Cincinnati and Charleston was chartered by the states of South Carolina, Tennessee and Kentucky, but construction was checked in 1839 after a general shortage of funds was compounded by disagreement over the route. A series of short roads intended to link Memphis and Charleston had produced only eight miles of track when the 1837 panic halted work. Vicksburg in Mississippi planned an eastward route to Charleston, but the completion of the line to Jackson in 1840 was followed by the collapse of the other roads in the link. The lines proposed from Mobile to Chattanooga and from New Orleans to Nashville also came to a standstill with only small sections completed.

Such reverses transformed the early enthusiasm for railroads into hostility. High taxes levied to pay for the loans had resulted in little actual construction, state legislators had become wary, and the 1837 crisis resulted in a shortage of funds for investment that virtually ended construction for several years.

The Mohawk and Hudson's *Experiment* (far left) was designed by John B. Jervis and built by the West Point Foundry in 1832. The reconstruction of the Albany and Hudson's *De Witt Clinton* (center) was made in 1893, while *Old Ironsides* (below) was Matthew Baldwin's first locomotive.

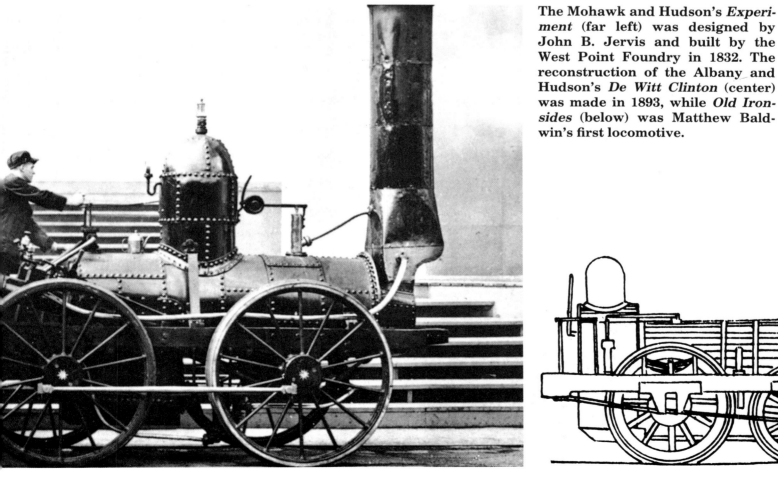

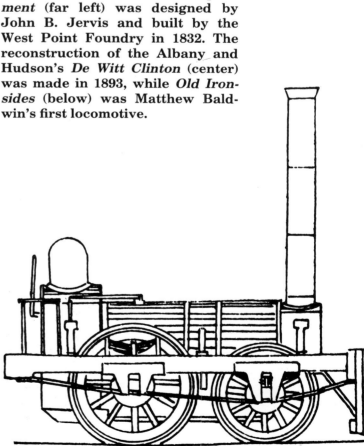

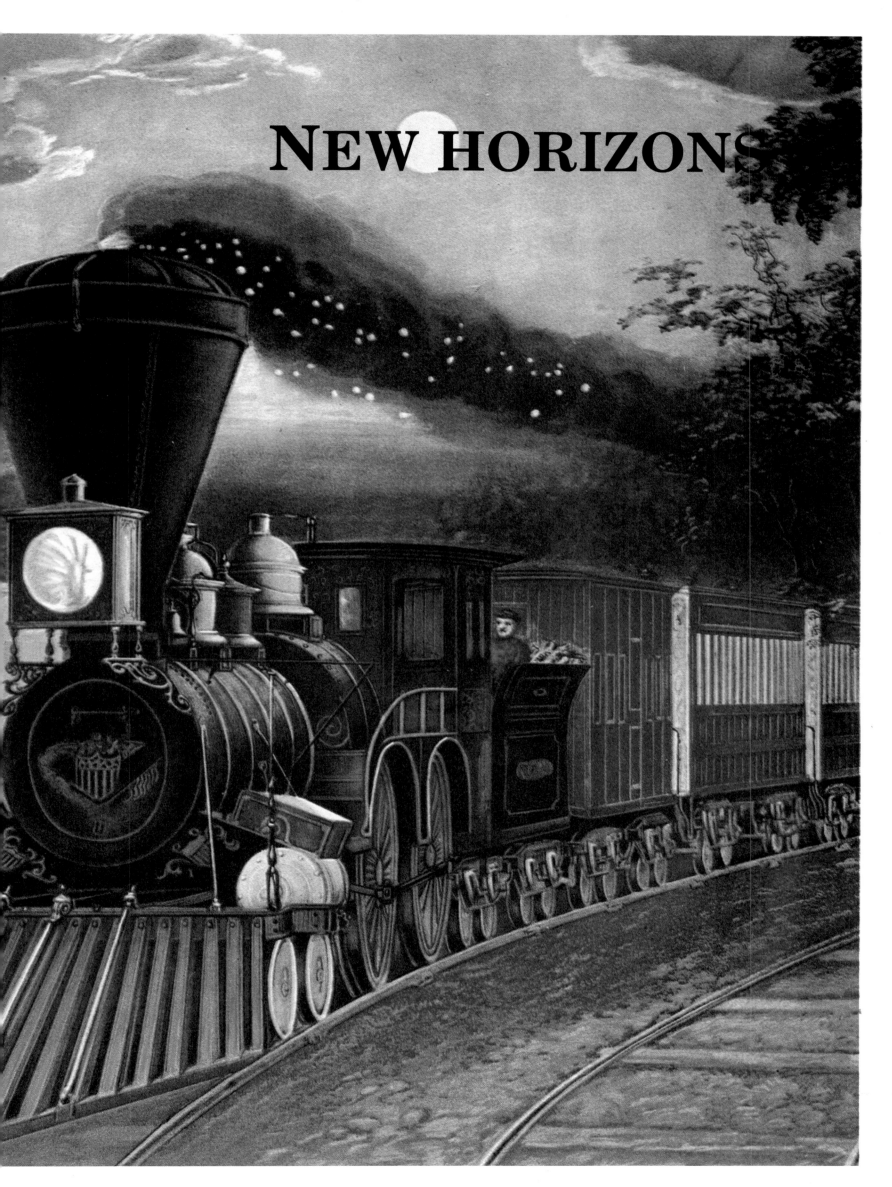

NEW HORIZONS

The state-backed railways begun in the 1830s might not have lived up to the expectations of their planners, but they provided the foundations for a new stage of building. The experimental stage had been completed with public backing, but the huge debts incurred in the process had made the politicians wary, and new construction was generally left to private builders. The southern states had little spare cash, but the growing manufacturing industries of the northeast provided the capital for a new era of expansion.

The Baltimore and Ohio had ground to a halt at Cumberland, barely halfway to its goal, in 1842, but in 1848, having survived the depression, it began to be extended again, and in 1853 the line reached Wheeling on the Ohio. A proposed connection to Pittsburgh provoked Philadelphians to begin the Pennsylvania Railroad in 1847, and by the end of 1852 this had been completed to Pittsburgh.

In the state of New York, the pioneering Mohawk and Hudson had been joined in 1836 by the Utica and Schenectady, and in the 1840s further links between the towns along the route of the Erie Canal linked Albany with Buffalo. The completion of the Hudson River Railroad in 1851 and of the New York and Harlem early in 1852 provided connections between Albany and New York; and this was followed in 1853 by the merger of the individual lines along the Erie to form the New York Central, thus obviating the need for passengers to change trains at each junction. At the same time, the New York and Erie Railroad across the southern part of the state, which had been formed in 1832 but had gone bankrupt in the depression, was reorganized, and by 1851 reached from Piermont on the Hudson to Dunkirk on Lake Erie.

It was not long before the builders of these lines realized that connections in the western states must be provided if trade was to be diverted away from the waterways to the south; and investment west of the Ohio led to a revival of the foundered railway project in the 1840s.

Ohio again took the lead. The Mad River and Lake Erie was revived in 1846 and within two years was completed to Sandusky; and the simultaneous completion of a line from the port to the Ohio Canal led to the formation of new railroads to link the rival port of Cleveland with Cincinnati and Columbus. These lines were completed in 1852, and the following year saw the opening of westward extensions of the New York Central and Erie systems to

The main photograph shows an excursion train on the Baltimore and Ohio in 1858, while the Buffalo and Albany timetable was issued in 1843.

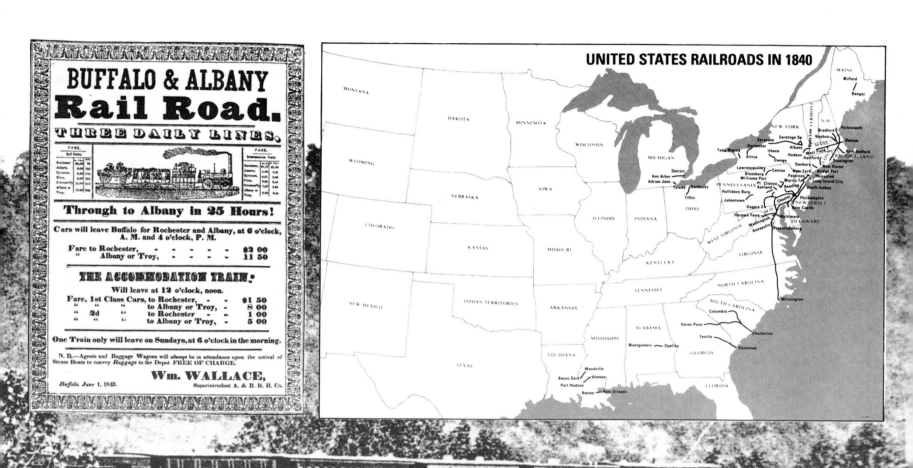

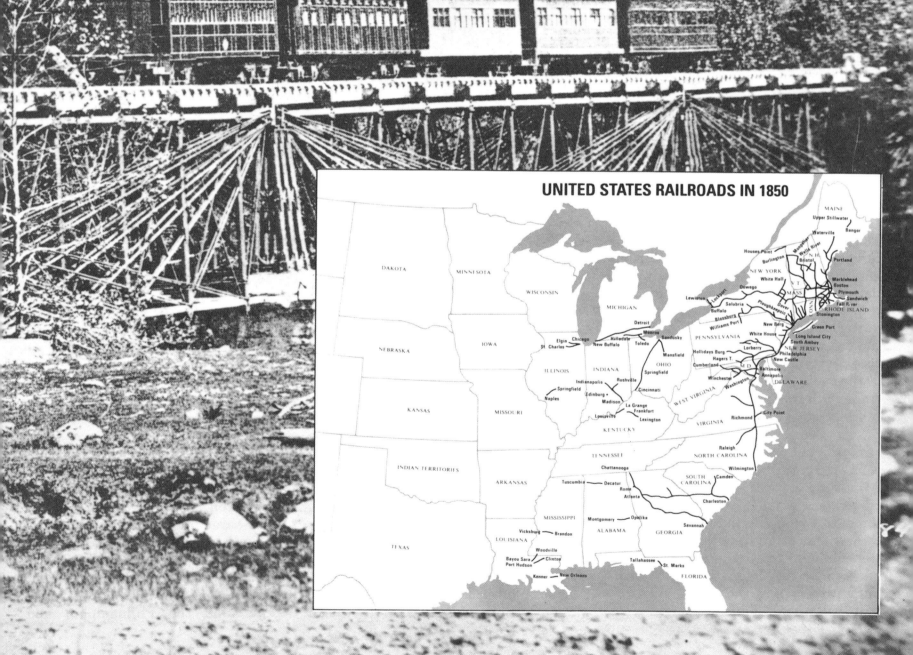

Cleveland and Toledo. The Pennsylvania Railroad was also pushed west from Pittsburgh towards Chicago.

Chicago's growing importance was reflected in the founding of the Chicago and Galena, the Chicago, Burlington and Quincy, and the Chicago and Rock Island Railroads, which would spread out west from Chicago. Most important of all, however, was the resumption of the Illinois Central, which was now planned to run from Cairo, at the confluence of the Ohio and the Mississippi in the extreme south of the state, to Chicago and Galena. The main significance of the Illinois Central lay in the land grants which were made to facilitate the building of the line: alternate sections of land six miles on either side of the track were allocated to the railroad by the state, and the proceeds from the sale of this land were to be used to finance construction. The links to Galena and Chicago were completed in 1855 and 1856 respectively, and the land grant principle thus established was to be a major factor in the future development of the railroads. Equally important were the effects on trading patterns, with the iron rails now linking the western states to the northeastern ports replacing the old river routes

to the south as the main arteries of the trade with the interior.

The southern railroads that had been begun before the depression were resumed, but progress was slow. Routes connecting the Mississippi, Gulf and Atlantic ports with the leading inland cities were pursued without much attempt to any link with the north. Moreover, most of the southern railways were built to the 5 ft gauge originally adopted by the Charleston and Hamburg rather than the 4 ft 8½ in gauge that was more common, though by no means universal, in the north.

The northern railroads continued their advance to the west in the 1850s. In 1854 the Rock Island Railroad reached the Mississippi, to the accompaniment of great ceremony and celebration, and speeches that only partially exaggerated the significance of the occasion. A bridge across the river, using the island that had given its name to the enterprise, was the Rock Island's next objective, and despite opposition from the steamboat operators who saw it as a threat to their livelihood, the bridge was built to connect Rock Island, Illinois and Davenport, Iowa. The bridge itself was destroyed by fire shortly afterwards when a steamboat

collided with one of the piers in somewhat mysterious circumstances. A series of court battles followed, but ultimately the Supreme Court decided that railroads had as much right to cross rivers as boats had to use them.

Already, though, the Rock Island's president, Henry Farnam, had his sights set farther west. A new company was formed, the Mississippi and Missouri Railroad, to build across Iowa, and others were following. The Missouri Pacific was begun from St Louis toward Kansas City, while the Chicago and Northwestern crossed the Mississippi at Clinton, Iowa, and was pushed on toward Council Bluffs on the Missouri. Both were beaten to their goal, however, by a Missouri road, the Hannibal and St Joseph, whose promoters were inspired by the example of the Illinois Central to demand federal land grants for their project. The demands were met, work was begun in 1851, and early in 1859 the sections building east and west from opposite ends met to complete a further lap in

Some of the most elegant 4-4-0s were the work of William Mason. This B&O was built in 1857.

the westward march of the rails.

The overall extent of this spate of construction is shown by the statistics. The 2800 miles of railroad in operation in 1840 had increased to 9000 miles by 1850, and during the ensuing decade that total was more than trebled to over 30,000 miles. From the trading viewpoint, by 1850 New Orleans was no longer the country's leading port for export: Britain's repeal of the Corn Laws in 1846, lifting the prohibition on the importation of wheat, coupled with the new railroad connections, made New York and the northeastern ports the main markets for western grain.

The motive power for all this activity had taken on a distinctive form that was to last through most of the century. There was some experimentation with new wheel arrangements, such as Baldwin's eight-coupled freight locomotives, first built in 1842 for the Central of Georgia and the Philadelphia and Reading Railroads. These succeeded in combining the increased tractive effort of more driving wheels with the flexibility demanded by the irregularities of the track by mounting the front two pairs of driving on flexible beams and using ball-and-socket couplings to the rear wheels in their rigid frame. Less successfully, John Stevens tried a 6–2–0 arrangement in 1848 which incorporated 8-ft driving wheels.

But by far the most common locomotive, so nearly universal that it came to be known as the American type, was the 4–4–0, with its leading bogie and equalized driving wheels providing the optimum combination of tractive force and flexibility. The basic formation evolved in the 1830s was soon given its familiar guise by the addition of the wide firebox for burning the wood that was commonly used in the early days; the rear of the boiler was made conical in shape to fit the firebox; headlamp, big 'balloon stack' chimney, sandbox and bell took their places on top of the boiler and smokebox, and a cab at the rear provided protection for the engineer and fireman who manned the machine. Equipped in this way, the American locomotive was ready to begin its journey, a journey that would ultimately take it to every corner of the continent, from the Gulf of Mexico to the northern wastes, and from the Atlantic Ocean clear across the plains and mountains to the Pacific.

For it was during the 1850s that the railroads began adding the word Pacific to their titles, and that the most ambitious plans yet began to take shape: the transcontinental railroad was becoming a possibility.

By 1846, when California and the Oregon Territory were ceded to the United States by Mexico and Britain, there had been a number of proposals for a transcontinental railroad, but

those who made them were generally greeted with ridicule. One of the most practical suggestions had come from a New England merchant, Asa Whitney, who saw such a road as a trading link with China and the East Indies. In 1845 Whitney proposed that the government should grant him a strip of land 60 miles wide from the Great Lakes to Oregon, in return for which he would build the railroad. His idea aroused fierce opposition, primarily from those who wanted any railroad to the Pacific to start from their own city, and a Congressional bill based on Whitney's plan was narrowly defeated in 1848.

Public pressure for a transcontinental railroad continued to grow, however, and in 1853 Congress instructed the U.S. Army to make a survey of possible routes.

The army's proposed routes comprised two in the north, from Lake Superior to Portland and through South Pass to San Francisco, and two in the south, along the Red River or through southern Texas to southern California. At this point Illinois senator Stephen A. Douglas, who had been instrumental in arranging the land grants for the Illinois Central, proposed that three routes should be followed, one in the north, a central line to San Francisco, and another in the south from Texas to southern California. Still another proposal came from the promoters of the Leavenworth, Pawnee and Western, a railroad in name only but one which had secured rights to large tracts of Indian land in Kansas on its planned route west from the Missouri border; and the supporters of the Hannibal and St Joseph were naturally keen to extend

A typical American type 4-4-0 of the Chicago and Eastern Illinois Railroad, photographed in 1854.

their line west in the wake of the Pony Express service which had begun operations from St Joseph in 1860.

Meanwhile, on the other side of the continent, Theodore Judah, a civil engineer from Connecticut who had traveled to California to supervise the building of a short railway from Sacramento to the mines around Placerville, held a series of public meetings to promote the idea of building a railroad east from California. He attracted the attention of a consortium of businessmen – Collis P. Huntington, Mark Hopkins, Leland Stanford and Charles Crocker – who decided to back him in his scheme; and in 1860, after Judah returned from an unsuccessful lobbying trip to Washington, it was decided that they should conduct their own survey.

Judah, Huntington, Crocker and Stanford spent the summer of 1860 in the Sierra Nevada plotting the course of their road. They mapped out a route through the Donner Pass that clipped over a hundred miles off the army surveyors' route, and would take the railroad into the vicinity of the new mines in the Carson River valley. The next step was to obtain government approval for their scheme – the anticipated federal subsidies were a prime motivating factor – and in 1861, having incorporated the Central Pacific Railroad of California, Huntington set off with their combined funds of $200,000 to join Judah in presenting their case to Congress.

23

WAR AND THE WESTWARD TIDE

Washington in 1861 was the capital of a nation at war. The spreading railroads had united the northern states from New England to Iowa in economic interdependence, while the southern states had extended the slavery principle into Arkansas when that state was formed in 1836. The Missouri Compromise of 1820 had already admitted slavery in the region, but on condition that it would not be allowed in the remaining western lands north of the Arkansas border. By the 1850s the continuing westward movement of the frontier made the organization of that land a matter of urgency, and one that would influence the location of the transcontinental railroad.

Stephen Douglas, the senator from Illinois, quickly realized this fact. A single territory west of the Mississippi would be settled first by migrants from Missouri and Arkansas, who would almost certainly establish a southern capital, drawing the railway south with it. Douglas was intent on making Chicago the eastern terminus of the transcontinental, and his solution was to divide the region into two parts; and to render the scheme attractive to both northern and southern interests the question of slavery would be left to the eventual inhabitants.

A bill to this effect, repealing the Missouri Compromise and establishing the new territories of Kansas and Nebraska, was passed by Congress in 1854, but its results were not entirely what Douglas had anticipated. The northern opponents of slavery were appalled at the repeal of the compromise, southerners delighted, and in Kansas the two factions became embroiled in increasingly bloody conflict. The presidential elections in 1860 reflected the bitterness, and the victory of Lincoln and the Republican party was the signal for the southern states, led by South Carolina, to secede from the Union. By the spring of 1861 Union and Confederacy were at war.

The frontier between the two lay along the northern borders of Virginia, Tennessee and Arkansas. North of that border were concentrated more than two-thirds of the nation's 31,000 miles of railroads, and those railroads formed much more of a coherent network than the south's disjointed system that was a legacy of slow and piecemeal development. Indeed, to a large extent it was only the railroads that allowed the war to be fought, the huge armies being dependent on them not only for transport but also for the enormous quantities of supplies that had to be distributed over vast distances.

Initially, therefore, the railroads

Locomotives of the United States Military Railroads at the field hospital at City Point, Virginia.

were targets for raids from both sides. The Baltimore and Ohio's bridge at Harper's Ferry had been destroyed by John Brown's raid on the town in 1859; rebuilt, it was destroyed again by Stonewall Jackson in 1861. Another raid by Jackson on Martinsburg resulted in the destruction of 44 B & O locomotives, and the line was subject to repeated sabotage by the Confederate forces.

Slightly farther south, the Norfolk and Petersburg and the South Side Railroads that later formed part of the Norfolk and Western system were subject to systematic destruction, with major battles fought up and down their length. Elsewhere, raiding parties attacked rolling stock and installations, destroying bridges, cutting telegraph lines and tearing up tracks in order to disrupt opposition communications.

On a broader front, the railroads became invaluable for large-scale

transportation of troops, ammunition and supplies. The first major battle of the war, at Bull Run in July 1861, was swung in the Confederacy's favor by the timely arrival by rail of reinforcements. Thereafter the Federal use of railroads grew progressively more organized and purposeful, while the southern armies remained hamstrung by their incomplete and underdeveloped network.

The south's disadvantage in the matter of railroads was demonstrated

in July 1862, when Braxton Bragg's 35,000-strong army was transported by rail from Tupelo, in northeastern Mississippi, to Chattanooga; the transfer was accomplished successfully, but only at the cost of a detour via Mobile, on the Gulf coast of Alabama, that virtually trebled the distance. Moreover, production of rails, locomotives and rolling stock was concentrated almost exclusively in the north, while rivalry between the various companies often

amounted to outright obstruction of the military authorities.

The northern network at the start of the war, while more comprehensive and much better equipped, was far from perfect, with widespread variations in gauge reflecting continuing inter-company rivalry; but whereas the southern railroads were not brought under full military control until 1865, when it was far too late, President Lincoln was authorized by Congress in 1862 to commandeer any railroad he considered vital to the war effort. Even more significant was the creation of the United States Military Railroads as a subsidiary of the War Department. Under Daniel C. McCallum the USMR laid nearly 650 miles of track during the war as well as building many bridges, and ultimately controlled more than 2000 miles operated by over 400 locomotives and 600 cars.

By the later stages of the war it had become possible to carry out rapid troop movements on a massive scale. In September 1853, after the battle of Chickamauga had left Rosencrans and his army bottled up in Chattanooga, more than 20,000 men, along with the enormous quantities of equipment they required, were moved from their defensive positions near Washington to Chattanooga, a distance of some 600 miles, in only 12 days.

While the opposing commanders came to realize the potential of the railroads in war, they also became aware of their main drawback, namely vulnerability to sabotage: once they allowed themselves to become dependent on the iron rails, they were also forced to dissipate their resources in defending them.

This fact was grasped by Sherman in his 1864 campaign. After assembling ample supplies at Nashville and Chattanooga, he drove the southern forces back along the rails to Atlanta, cutting the rail links from Atlanta to Macon and Montgomery and forcing Hood's army to retreat to the southeast, while repairing the wrecked track behind him to keep his army supplied. But having taken Atlanta, he found that the defence of his supply line to Chattanooga was occupying half the army, and toward the end of the year he reversed his policy. Deliberately cutting the rail link behind him, he set off on a march to the sea, his men destroying railroads and anything else in their way. Living off the land, and freed of the need to defend supply lines, Sherman's army reached Savannah just before Christmas to complete one of the most significant campaigns of the war.

The end of the war the following year left the southern railroads in chaos. Those roads that had escaped outright destruction had suffered, like the whole southern economy, from years of ne-

Locomotives in the ruins of the Atlanta engine shed after Sherman's capture of the city in 1864.

glect and abuse. In the north, on the other hand, they had benefited from the enormous increase in traffic caused by the war: progress had been made toward standardization of gauges, and track and rolling stock had been improved as the first steel rails were laid and coal began to replace wood as the normal fuel.

Perhaps most significant of all, the outbreak of war had galvanized the administration into action over the vexed question of the transcontinental railroad. For in Washington the rival proponents of the various schemes had not allowed even civil war to deflect them from their goals. Throughout 1861 the rivals pressed their cases – but war had changed the circumstances.

While the construction of the transcontinental was now regarded as a matter of national importance to deter any further secessionist movements, especially in the west, the southern routes were out of contention, since they would cross states that were even then attempting to leave the Union. Missouri was also ruled out by the fighting there, with trains, track and bridges being systematically destroyed. The claims of the Hannibal and St Joseph could hardly be taken seriously when its president had been kidnapped by rebels in support of their demand for the halting of all trains.

Accordingly, it was hardly more than a formality that the eventual legislation – officially the Act to aid the construction of a railroad and telegraph line from the Missouri River to the Pacific Ocean – signed by Lincoln on July 1, 1862, should specify a starting point on the Iowa border. Nor was it likely that the western part of the job would be assigned to anyone but Huntington, Judah and the Central Pacific. The eastern section, meanwhile, would be built by a new company, designated the Union Pacific.

USMRR work gang with Brig-Gen Herman Haupt, head of construction and transportation.

THE PACIFIC RAILROAD

The conditions laid down by Congress for the building of the railroad to the Pacific were numerous. The builders were required to lay a single-track railroad and a telegraph line. The California-Nevada border was designated as the dividing line between the two companies, with the Central Pacific building west of this point and the Union Pacific the remainder. For land they were given a right of way 400 ft wide, plus five alternate sections of land on each side of every mile of track laid.

As for finance, the two companies were promised loans of $16,000 per mile of track, rising to $32,000 per mile in the foothills and $48,000 in the mountain sections. With the help of some imaginative classification of terrain, this gave the Union Pacific $27,000,000 and the Central Pacific $24,000,000, granted as first mortgages on the railroads. They were also allowed to sell 100,000 shares of $100 each to the public, with no individual allowed to buy more than 200 shares and no work permitted until one-fifth of the shares had been subscribed. In order to benefit from these terms the Union Pacific was required to complete 100 miles of track within two years and 100 miles per year thereafter; half those totals were required on the more difficult western sections.

Another stipulation was that only American iron was to be used. Finally, in order to spread the benefit of the road, a series of eastern connecting lines were authorized between the 100th meridian and Omaha, Leavenworth, St Joseph, Kansas City and Sioux City.

While Huntington was busy securing the charter to build the Central Pacific, his colleague Leland Stanford was elected governor of California, and the CP was given an early boost by a state loan of $1,659,000. More funds were raised by selling bonds to the communities along the route, such as the million dollars' worth subscribed by San Francisco, sales made considerably easier by the potentially fatal effects on towns the railroad chose to bypass. Sacramento and Placer County set the ball rolling with a total of $848,000, and on January 8, 1863, with the customary ceremony, ground was broken by Stanford on the east bank of the Sacramento River.

Already, another of the CP consortium, Charles Crocker, had been busy accumulating materials at Sacramento. Now he took charge of building as general superintendent, and within six months 18 miles of track had been graded ready for rails to be laid, while a 400-ft trestle bridge spanned the

Chinese laborers on the Central Pacific Railroad's Secrettown trestle in 1867.

American River, first of many formidable obstacles to the railroad's progress. For the first 20 miles or so, to Roseville, the rise in altitude from the near sealevel of Sacramento was negligible, but from that point the builders had to contend with rapidly steepening grades, the climate becoming harsher as the altitude increased.

One of the main requirements for the enterprise was ample supplies of labor to chop out the rock and cart it away, to level the roadbed and to lay the ties and rails. Bridges up to 500 ft long and 100 ft high were to be built across the steep ravines that intersected the route, tunnels a quarter of a mile and more long had to be bored through the granite ridges – and for this dangerous and demanding work the Central Pacific was offering no more than two or three dollars a day, paltry by comparison with the lucrative wages offered by the gold and silver mines in the region.

The problem was solved by Crocker's

A Union Pacific track-laying gang in August 1866 placing rails in position on the sleepers laid ready on the roadbed by earlier gangs.

idea of recruiting from the Chinese colony in San Francisco, and though his construction superintendent was at first reluctant to follow this course, a trial of fifty Chinese laborers convinced him of their ability; moreover, they were prepared to work for only a dollar a day. After recruiting all the Chinese labor available in California, the company began signing up workers in China itself and shipping them across the Pacific to work on the road. In fact, so able and industrious did the Chinese prove that 90 per cent of the 4000 men employed by the summer of 1865 were Chinese, and plans were in hand to double that number.

Along with this novel labor policy, the CP's founders pursued an imaginative financial scheme. In order to maintain control over the finances that were, after all, their primary concern, Huntington and his partners formed the Contract and Finance Corporation which the Central Pacific company proper employed to build its road. An eventual total approaching $80,000,000 was paid by the railroad to the construction company, something in the region of twice what it should, by reasonable estimates, have cost. Huge sums of

government and shareholders' money were thus, effectively, lost by the railroad to the consortium's Contract and Finance Corporation.

An early reward for this approach came in 1866, when Congress passed amended legislation to allow the Central Pacific to continue building beyond the state line that was to have been the limit of its activities.

As the labor force grew and the carefully managed flow of money was stimulated by the initial achievements, so the rate of construction was accelerated. In June 1864 the CP was able to issue its first timetable, over the 31 miles from Sacramento to Newcastle: three trains a day, one carrying passengers and mail, the others passengers and freight, were slotted in among the other trains carrying laborers and materials to the railhead. The next 12 miles, over an 800-ft rise to Clipper Gap, took a month each, but another two months saw a further 11 miles in operation. Grading continued through the winter as the rate of climb reached the maximum permitted by the Pacific railroad act. By the end of 1866 they had reached Cisco, only 92 miles from Sacramento, but nearly 6000 ft above

sea-level.

The ensuing winter was one of the worst on record: from February to March the average depth of snow was over ten feet, while blizzards swept the peaks for days on end and 50 degrees of frost became routine. Work, however, was not suspended. The railroad could afford neither to pay its men to remain idle, nor to lose the skilled labor force it had built up. Instead, while a massive snowplow toiled to keep the line from Sacramento open, snowsheds were built to protect the track behind and the newly graded roadbed ahead, and tunneling began in earnest.

The 1659-ft Summit Tunnel, through the final peak 7017 ft above sea-level, was dug and blasted inward from both ends and outward in both directions from a central shaft, 8000 men working in shifts around the clock. When the snow finally defeated the efforts of a dozen locomotives to drive the plow through the mounting drifts, teams of oxen were used to keep the timber, explosives and supplies coming.

Pressing on, they came to the Donner Pass, named after a party of emigrants who had been marooned there by the snows and died a few years earlier: in

1867 the last snow in the Donner Pass did not thaw until June. As the snow finally cleared, rails were laid on the new roadbed and by the middle of 1867 the laborers had completed some 130 miles from their starting point, though the rails through Summit Tunnel itself would not be laid until the end of the year. Three locomotives and 40 railcars were hauled over the summit, to be followed by all the materials needed for another 50 miles of track, ox-teams bridging the gap in the rails. Even so, only 40 miles, albeit in unimaginable conditions, were completed in 1867: the Nevada state line was reached in December, but a seven-mile gap in the rails remained near Donner Lake, where snow had again halted work. Still they pushed on, reaching the new town of Reno in the spring of 1868 before closing the gap behind them and pressing on across Nevada, aiming toward Utah and determined, with the revenue from the rich traffic of the Nevada mines now boosting their other sources of income, to beat their eastern rivals to Ogden.

Those rivals had been slower to start building. The Union Pacific Railroad was chartered by Congress in the 1862

Act, which named 158 commissioners, and a number of these held an inaugural meeting at Chicago in September 1862 to elect William B. Ogden president. But Thomas Durant, financial brain behind the Rock Island line and its Mississippi and Missouri subsidiary, had other ideas.

When only 150 shares had been sold by March 1863, Durant, using the names of a number of friends to circumvent the rules on share sales, bought the 20,000 shares that had to be sold before work could begin, financing the transaction by selling his holdings in the Mississippi and Missouri. Durant then proceeded to remove Ogden in October 1863, replacing him with John A. Dix, who had served as figurehead president of the M & M. A few weeks later, on December 2, the familiar round of speeches – equating the Pacific railroad and the nation – bands and cannon fire accompanied the groundbreaking ceremony at Omaha. But by the following spring only a few miles of preliminary grading had been carried out and work was at a standstill: with

A UP construction train at Bear River City, southern Wyoming, in 1868.

the Civil War still in the balance, money was short, and short money did not build long railroads.

Durant soon remedied that. After forming a holding company, the Credit Mobilier of America, he persuaded Congress to double the Union Pacific's land grant and include any mineral deposits the land might contain, convert the government loans into a second mortgage and increase the permitted number of shares to a million – ten times the original stipulation. The final refinement of the scheme involved the replacement of Peter Dey, who had been appointed chief engineer and had estimated construction costs at between $20,000 and $30,000 per mile, with Colonel Silas Seymour, who had prepared a more meandering route, and arranging for the Credit Mobilier to contract for construction at $50,000 per mile.

With the financial details under control, it was time to build the railroad: already the Leavenworth, Pawnee and Western, with its own federal land grant and a new name – Union Pacific, Eastern Division – was building west from the Missouri, and Cyrus K. Holliday's Atchison and Topeka road had been granted land for its line, originally intended to run only from Atchison on the Missouri to the Kansas state capital of Topeka, but now with ambitions to follow the old Santa Fe Trail to the Pacific.

Unfortunately, Seymour proved less than effective at building railroads, and by October 1865 only 15 miles of track had been laid. At this point General Grenville Dodge, who had been Peter Dey's assistant on the Rock Island line, had assisted in the Mississippi and Missouri surveys, and had gone on to distinguish himself under Sherman during the Civil War campaign in Georgia, was selected as Seymour's replacement. And at the same time, in the spring of 1866, General John S. Casement and his brother Daniel were hired to oversee construction.

The new men soon had an effect on

the railroad. The ferry landing at Omaha became a thriving industrial town as workshops were erected and fleets of boats began to arrive with the required materials. The work force was built up rapidly to 10,000, and as many draft animals were employed in hauling the rails, ties and supplies from Omaha to the railhead. As the line progressed a boarding train was built, with triple-deck bunks to accommodate the laborers at night. More trains followed, loaded with ties and rails, from which they were transferred to their ultimate resting places by horse-drawn wagons. Ahead of the tracklayers supplies were hauled to the graders by ox-teams, while yet farther ahead surveying parties mapped out the route. Before long the mile of track that had taken Seymour's men a week was being laid in a day. In October 1866 the rails reached the 100th meridian, 247 miles west of Omaha, and a few weeks later winter quarters were built at North Platte.

In the spring of 1867 the Chicago and Northwestern Railroad reached Council Bluffs, easing supply problems considerably, and at the same time the UP resumed its westward progress. By the following winter the rails had reached a

new camp at Cheyenne, already grown from nothing to a town of some 4000 inhabitants.

The next stage of the Union Pacific lay through the Black Hills, while the Central Pacific had conquered its mountain range and was building across Nevada. Both were now aiming to be first into Utah, and Dodge declared his intention of doubling the 500 miles already laid and reaching Ogden by the end of 1868. In pursuit of this objective both UP and CP contracted with the Mormons in Utah to start grading routes far ahead of their rails, and many miles of parallel routes were graded before the government decreed Ogden as the meeting place.

The tracklaying operation was now organized on a massive scale. Before the 1868 season began 3000 men were at work felling trees and laying them ready along the Union Pacific's route; the work train was expanded to make room for bakers, butchers and even an occasional newspaper publisher; and Hell on Wheels, as the camp followers with their portable saloons had become known, followed the tracks through Laramie, Benton, Red Desert, Black Butte, Green River, Salt Wells, Bitter

CYRUS K. HOLLIDAY
1826—1900
PIONEER AND BUILDER
FOUNDER AND MAYOR OF TOPEKA.
INFLUENCED THE SELECTION OF THIS CITY
AS THE CAPITAL OF KANSAS.
ORGANIZED THE ATCHISON, TOPEKA AND
SANTA FE RAILROAD COMPANY. OBTAINED
THE ORIGINAL CHARTER IN THE YEAR 1859.
PROMOTED THE EARLY DEVELOPMENT OF
KANSAS AND THE ENTIRE SOUTHWEST.

Locomotive No 5 of the Atchison, Topeka and Santa Fe Railroad was built by William Mason's Taunton Locomotive company in 1870. The plaque commemorates the railroad's founder.

Creek: the names of the temporary camps reflected the nature of the alkaline desert of southern Wyoming.

When winter again intervened the railhead had reached Wasatch in the mountains of the Wyoming-Utah border, only 67 miles from Ogden and 995 miles west of Omaha: on the other side the Central Pacific had reached 446 miles east from Sacramento to Carlin, in northeastern Nevada. With Ogden so close, there was to be no winter break,

despite appalling conditions in the mountains. Wages were doubled, work continued, and by the spring both railroads were racing across the plains of Utah. The Union Pacific was first to reach Ogden, on March 8, and by this point barely 50 miles separated the two roads. Even so, it was only as a result of pressure from President Grant that they would agree on a meeting place. They finally settled on Promontory, 53 miles west of Ogden.

By now the telegraph line had been completed, and daily newspaper reports of the rivals' progress were absorbing the interest of the whole country. Crocker and the Casements responded by doubling and redoubling the daily milage until six, seven and eight miles of rails were being spiked down by one side or the other between dawn and dusk. Rivalry between the CP's Chinese and the predominantly Irish laborers of the UP became so intense that there

were instances of work gangs deliberately setting off explosive charges both above and below each other's positions.

The climax came on April 28. With only some 20 miles of track remaining to be laid Crocker settled a bet of $10,000 he had made with Durant by having a specially selected team of his men lay ten miles of rail in twelve hours.

Another few days and it was all over.

On Monday May 10 officials and workers of the two railroads gathered at Promontory for the placing of a silver-wreathed laurel tie and the driving of a golden spike to mark the junction of the rails. The Union Pacific locomotive *Jupiter* and the Central Pacific's No 119 inched forward to touch each other, champagne bottles were broken, and the telegraph signaled the completion of the first transcontinental railroad.

The celebrations of this epic achieve-ment engulfed the country. A 100-gun salute in New York was echoed by the ringing of the Liberty Bell in Philadelphia; a procession in Chicago grew to seven miles in length. But all the celebrations would be followed by the bitterness of disillusion, and a day of reckoning that would rock the nation.

In late 1868 Hell on Wheels reached Bear River City, Wyoming, as UP tracks neared the Utah state line.

News of the completion of the transcontinental railroad was awaited eagerly throughout the country: while officials and their wives posed with a throng of onlookers (below), the telegrapher at the table on the right sent out the single word 'Done' to signal the start of nationwide celebrations.

Left: The Central Pacific locomotive *Jupiter* with bandsmen of the 21st Infantry Division who provided the music for the occasion. Opposite: The Union Pacific paymasters' car (right) with a small group of the 10,000 men employed in the railroad's construction, and (left) railroad workers slake their thirst aboard a caboose.

THE WESTERN RAILROADS

The final cost of the first transcontinental railroad was fantastic. The Union Pacific had collected land grants totaling 24,000,000 acres, the Central Pacific another 9,000,000 acres – a combined total of over 50,000 square miles. Government grants to the two companies amounted to $27,000,000 and $24,000,000 respectively, quite apart from the further huge sums raised from the sale of stock.

In 1869, few doubted that this was money well spent. Even the fact that the actual railroad, especially that built by the Union Pacific, was of poor standard was at first overshadowed by the immensity of the achievement. Randomly spaced ties placed unballasted on the ground, and fashioned of soft pine that would rot almost as soon as they were laid; rickety bridges and insubstantial embankments; poor rail joints and a deliberately meandering route apparently selected to maximize land grants: all these and other faults could be explained by the speed of construction. At least the trains were running: there would be plenty of time to improve the track and straighten out the route.

The real shock came a few years later, in 1873, when it was revealed that numbers of congressmen had received stock in the Credit Mobilier, which had been able to pay huge dividends on the basis of its fraudulent transactions with the Union Pacific. The Credit Mobilier became a national scandal that quickly eroded public faith in the railroads. In the words of one senator, 'I have seen our national triumph and exaltation turned to bitterness and shame by the unanimous reports of three committees of Congress that every step of that mighty enterprise had been taken in fraud.'

One immediate consequence of the scandal was a disastrous fall in the value of Union Pacific shares: by the end of 1873 they had dropped from $100 to $14, and at this point they attracted the attention of a new operator in the person of Jay Gould. Gould had established himself as a powerful and ruthless businessman in his battles with Cornelius Vanderbilt over the New York railroads.

Railroads, as virtually the only large industrial concerns before the Civil War, had been popular with speculators in stocks and shares since the 1830s. During the war Vanderbilt and others had made large sums from such speculation, and by the time it ended Vanderbilt had used his holdings in the Harlem Railroad to force the directors of the New York Central, who depended on the Harlem for their New York connection, to surrender control to him.

At the same time two younger adventurers, Jay Gould and Jim Fisk, had managed to take control of the Erie system from Daniel Drew, one of the original railroad speculators, who had taken over the Erie in the 1850s purely to facilitate speculation in its shares. Vanderbilt's New York Central system was at least soundly organized and well run: the Erie, by contrast, had become notorious for its neglected condition and high accident rate, since shares were issued for the profit of its controllers and hardly any of the proceeds were spent on track or rolling stock.

Gould and Fisk continued and expanded on Drew's manipulation of the Erie, and in the late 1860s their battles with Vanderbilt reached quite unbelievable heights of drama. At one point, early in 1868, they were forced to flee New York to avoid arrest and set up headquarters in Jersey City; after a series of legal and political battles, in the course of which judges and state legislators were bribed liberally, and often by both sides, Fisk and Gould were able to return to New York. Here they established themselves in a vaudeville theatre, while a printing press in the basement churned out a constant flow of Erie stock certificates.

The Erie battle finally ended in compromise, and Gould, now known as the Mephistopheles of Wall Street, began to turn his attentions further afield. He

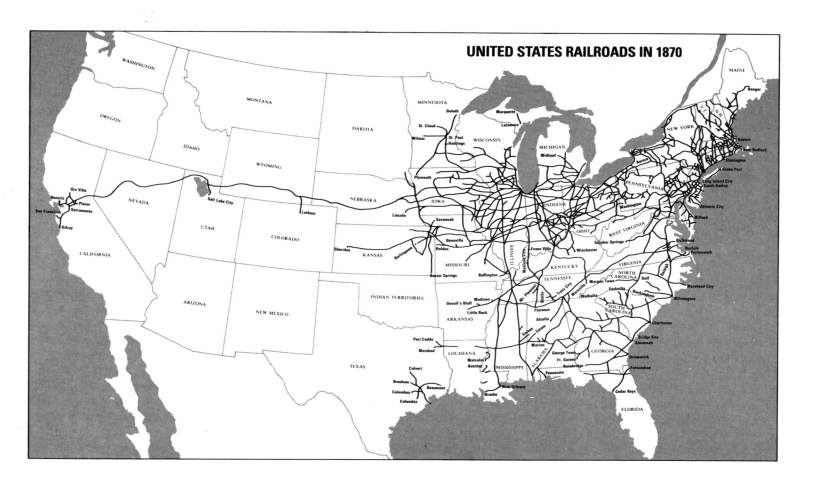

UNITED STATES RAILROADS IN 1870

began by speculating in the Wabash and Lake Shore lines that skirted the southern reaches of the Great Lakes. His attempt to corner the nation's entire gold supply as a means of bring-

ing down the export price of grain, thus stimulating traffic on the grain-carrying Wabash, was foiled by government intervention; but Gould managed to sell out just in time, and after the

An early passenger train on the transcontinental, headed by UP locomotive No 945, built in 1870.

Credit Mobilier scandal he began buying up Union Pacific stock at its new low price.

As with his Erie operations, this was purely a speculative measure. Gould controlled the Union Pacific only long enough to enrich himself by declaring ridiculously high dividends, then selling out at the inflated prices this produced. In 1878 he turned to the bankrupt Kansas Pacific, and after settling with the bondholders he announced his intention to build a line from Denver to the west coast. By this measure he forced the new UP directors to take over the Kansas Pacific in order to protect their monopoly of the route: again, the price of his holdings soared, and again he sold out.

Compared with these scandalous maneuvers, Collis Huntington's financial affairs had been as soundly constructed as his railroad's tunnels through the granite of the Sierra Nevada. His horizons stretched far beyond Durant's exploitation of a single railroad, and whereas he was as concerned as Gould with making money, he did so as a businessman in the conventional sense rather than by simply manipulating the prices of securities. He was determined to hang on to the enterprises he created; and in addition to expanding his interests to include west coast shipping and various other industries, even before the golden spike was driven at Promontory, he was moving toward nothing less than a second independent transcontinental railroad.

In 1868 Huntington and his associates acquired the charter for the Southern Pacific Railroad in order to consolidate their position in California. The Contract and Finance Company, having absorbed some $79,000,000 — not far short of double the estimated actual cost — for its part in building the Central Pacific, was quietly buried. In its place, the Western Development Company was formed to further their exploitation of the richly fertile and as yet sparsely populated golden state.

The first stage was the construction of a railroad through the San Joaquin valley from San Francisco to Los Angeles, and with the help of generous grants from the latter town this line was completed in 1876. The next step was to fight off others who were interested in building a southern railroad to the west coast.

Principal among these was the Texas and Pacific Railroad, which had been chartered with a federal land grant of some 18 million acres along the Mexican border. The Texas and Pacific was headed by Thomas A. Scott, president of the leading eastern railroad, the Pennsylvania. Scott had previously tried his hand at running the Union Pacific, but had abandoned that sorry enterprise, and had hired Grenville Dodge to build the new road. Problems arose in 1873, when Dodge was implicated in the Credit Mobilier scandal, funds being dried up as a result of the financial crisis that enveloped the country. The Texas Pacific reached Dallas in 1873, but by 1876 it had progressed only as far as Fort Worth, less than 200 miles from its starting point at Marshall.

In 1877 an agreement was reached between Scott, Huntington and the federal government whereby the Southern Pacific would retain control of the California end of the new transcontinental route, while Scott would continue the Texas Pacific to Yuma on the California-Arizona border and provide a connection to the east.

This did not stop Huntington. Having built the Southern Pacific as far as Yuma, he obtained charters from the territorial governments of Arizona and New Mexico to circumvent the lack of federal backing. Bridging the Colorado River and presenting the government with a *fait accompli*, he won presidential approval for his plan to continue building eastward.

Ultimately, the competing railroads agreed on a junction at El Paso on the Texas-New Mexico border, and this was achieved in 1882 to complete a second transcontinental railroad. The following year the Southern Pacific acquired its own route across Texas by taking over the Galveston, Harrisburg and San Antonio Railroad which, along with other small lines, eventually gave the SP access to New Orleans. And in 1895 the Central Pacific itself was absorbed into the new system.

Nevertheless, there were other railroads building toward the Pacific through the southwest. The Denver and Rio Grande Railroad was established by the citizens of the state capital to exploit the new mines in the Colorado Rockies. The Kansas Pacific had been built to Denver from Kansas City, with a branch north to a junction with the Union Pacific at Cheyenne. The new line was aimed south toward Santa Fe, which was also the objective of another ambitious western project, the Atchison, Topeka and Santa Fe Railroad.

The AT & SF had made little progress, since receiving its Kansas land grant in 1863, until 1870, when it began building across Kansas, establishing itself on the strength of the thriving cattle trade based on Dodge City, which it reached in 1872. A year later it reached La Junta in southeast Colorado, at the same time as the Denver and Rio Grande reached Pueblo, some 70 miles to the west. Both lines were then held up by the financial panic, but by 1876 the tracks of the Santa Fe had also reached Pueblo.

At this point the financial and politi-

Cornelius Vanderbilt, the Commodore's grandson, and President of the NY Central until 1899.

cal battles that had punctuated the progress of the western railroads erupted into armed battles. The only route south to Santa Fe lay through the Raton Pass on the New Mexico border, while the other objective of the rival railroads, the mining area around Leadville, to the west of Pueblo, could only be reached through the Royal Gorge of the Arkansas River. With the permission of the operator of a toll road through the Raton Pass, the Santa Fe construction gangs arrived to begin grading work in February 1878. They were opposed by

Thomas A Scott, President of the Pennsylvania Railroad and promotor of the Texas Pacific.

Oakes Ames, Congressman, shovel manufacturer and one of the Credit Mobilier ringleaders.

armed employees of the Rio Grande, but local feeling had been turned against the Denver company by some scandalous real estate operations, and the Santa Fe men fought off their rivals to secure the route to the south. Further battles followed over the Royal Gorge right of way, but the eventual court settlement went in favor of the D & RG.

The Santa Fe now turned its attention farther west, and in 1880 acquired the old charter for the Atlantic and Pacific Railroad; this was intended to

Frederick Billings lost control of the Northern Pacific to Henry Villard in 1881.

connect St Louis with southern California, but had so far hardly progressed beyond the Missouri state line. In the east a line was built from the Santa Fe tracks at Wichita to a junction with the Atlantic and Pacific at Pierce City, near Springfield, Missouri, giving the AT & SF an eastern outlet at St Louis. In the west, meanwhile, the Atlantic and Pacific charter brought with it substantial land grants in New Mexico and Arizona, and by virtue of these the Santa Fe built a new line to Albuquerque. This left the city of Santa Fe to be served by a branch line, while the main line carried on to the California border at Needles, one of the few possible bridging points on the Colorado River. The Southern Pacific had already built its own line to Needles, and an agreement between the two companies allowed the Santa Fe to run its trains to Los Angeles and San Francisco to complete a third transcontinental line.

Meanwhile, far to the north, yet another Pacific railroad was under way. This was the Northern Pacific, along the route from Lake Superior to Portland that Asa Whitney had advocated back in 1845. During the Civil War, when the Pacific railroad charters were compiled, the Northern Pacific had been granted 47,000,000 acres in the northwest from Minnesota to Washington, but the lack of any cash subsidies to go with it had delayed construction for five years. In 1869, however, Jay Cooke, the Philadelphia financier who had amassed the bulk of his fortune selling the government bonds that financed the Union during the Civil War and had reinvested much of it in large areas of land in Minnesota, came on the scene.

After conducting his own surveys of the Northern Pacific's territory, Cooke became the company's financial agent. With his unmatched expertise at selling bonds, Cooke hired newspaper editors and public figures to broadcast the virtues of the northwest; and indeed the advertisements circulated were larded with so much hyperbole that the curving swathe of land which appeared in the accompanying maps received the popular name of Jay Cooke's Banana Belt. This publicity campaign aimed to sell 100 million dollars' worth of bonds in order to finance the building of the railroad.

Work was started in 1870, and soon branches from Duluth and Minneapolis met at Brainerd and carried on across Minnesota and Dakota to the banks of the Missouri River, where in 1873 the new town of Bismarck was established. The naming of this city after the German chancellor was part of an attempt to lure both emigrants and investment from Germany; but unfortunately for Cooke the railroad had been spending money faster than he could sell the bonds, which were in any case sold at a massive discount to reimburse him for his efforts, and Cooke's own bank was subsidizing the railroad to the tune of $5,500,000. An attempt to bolster his financial empire by selling a new issue of government bonds failed when these proved difficult to shift. The Credit Mobilier scandal and rumours of the Northern Pacific's difficulties, allied to a number of less rosy reports of conditions along the Banana Belt, made it even harder to dispose of new railroad bonds. Furthermore, European capital was scarce as a result of the Franco-Prussian war; and on September 18, 1873, the closure of the New York offices of Jay Cooke's bank sparked off the biggest of the crashes and panics that had already punctuated the short history of Wall Street.

The railroads at this point had absorbed some three billion dollars from government and investors. Between 1865 and 1870 their combined length had grown from 35,000 to 53,000 miles. But whereas in 1860 there had been 1026 investors, on average, to support each mile of railway, by 1873 that figure had fallen to only 590, which was not nearly enough. The result was the collapse of the financial system, and with it went railroads all over the country, though the Northern Pacific itself managed to survive until 1875 before going bankrupt.

To add to the problems in the northwest, the Indians who had been driven steadily north as the railroads carved up their old hunting grounds, were refusing to move any further or to allow any more building. The military expedition to 'pacify' them ended in Custer's defeat at Little Big Horn in 1876; but after that final victory Sitting Bull led the tribes north into Canada. As the financial debris settled, interest in the northern route revived.

Henry Villard, originally a German journalist, had represented German bondholders in the bankruptcy of the Kansas Pacific, and had established a reputation at that time by his determination to hold out for the repayment of the debts rather than connive in Gould's scheming. He was now commissioned to protect the interests of a similar group who had invested in the bankrupt Oregon and California Railroad. Deciding to become involved in his own right, Villard began by incorporating the Oregon Railway and Navigation Company, and soon came to dominate transportation in the region. He built railroads along the Columbia and Willamette river valleys, and soon became interested in building his own transcontinental railroad. The moribund Northern Pacific, however, still possessed the land grants. After 1875 it had been reorganized by

Frederick Billing and had resumed building toward Tacoma, on the natural harbors of the Puget Sound, rather than to Portland, a hundred miles inland from the sea.

When the Northern Pacific refused his offer to use his Columbia River valley tracks as its western terminus, Villard organized a 'blind pool,' raising money from a number of investors without disclosing its purpose, and managed to secure control of the Northern Pacific. But having begun his railroad career protecting the interests of investors, Villard now over-reached himself. Construction costs, especially over the Rocky Mountain sections, escalated beyond the railroad's resources; and his neat stunt of using a rusty old spike from one of the first sections of rail laid in place of the customary golden spike to mark the road's completion in September 1883 was to prove more than a little ironic. By the end of the year the Northern Pacific was bankrupt and Villard resigned. Once he

was out of the way, the railroad was completed to Tacoma.

The Northern Pacific, with its huge land grants, seemed to have a monopoly on the northern route to the Pacific, but another great financier, James J. Hill, who had made his fortune in the grain trade in St Paul, also had designs on the region. His opportunity came in the form of another of the bankrupt railroads that littered the country after the 1873 panic.

The St Paul and Pacific Railroad had been chartered in 1862 with a land grant of five million acres of Minnesota Territory, but had reached only as far as a junction with the Northern Pacific at Brainerd, while another branch ran up toward the Canadian border. In 1878 Hill succeeded in gaining control of the St Paul and Pacific by buying its stock for a fraction of the face value; and by selling off the land that was included he managed to make a substantial profit. After changing its name to the St Paul, Minneapolis and Manitoba, Hill began

extending his line toward the Canadian border and a junction with the new Canadian Pacific railway at Pembina.

As immigrants flocked to northern Minnesota, and bumper grain crops were produced, Hill gradually extended his railroad. Unlike some of the speculators who had preceded him, Hill built his line slowly and prudently, operated it efficiently, and charged lower rates than the Northern Pacific,

Previous page:
A passenger train on the Northern Pacific Railroad near Taylors Falls, Minnesota, during the 1880s.

Construction of the Northern Pacific in western North Dakota in 1880, when Henry Villard had taken over; and (inset) James Jerome Hill, who ultimately added the line to his railroad empire.

his competitor, in order to ensure a continuation of traffic. During the 1880s the railhead progressed slowly westward, through timber country and the copper mines of Montana, his competition helping to drive the Northern Pacific down the road to ruin.

In January 1893 the Great Northern route to the Puget Sound at Seattle was completed, and before the year was out the Northern Pacific, of which Villard had, astonishingly, managed to regain control in 1889, was bankrupt again. The second failure ousted Villard for good, and by 1896 Hill had gained control of the parallel route. But even with two transcontinental railroads under his control he was not satisfied: his ambition now was to expand into Chicago and the Midwest.

There were two possible means to this end. The Chicago, Burlington and Quincy Railroad was formed in 1856 by the amalgamation of a couple of small lines in the Chicago area, and over the years it had grown by extensions and takeovers into a system of over 6000 route miles reaching from Chicago as far afield as St Louis, Kansas City and Denver, north to Minneapolis and northwest into Montana. The other system that would have answered Hill's needs, the Chicago, Milwaukee and St Paul, had the backing of Standard Oil founder William Rockefeller, and was not for sale; so the Chicago, Burlington and Quincy was added to Hill's empire.

By this time the term 'transcontinental' had lost much of its meaning. There was no through line from the Atlantic to the Pacific, although one man did almost bring it about a decade or so later. This was George Gould, heir to the Mephistopheles of Wall Street. Until the panic of 1907 Gould had included the Denver and Rio Grande Western, the Wabash and the Western Maryland among his extensive railroad interests; and when his Western Pacific was completed in 1909 between Ogden, Iowa, and San Francisco, he came close to achieving a system that actually did span the continent from coast to coast.

The transcontinentals were by no means the be-all and end-all of railroading in the west. Railroads were built wherever there was a need, and often where there was none, as the old frontier was tamed and disappeared under the advancing rails. In the Colorado Rockies, for example, the Denver and Rio Grande was only one, albeit by far the biggest, of several railroads serving the mining towns of the area. Much of the D & RG's track was originally built to the 3-ft gauge that became popular in the west after 1870, although narrow-gauge railroads always had the disadvantage of being unable to exchange traffic with standard-gauge lines. The Rio Grande soon began to convert most of its track to standard gauge, though

the narrow-gauge branch from Durango to Silverton was preserved as a tourist attraction, and steam-hauled excursion trains have continued to be operated over that branch.

There was, however, one transcontinental line still to be built, one which epitomized the wastefulness of much nineteenth-century construction in that it competed directly with two existing systems, yet which in its operation was to become one of the most advanced in the country.

As outlined above, James Hill had been baulked in his attempt to acquire the Chicago, Milwaukee and St Paul Railroad to complement his twin Great Northern and Northern Pacific transcontinental routes, but had succeeded in gaining control of the Chicago, Burlington and Quincy. The reaction of the Milwaukee road's management was a decision, taken in 1905, to build its own northwestern road to the Pacific. With none of the land grants that had helped its predecessors complete their lines, the Milwaukee nevertheless built its line in the remarkably short space of three years, and over a route shorter than either of its competitors, between Chicago and Seattle.

This was only achieved at considerable expense, and by following a route that included some very severe grades through a series of mountain ranges. As a result of the operational difficulties and challenges, the Milwaukee, which now added the word Pacific to its full title but which became known universally as the Milwaukee Road, was induced to embark on an ambitious electrification scheme in the Rocky and Bitter Root Mountains. Two sections were equipped with overhead supply of 3000-volt DC current, that between Harlowtown and Avery being opened in 1917 and the other, from Othello to Seattle, in 1920. Together they represented 656 miles of electrified main line, the longest in the world at the time and using the most advanced system available. The eventual replacement of steam power by diesel locomotives, and the inconvenience of the 110-mile gap between the two electrified sections, led the Milwaukee to decide, in 1973, to abandon its electric operations, which had proved a thoroughly economic exercise.

Previous page: A snow clearing gang pose with their equipment on the Northern Pacific in 1886. The Denver and Rio Grande adopted a gauge of 3ft for its original lines in the Rockies, as on this section (left) in 1875. The Milwaukee Road turned to electrification for its mountain sections: here, three electric locomotives head a heavy freight out of Harlowton, Montana.

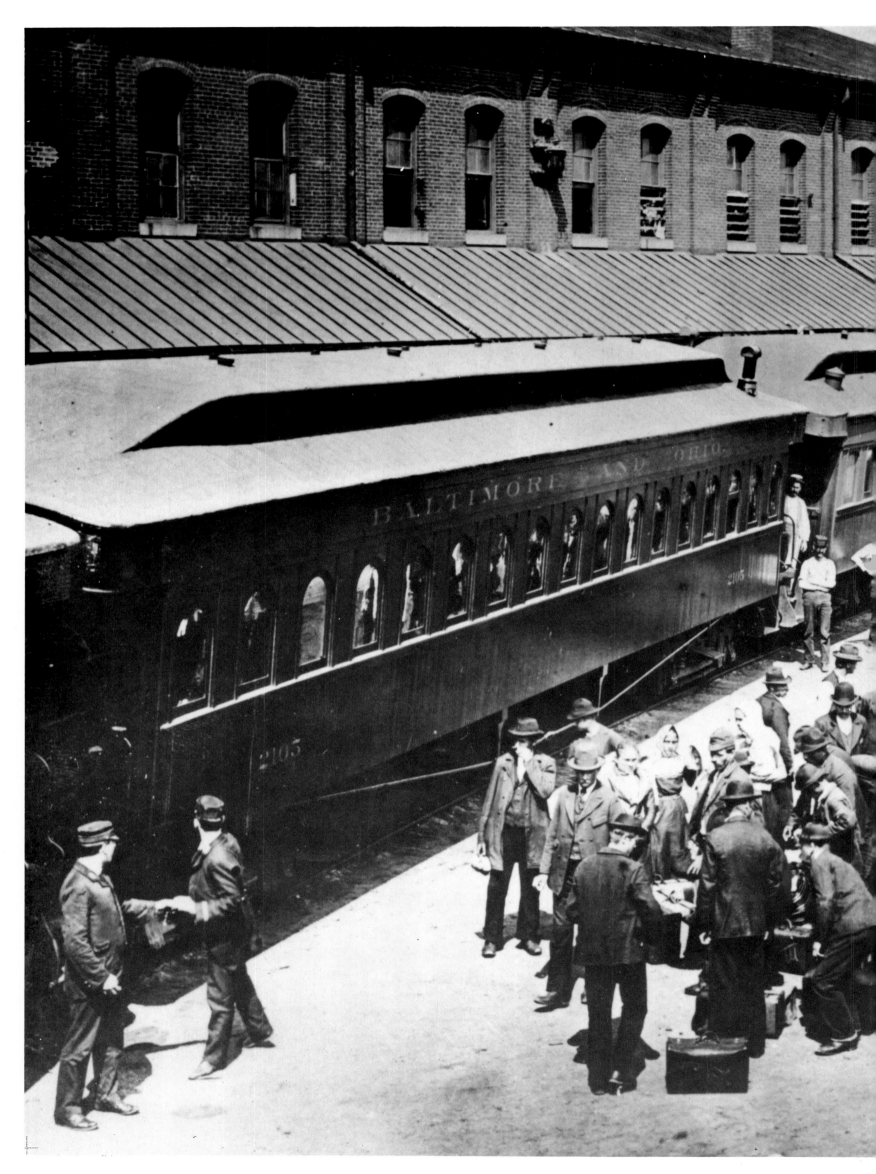

REGULATING THE RAILROADS

The major railroads and the sorry catalog of scandals that blackened their name, only constituted part of the story. There were, in fact, railroads of every size, from the massive systems that measured their extent in thousands of miles to single-track lines a few miles long and operated by a single locomotive; there were specialized freight operators concentrating on a single product – coal, mineral ore, chemicals or lumber; and there were suburban railroads catering almost exclusively for commuters. But it was clear that, whatever their individual forms, the railroads as a whole had become too important to be left to the vagaries of market forces and the whims of tycoons.

Many of the troubles that beset the railroads were a consequence of their origins. Before the Civil War railroads were chartered by individual states, which could have important effects on their routes. The Erie, for example, followed a route across southern New York that was governed more by the location of the state line than by any more practical consideration. The Congressional land grant system, applied first to the transcontinental railroads and later to new railroads in the Territories, produced systems that were dependent on through traffic, rather than local demand, and this in turn tended toward consolidation of individual roads into interstate systems.

At first this process was left entirely to the initiative of individual managements, and the results were largely dependent on their characters. Thus the Pennsylvania Railroad, under the presidency of J. Edgar Thompson and his successor, Thomas A. Scott, became the premier system of the world, the standard against which all others were measured: its track was the finest, its locomotives outstanding, its services so impressive that Henry James, returning to the United States in 1904 after twenty years in Europe, was moved to single it out for special praise. In *The American Scene* James recorded his impression that the Pennsylvania was actually designed to serve another world, and that by staying on board beyond his destination he might be carried to some ideal city not mentioned in any timetable, passengers being merely a vulgar intrusion on its more sublime operations.

Allowing for such fanciful exaggeration, there is no doubt that other systems existed which, to say the least, compared unfavorably with the Penn. The nature of the competition between the railroads that arose from the growth of interlocking systems was such as to reward outstanding unscrupulousness and outstanding managerial skill alike. Nor was it only investors who suffered from highly unscrupulous management techniques. For many years safety standards were appallingly low, with accidents commonly caused by defective track.

Freight rates were an area of competition which had more widespread consequences. The essence of rate competition lay in the two types of costs incurred by the railroads, namely the fixed costs of maintaining the system and the running cost of conveying a particular load over a particular distance.

Over a route where competition existed, it was tempting for a railroad to calculate its rates on the basis of running cost alone, leaving the fixed costs to be met from other sources – such as another route where it enjoyed a monopoly, and where rates would be correspondingly higher.

Other abuses included discriminatory rates charged for different commodities, or for different journeys. In practice this meant that influential customers, such as those who supplied a large volume of freight, could demand lower rates: it was tempting for the railroads, as long as they could cover their running costs, to comply with such demands, if only to deprive their competitors of the business. But its effect, in leaving the fixed costs to be met from other sources, was to subsidize big customers at the expense of small. And where the railroad had no competition it would be free to charge whatever it thought fit. Again, there was the formation of rate pools, whereby competing railroads, finding the cost of competition ruinous, might agree on

uniformly high rates.

The customers who were most susceptible to such practices, and those who were liable to suffer the most, were the farmers, whose products were worthless without transportation, and in many cases immediate transportation, to the markets. And it was the farmers who were first to organize their

Union Pacific fruit train, and (inset) itinerant harvest workers in 1890.

Austere elegance in the dining car of the Great Northern Railroad's Oriental Limited in about 1910.

resistance to such sharp practices.

In 1867 an organization was founded known as the National Grange, officially the Patrons of Husbandry. It originated as a social and educational institution, but during the 1870s, when nearly a million farmers, predominantly in the Midwest, became members, the National Grange rapidly evolved into a political force, co-ordinating the votes of its members to ensure the election of state legislators sympathetic to their cause, and the consequent enactment of legislation to outlaw the most common abuses.

The railroads had grown used to controlling political and judicial processes to their own advantage: and, the Grangers were encouraged when, at first, the railroads' appeals against the new measures were dismissed by the Supreme Court. However, in 1886 the same court reversed its earlier decision when it ruled that states had no power to regulate rates charged on traffic that passed beyond their own borders, thus undermining the Granger cause, and providing another illustration of the need for federal regulation.

The process of consolidation of individual routes into ever larger systems, which had been the principal cause of the competition that engendered the rate wars and their accompanying evils, was only hastened by the

mounting attacks to which the railroads found themselves subject. In fact, the main force behind the co-operation between railroads that gradually replaced much of the competition toward the end of the nineteenth century was the leading banker of the day, J. Pierpont Morgan.

Morgan had become involved in railroads in spectacular fashion during one of the skirmishes in the 'Erie wars' of the late 1860s. After reaching a compromise with Vanderbilt, Gould and Fisk found a new outlet for their acquisitive tendencies in the growing traffic from the coalfields of northern Pennsylvania. A new line from Binghamton to Albany, the Albany and Susquehanna, was about to be opened in 1869, and Gould and Fisk, acting through the agency of the Delaware and Hudson Canal Company, attempted to buy out the A & S. They found themselves opposed by Morgan, in alliance with the Lackawanna and Western Railroad, and after reaching a stalemate the conflict was eventually settled by a trackside battle, in which Morgan's 'army' prevailed, and a bitter legal and political struggle which the Erie men finally abandoned as fruitless.

As his banking interests grew, Morgan found himself increasingly caught up with the railroads. By 1879 he was a director of Vanderbilt's New York

Central, and in 1880 he was instrumental in raising $40,000,000 for the tottering Northern Pacific. During the 1870s railroad construction, funded by private investors or by the local communities that were enabled by the General Bonding Law of 1869 to raise money to buy railroad securities, had far outstripped demand: many new lines were built without any hope of immediate financial return, and by the end of the 1870s bankruptcies were common. In 1879 alone, 65 railroads with a combined capitalization of well over $200,000,000 were foreclosed. Even those railroads that avoided outright insolvency found themselves paying annual interest charges on existing debts that could amount to half or more of their net earnings.

Nevertheless, each panic, after a few years while the markets recovered, was followed by a new outbreak of uneconomic building. Nowhere were the consequences of this felt more acutely than in New York, which in 1880 had nearly 6,000 miles of main line, and where almost 2,000 more were added in the ensuing decade.

The competition was fiercest between the major trunk routes. The New York Central and the Erie, both with exten-

Cartoonist's view of Cornelius Vanderbilt and Jim Fisk in 1870.

sive networks of feeder lines, were also subject to competition from the Baltimore and Ohio and the Pennsylvania for traffic to the Midwest. In the early 1880s the Pennsylvania, which dominated traffic in its native state, was expanding most rapidly, at the expense of the other three.

The same period saw the appearance of new railroads whose sole purpose seemed to be to duplicate the existing routes and force the incumbents to buy them out. In 1878 Vanderbilt had been forced to buy the new Nickel Plate – the New York, Chicago and St Louis Railway – to protect his Lake Shore route to Chicago, and in 1883 the West Shore Railroad began building up the Hudson in direct competition with the New York Central. William Vanderbilt, believing the Pennsylvania to be behind these encroachments, responded with his own counterattack, selecting the small but prosperous coal-carrying Philadelphia and Reading Railroad as the basis for a new venture, the South Pennsylvania Railroad.

By 1885 Morgan, whose own reputation as a financier of the railroads was suffering by association with such suicidal competition, concluded that 'something should be done.' His solution was that Vanderbilt and the Pennsylvania should buy each other's competing railroads, Vanderbilt taking over the West Shore and the Penn the South Pennsylvania. Morgan was able to impose this compromise on the reluctant rivals, and in the process took charge of reorganizing the South Pennsylvania, West Shore and Philadelphia and Reading, being named as owner of the South Pennsylvania to circumvent a state ordinance prohibiting the Penn itself from buying competing railroads.

Morgan, like others before him, then found his interests spreading to the west: and, like his predecessors, he found himself in conflict with other powerful and ambitious men. Attempting to extend the Vanderbilt system into Iowa from Chicago, he was blocked by Edward Harriman, who in 1881 had gained control of the Illinois Central and had guided it through prosperity toward expansion. That first clash in 1886, over the obscure Dubuque and Sioux City Railroad, was won by Harriman: soon they were contesting more substantial spoils.

In 1893 the Erie finally collapsed and Morgan, charged with restructuring the company, again found himself opposed by Harriman, who succeeded in imposing some of his own conditions on the process of reorganization. Two years later another railroad which had suffered in the past from the dead hand of Jay Gould – the Union Pacific – collapsed along with over 150 others. The state of the UP by then was such that not even Morgan was interested in attempting to salvage it, and Harriman, now enjoying the backing of the Standard Oil concern, assumed control. Within five years Harriman transformed the Union Pacific into a booming business, and on the death of Collis Huntington in 1900 he raised $50,000,000 to take control of the Southern Pacific.

Morgan, meanwhile, had formed an alliance with James Hill to establish the common ownership of the Northern Pacific and Great Northern monopoly in the northeast, and had seen the Chicago, Burlington and Quincy added to this system. In New England he extended his control of the New York, New Haven and Hartford Railroad to incorporate many of the smaller operations in the area; and he used his influence in the region to block the planned expansion of the Philadelphia and Reading (which, since its part in the Penn-New York Central standoff, had grown to a 5000-mile system) until he could assume control. In the southeastern states, where the depradations of the Civil War had been followed by spurious constructors appropriating state funds with little attempt to construct the railroads they were intended to finance, Morgan applied his organizational skills to the creation of the 9000-mile Southern Railways system.

He was also able to exercise authority over all the New York trunk routes and their associated feeders, so that coal traffic was evenly distributed and uniform rates were charged.

Nor was this the limit of Morgan's activities, for he was active in every area of major industry, imposing his own brand of order on the financial workings of half the country, epitomized by his part in the formation of the mammoth US Steel trust. But such an empire can only be fueled by its own growth, and the growth of the Morgan railroad empire led inevitably to a final conflict with Harriman.

The area of conflict was the north-

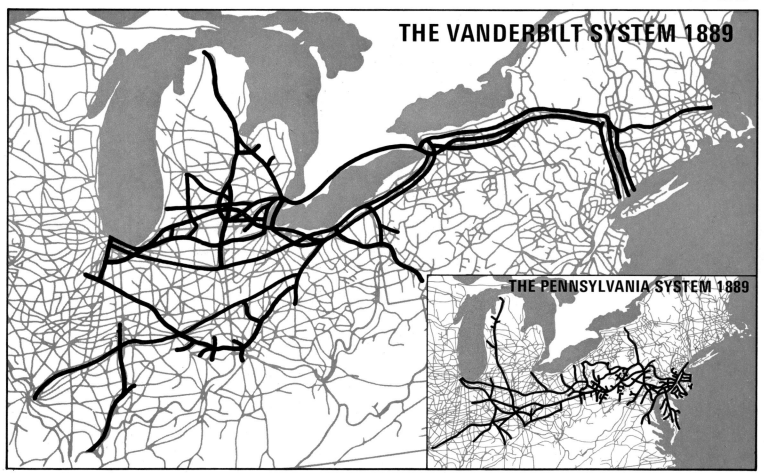

THE VANDERBILT SYSTEM 1889

THE PENNSYLVANIA SYSTEM 1889

By the beginning of the century Edward Harriman was one of the leading railroad operators. At the time the Union Pacific train (below left) was photographed at Genoa, Nebraska, in 1894 the railroad was close to collapse, and the following year Harriman took it over. Under his administration the Union Pacific was transformed into one of the country's most successful railroads, and on the death of Collis Huntington in 1900 he was able to add the Southern Pacific to his other interests. The simultaneous growth of the powerful railroad interests of J. Pierpoint Morgan, in alliance with the northwestern empire of James Hill, represented (below) by a passenger car on the Northern Pacific's North Coast Limited in April 1900 featuring the first electric lights to be used on a northwestern transcontinental train, led to inevitable conflict between the two. The resulting battle for control of the Northern Pacific ended in a national financial panic.

west, where the takeover by James Hill, Morgan's ally, of the Chicago, Burlington and Quincy provoked Harriman, who was also seeking a rail entry into Chicago for his Union Pacific-Southern Pacific system, into a fantastic scheme of his own. Refused a share in the Burlington by Hill, he decided to buy control of the Northern Pacific itself in order to obtain its Burlington holdings.

The resulting battle took on epic

proportions. As the financial might of Morgan and Hill was ranged against that of Harriman and his ally, Rockefeller, outsiders joined in, but their short selling of the soaring Northern Pacific stock backfired when the price kept rising and there was no more stock to buy. The resulting financial panic could only be ended by a truce between the two factions, and eventually a new holding company was established in which both sides had an interest – the Northern Securities Corporation. In the course of the affair Morgan gave the game away with his reply to a reporter who asked for a statement in the public interest, asserting 'I owe the public nothing.'

Meanwhile, the representatives of the public to whom Morgan felt himself under no obligation had made some efforts to impose their own control. Following the Supreme Court's decision of 1886 that states could only regulate rates within their own boundaries, the Interstate Commerce Act was passed by Congress in February 1888. This Act banned pools, discriminatory rates, preferential treatment and the other common abuses, laid down that rates must be 'just and reasonable,' and established the Interstate Commerce Commission to enforce its provisions. But the ICC was virtually devoid of any power to enforce them, and public skepticism was not diminished when 15 of the 16 rate cases in which the Supreme Court adjudicated between the passing of the Act and 1905 went in the railroads' favor.

Governments had been slow to act in other areas of railroad operation too. The standard gauge was not legally established until 1886. The Westinghouse airbrake, which made possible dramatic improvements in efficiency as well as safety, was adopted only slowly; and the universal coupling, another device which was to save the lives of hundreds of railroad brakemen annually, was not made a legal requirement until 1893, when the airbrakes were also made mandatory.

Finally, after the Northern Pacific debacle of 1901 the government was compelled to act. The railroads themselves were ready for legislation by this time, as the years of competition had taken their toll and they were now suffering from the abuses they had imposed on others, with the biggest shippers able to demand covert rebates on the published freight rates. Accordingly, the Elkins Act of 1903 strengthened the Interstate Commerce Act by making any deviation from the published rates illegal, without any need for customers to take court action to prove their case.

The ICC was further strengthened in 1906 by the Hepburn Act, which extended its powers to cover activities of the railroads other than the purely operational, increased the size of the commission, gave it powers to establish maximum rates and made the commission's decisions binding. In 1916 the eight-hour day was made standard.

In 1917 there was more dramatic government intervention. The increased labor costs brought about by the imposition of the eight-hour day, and rates that the ICC had steadfastly refused to increase, brought the entire

system to the brink of collapse as the nation's involvement in the First World War brought record freight movements to the east coast. For just over two years from the end of 1918 the railroads were placed under government control.

Conditions after the First World War, when the railroads were returned to their owners, were to prove very different from the years which had seen their growth. New forms of competition would erode their monopoly of transport, and the quarter of a million miles they reached in 1916 would prove to be a peak from which, slowly and painfully, they would be forced to recede.

The Westinghouse air brake was first fitted to this locomotive of the Pennsylvania in 1869, but was not a legal requirement until 1893.

PRIVATE ENTERPRISE AND PUBLIC SERVICE

By the time the federal government assumed control of the railroads at the end of 1917, the men who had dominated the scene during the years of expansion had gone. Gould, Vanderbilt, Morgan, Jim Hill and Ed Harriman had followed their own visions, looting, empire-building or rationalizing as their tastes dictated, and had left their legacies in the systems they created or destroyed.

Increasing government control in the early years of the new century built on the order that Morgan had sought to impose, as the ICC's powers were extended, but the railroads themselves had welcomed the standardization of rates and had otherwise carried on more or less as they pleased. Traffic, revenue and earnings were more than doubled between 1900 and 1913, but depression in 1913–14 caused a small drop in traffic and a rather larger drop in income: there was still far too much spare capacity and in the two years to 1915 some 15,000 miles of track – about 6 per cent of the total – were in receivership. Too much money had been spent on corporate rearrangement of the kind which saw the Pennsylvania Railroad, acquire large holdings in the Baltimore and Ohio and other northeastern systems, at the expense of track and rolling stock maintenance and replacement, so that the large increase in traffic that followed the outbreak of war in Europe found the railroads unable to cope.

The main symptom of this inability was the breakdown of the system whereby freight cars run over 'foreign' roads were returned to their owners. The massive increase in freight traffic to the northeastern ports was more than the operators in the region could handle, and as the backlog of empty cars grew, the unloading of full cars at New York and New Jersey began to be impeded, while a nationwide shortage of cars increased to alarming proportions. The establishment of the Railroad War Board in 1917 had little effect, and ultimately the government was forced to take over.

The government's conduct of the railroads was subsequently the subject of much controversy. Industry propaganda held that efficiency had deteriorated, that the policy of rerouting traffic from the Pennsylvania and the Baltimore and Ohio onto the New York state trunk routes was misguided, and that railroad property was neglected: the Director General of Railroads contended that efficiency was improved by standardization of operation, and that new equipment purchased and compensation paid to the operators amounted to a large government subsidy.

Whatever the truth of these conflicting claims, price and wage inflation had certainly taken their toll, as a doubling of operating revenue to six billion dollars between 1914 and 1920 was accompanied by a fall in the associated net income from $500,000,000 to only one-fifth of that amount. Consequently, the Transportation Act of 1920, by which the railroads were returned to their prewar ownership, included provision for low-interest federal loans and

By the beginning of the twentieth century the railroads' provision of facilities for passengers included every modern convenience, such as the vacuum cleaner and telephone exhibited (below) in the observation car of the Oriental Limited. Washing facilities were standard on long-distance journeys, as in the scene on a Santa Fe express (opposite) at the turn of the century, though not all trips can have been quite as jolly as that being enjoyed by the ladies (opposite, below) on the same railroad a few years later.

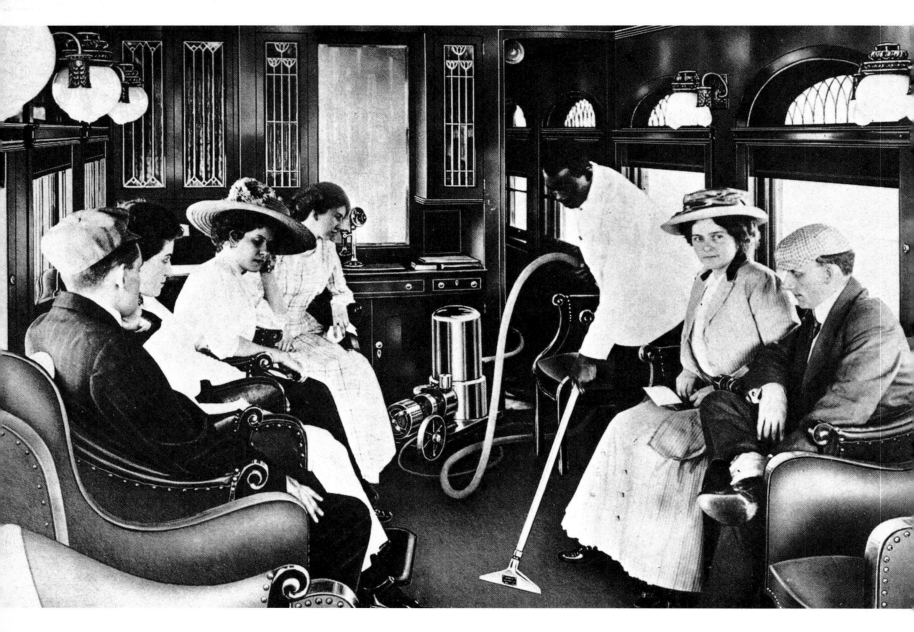

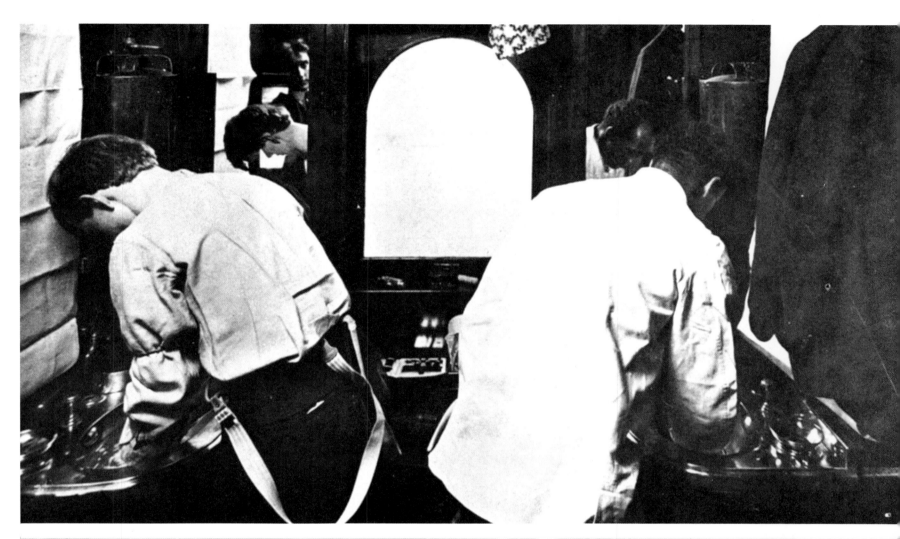

grants to be made available.

At the same time, the Act required the Interstate Commerce Commission to prepare a scheme for consolidation of the railroad network. Unfortunately, the plan was obliged to provide for the retention of existing routes, the maintenance of competition and preservation of uniform rates, and the ICC was given no power to enforce any merger it considered desirable, but allowed only to withhold its approval. Effectively, it was being asked to design a competitive system to be operated under monopoly conditions and to implement it with no instrument but a veto on mergers. The result was that the ICC was restricted to maintaining the status quo.

In fact, the ICC produced a plan along the lines laid down by Congress, but this was opposed successfully by the railroads, who then embarked on a process of consolidation, often by financial arrangements that avoided the outright mergers which the commission had the power to block. In the northeast, for example, the ICC wanted to set up a fifth trunk route by re-arranging elements of the existing Pennsylvania, New York Central, Baltimore and Ohio and Erie systems with a consolidation of the Delaware, Lackawanna and Western and the Nickel Plate roads so as to establish a balance of power between the five. the Penn and the NYC, which stood to lose most under this plan, managed to block it, but then failed to agree on an alternative scheme of their own.

Meanwhile the Van Swerigen brothers of Cleveland had acquired a series of railroads, including the Nickel Plate in 1916 and the Erie in 1923, while in 1924 the Pennsylvania bought a controlling interest in the Norfolk and Western, a big coal carrier based on Roanoke, Virginia. The Pennsylvania went on to gain majorities in the stock of the Lehigh Valley, the Wabash and the Boston and Maine. This use of holding companies to circumvent ICC regulations was imitated by the Van Swerigens, who used their Allegheny Corporation to build up a 30,000 mile system, and in fact became so popular that holding companies organized by the eastern trunk lines spent over

(Previous page) Missouri Pacific operations during and after the Second World War: a passenger train out of Little Rock, Arkansas in 1943, and a freight train in 1947 headed by locomotive No. 2118.

Two K4 Pacifics head the Pennsylvania Railroad's Rainbow Limited out of Canton, Ohio. First built in 1914, the K4s served through the boom years of the 1920s, and the depression of the next decade extended their careers until 1942.

The war brought a new period of booming business to the railroads, though the legacy of the 1930s, when expenditure on new equipment had been drastically curtailed, found many companies struggling to cope with the increase in traffic. One exception to this rule was the New York Central, whose streamlined 4-6-4 Hudsons hauled the 1000-ton Twentieth Century Limited on the four-track main line alongside the Hudson at average speeds of over 80 mph, covering the 930 miles between Harmon, New York, and Chicago in only 16 hours.

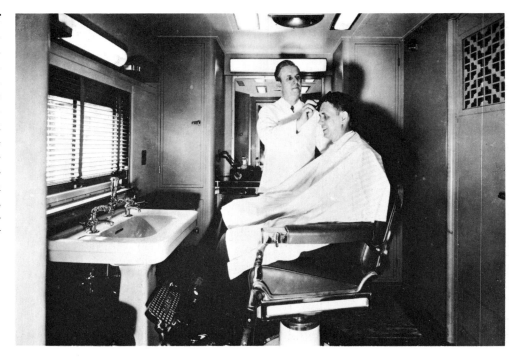

New York departure point for the Twentieth Century Limited was Grand Central Station, and the upper concourse (left) provided a suitably magnificent setting for the start of long-distance journeys. A lower concourse catered for suburban traffic. During the 1920s, when riding the Century was the ultimate in travel, the three sections would move out from adjacent platforms with their tail observation cars exactly in line, before taking up their positions in sequence in the tunnel. However, after the Second World War, even the attractions of onboard barber shop (opposite), secretary, telephone and other facilities could not halt the decline in traffic as competition from the airlines grew and comfort lost out to sheer speed of travel.

$300,000,000 on such activities in only eighteen months during 1928–29.

By now it was obvious, as even the president of the Baltimore and Ohio admitted to a commission member, that the situation was beyond the ICC's control. The railroads had benefited to such an extent from the general economic boom of the 1920s that the difficulties that had seemed so alarming in 1920 were forgotten, their existence masked by the general growth in traffic. Although route mileage declined slightly from its 1916 peak, track mileage increased by some 100,000 miles to reach 360,000 miles in 1928; and the railroads, though now acting corporately rather than – with the exception of the Van Swerigen operation – under the control of powerful individuals, appeared to return to the kind of anarchic power struggles that had caused such fatal weakness in the past.

A 'final' plan for the region, produced in 1929, took into account the mergers of the previous few years, and in consequence was unable to devise a viable fifth trunk system. In any case, the depression of the 1930s was to make such plans redundant. Revenues in 1930 were down 15 per cent on the year before, and by 1932 were down to half their 1929 level. The number of passenger miles had already dropped by a third from their 1920 level of 45 billion by 1928, largely as a consequence of the 15 million Model Ts that Ford had by then produced, and there were further large falls to come.

The railroads reacted with reductions in wages, numbers of employees and dividends; the government reacted with the National Transportation Committee, formed in 1932, which recommended co-operation to eliminate wasteful competition. In 1933, the new Roosevelt administration produced the Emergency Transportation Act, which endorsed the NTC's recommendations and called for eastern, western and southern co-ordinating committees to help a Federal Transport Commissioner carry them out, though at the same time it limited reductions in the workforce. In 1934 another important step was taken with the formation of the Association of American Railroads to act as a national policy-making body for the industry.

The AAR and the ICC soon reached agreement on a number of measures in what had become, for many railroads, a virtual struggle for existence: traffic continued to decline, and by July 1938 no less than 39 major roads, represent-

Steam on the Chesapeake and Ohio in the 1940s: an L2 Hudson ready to leave Cincinnati Union Terminal with the George Washington, and (inset) a 2-6-6-6 Mallet with a coal train at Allegheny Summit, West Virginia.

The introduction of streamlined trains in the late 1930s saw new standards of speed and comfort established. The Milwaukee Road's F7-class 4-6-4, introduced in 1938 and shown (below) with the Hiawatha leaving Chicago for Milwaukee in August 1941, could reach 120 mph with the 12-car Hiawatha trains on level stretches, and would have been able to complete the journey in only 60 minutes; but the competing Chicago and North Western and Burlington Route could not match such a pace, and the scheduled time was held at 75 minutes. By 1948 diesels had taken over the Hiawatha services, though the distinctive observation car at the tail (right) remained.

ing over a quarter of total mileage, were in receivership, the Van Swerigen empire having been among the first casualties.

One of the ICC's first moves in response to AAR recommendations was to bring interstate road traffic under its control, although the further acceptance of rates parity was to prove something of a two-edged sword, having the effect, in many instances, of limiting the railroads' competitiveness. There were also relaxations of the railroads' debt obligations, federal loans and widespread rejection of calls for public ownership.

Reeling out of the 1930s, the railroads were greeted with a new Transportation Act in 1940, and this went even further toward meeting their demands. The land-grant railroads' long-standing obligation to carry government traffic at reduced rates was abolished; water transport was added to the ICC's responsibilities; and a commitment was announced to a national noncompetitive transport policy, though almost in the same breath the new Act called for the preservation of inherent advantages in the various modes of transport. The 1940 Act also established new criteria for ICC approval of mergers – essentially consideration of both the public interest and the resulting debt position of the railroads involved.

Undoubtedly, a principal reason for the lenient treatment of the railroads in

1940 was anxiety over the war that was erupting round the globe, and the recognition of the need for a strong rail network should the United States become involved. Sure enough, by the end of 1941 the railroads were once again a vital part of a war effort. This time, apart from a token three-week nationalization at the end of 1944 to head off labor trouble, the railroads responded with a highly creditable display of co-operation with the Office of Defense Transportation that made the drastic action of 1917 unnecessary; and the two-way movement of war material and personnel helped avoid the crippling congestion at the ports that had been the trouble on the earlier occasion.

Moreover, the railroads showed sound financial judgement by applying the increased profits generated by the war traffic boom to reducing the fixed charges for interest on debts rather than squandering them on bumper dividends. The burden of debt had been a fetter on the railroads' financial freedom almost since their inception, and whereas formerly debts had been regarded as permanent fixtures, a concerted drive towards repayment saw annual fixed charges reduced by some $80,000,000 between 1940 and 1945. This was to stand them in good stead in the postwar years, when their improved credit enabled them to raise, without too much trouble, the two billion dollars that would be needed to finance the

By the start of the 1950s the postwar slump in passenger traffic was reaching alarming proportions, though freight continued to provide heavy traffic, and while the diesel takeover was well under way, some of the last great steam locomotives were still at work. The Norfolk and Western's J-class 4-8-4s, such as the example shown above with the Powhatan Arrow in September 1951, were the most powerful of their type, and on test recorded a speed of 110 mph.

wholesale dieselization that was found desirable.

Unfortunately, other factors in the postwar years were less favorable. By 1946 income was already 10 per cent down on that of 1944, and passenger traffic had embarked on a spectacular decline. By 1950 the railroads' share of intercity passenger milage was under 50 per cent of the national total, with buses taking nearly 40 per cent, but the buses' share also declined from that point. By 1960 buses and trains carried slightly over one-quarter each, as the airlines' share rose to over 40 per cent, and in 1970 the airlines took over three-quarters of the total. After the drastic reduction in passenger services in the early 1970s even private aircraft recor-

A Baltimore and Ohio streamlined President-class Pacific with the Cincinnatian at Athens, Ohio.

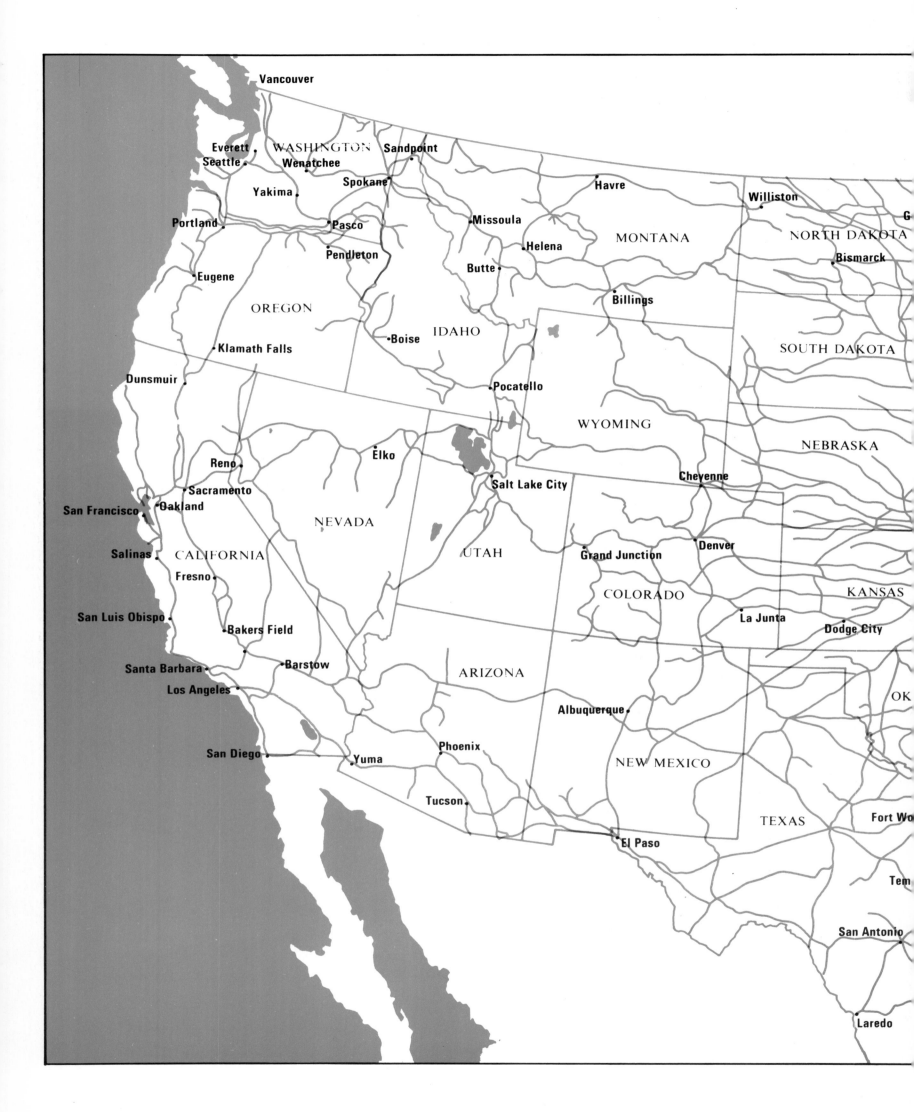

UNITED STATES RAILROADS POST WORLD WAR I

MAINE

MINNESOTA

Duluth/Superior

Cloud·

WISCONSIN

Minneapolis

Madison

Dubuque

Milwaukee

IOWA

Rock Island

Galesburg

Chicago

·Quincy

ILLINOIS

Springfield

Effingham

St. Louis

Kansas City

Jefferson City

MISSOURI

Poplar Bluff

ARKANSAS

·City

Little Rock

Texarkana

LOUISIANA

Baton Rouge

·Houston

New Orleans

MICHIGAN

·Port Huron

Detroit

Cleveland

Toledo

Ft. Wayne

OHIO

Pittsburg

Muncie

·Columbus

Indianapolis

INDIANA

Cincinnati

WEST
VIRGINIA

Charleston

Louisville

KENTUCKY

Charlottesville

VIRGINIA

Nashville

Raleigh·

TENNESSEE

NORTH CAROLINA

Charlotte·

Fayetteville

Greenville·

SOUTH
CAROLINA

·Memphis

Columbia

·Charleston

ALABAMA

Atlanta

Augusta

Birmingham

GEORGIA

·Savannah

MISSISSIPPI

Montgomery

Jackson

PENNSYLVANIA

Harrisburg

NEW JERSEY

Philadelphia

·Baltimore

DELAWARE

Washington

MARYLAND

·Richmond

·Newport News

Norfolk

Charlottesville

Rochester

Syracuse

VERMONT

NEW HAMPSHIRE

Boston

NEW YORK

Albany

MASS.

Buffalo

CONN.

Providence

RHODE ISLAND

New Haven

New York

Jacksonville

Tampa·

FLORIDA

·Palm Beach

·Miami

87

Mobilization of the armed forces for action in both Europe and the Pacific relied heavily on the railroads for transporting servicemen between training camps and embarkation points. G.I.s parade in front of a Union Pacific train (right), and new arrivals on a Santa Fe troop train at Los Angeles (above).

ded a higher number of passenger miles than the railroads could manage. Of course, all forms of public intercity transport had been overtaken by private automobiles in the 1920s, and all forms of public transport combined accounted for only 13 per cent of the total by the mid-1970s.

Freight traffic over the same period showed a steady decline taken as a percentage of the total. From nearly 70 per cent in 1944 it fell to 56 per cent in 1950, 44 per cent in 1960 and under 40 per cent during the 1970s, as trucks took over one-fifth from 1960, canals and rivers carried over 10 per cent by 1970 and oil pipelines increased their share to nearly a quarter. Actual tonnage was up slightly on the 1944 level in the mid-1970s, but the overall total had doubled during the period.

Faced with such trends, there was a limit to what the railroads could do. The introduction of diesel power increased efficiency but incurred massive capital

outlay. Mechanization and automation also promise improvements in operating efficiency, but again the initial costs are simply too high for many railroads. Diversification into other areas of activity has also provided a lifeline for some railroads, but unsuccessful business ventures can add to existing problems.

The reaction in many of the troubled railroads was a resurgence of the old tendency toward merger and consolidation. Of course, ICC approval was still required, and mere enhancement of individual roads' chances of survival is still not a valid criterion for that approval. Nevertheless, a number of mergers have been accomplished with successful results.

In 1959, the Norfolk and Western merged with the Virginian in a union of two coal carriers that brought complementary track layouts together. The 1960 combination of the Erie and Delaware with the Lackawanna and Western allowed some duplicated track

to be eliminated, but early results of the new Erie-Lackawanna were even worse than the pair's total pre-merger losses. On a larger scale, the Chesapeake and Ohio's takeover of the Baltimore and Ohio produced another big coal-carrying system reaching from Chesapeake Bay to the Great Lakes, and via the C & O's earlier acquisition of the Père Marquette into Canada. In 1967 the Seaboard Air Line and Atlantic Coast Line merged their east coast systems to produce the Seaboard Coast Line; and the subsequent acquisition of the Louisville and Nashville, and the lease of some other southern railroads extended the network of the new Family Lines System from Miami and Washington, D.C., in the east, to New Orleans, Memphis, St Louis and Chicago.

NYC's Niagara-class 4-8-4s attempted the highest possible use of steam locomotives.

The Union Pacific's contemporary 815-class 4-8-4s (below) were introduced for fast passenger services in 1937, but by 1952 were working freight trains.

The most surprising of the mergers, however, was undoubtedly that of the old rivals, the Pennsylvania and the New York Central in 1968. Unfortunately, the persistence of corporate hostility and the dissipation of the resulting savings found the new Penn-Central running out of credit only two years later. It was followed into insolvency by the Ann Arbor, the Boston and Maine, the Erie-Lackawanna, the Lehigh Valley, the Central of New Jersey and the Reading, all suffering more or less from the steep decline in coal traffic in New York.

The bankruptcy of virtually the whole northeastern rail network called for drastic government action, and this came in the form of the 1973 Rail Reorganization Act. The RRA established the United States Railroad Assocation as a fully representative body to plan the rationalized network that the ICC had been prevented from implementing

fifty years earlier, and the Consolidated Rail Corporation, or Conrail, to administer the resulting system. When Conrail began operations with a six billion dollar subsidy in 1976, it was the second biggest in the country, but before the decade was out it was asking for more government money to help it cope with the perennial problems of dilapidated equipment and crippling overheads, made worse by the remarkable severity of the winter weather twice in the late 1970s.

Nor was Conrail the first section of the industry to be bailed out by the government. The collapse of intercity services by the end of the 1960s led to a drastic federal operation whereby the remaining intercity passenger operators were given the option of handing over their passenger rolling stock and motive power, plus a cash forfeit based on a forecast of their losses, to a new National Railroad Passenger Cor-

poration, operating under the name Amtrak. If they preferred to carry on with their passenger services, they were bound to maintain them for at least two years. The only notable exceptions to the general acceptance of the offer were the Southern's 'Southern Crescent' Washington-Atlanta-New Orleans service and the Denver and Rio Grande Western's 'Zephyr'; and in 1979 the Southern, faced with annual losses approaching $7,000,000 gave in.

Amtrak was faced with a host of problems. Its antiquated stock, and the absence of any newer models of coach due to the lack of demand, had to be run over track which it did not control. With mounting losses, its future looked bleak until the gasoline shortages in 1979 induced Congress to substitute a 50 per cent increase in subsidy for President Carter's proposed cuts in both cash and services. Progress made in modernizing the northeast corridor route be-

tween Boston and Washington, which Conrail was made to hand over, and some impressive new rolling stock designs point to an interesting future.

Meanwhile, the more conventional mergers continued through the 1970s. The first year of the decade saw the logical consolidation of Jim Hill's old empire in the northwest as the Chicago, Burlington and Quincy, the Great Northern, the Northern Pacific and the Spokane, Portland and Seattle combined to form the Burlington Northern, the biggest network in the country. Elsewhere, grass was growing in the tracks of the Milwaukee Road and the Rock Island line, as the ICC vetoed their proposed mergers with Union Pacific and Chicago and North Western respectively. Suggestions for the creation of a western version of Conrail were ruled out by the potential cost to the government, leaving the ICC to adjudicate on the Southern Pacific's at-

tempts to buy the New Mexico-St Louis section of the Rock Island in the face of objections from the Santa Fe.

Even bigger deals awaited ICC decisions at the end of the decade, as the Chessie System – the old Chesapeake and Ohio – proposed to merge with the Family Lines, and the Union Pacific, Missouri Pacific and Western Pacific became embroiled in merger discussions.

The perennial problems are to balance the legitimate expectations of private enterprise with justifiable demands made on a massive industry (constituting a vital element of the nation's economic life) that grew up in anarchy and has had to live with unpredictable demands and sporadic, unco-ordinated policy decisions. These problems appear to be as far from solution as ever.

The example of the Union Pacific, once thought beyond salvation but now

a glittering example of efficiency and success, can be of little comfort to struggling managements. The UP's outside interests in such resources as coal and oil, which are not only profitable in themselves but provide profitable traffic for its modern railroad, have not proved readily capable of duplication; and the investment required to bring less prosperous roads up to the standard of the UP, with its exemplary track, computer train control and up-to-date motive power and rolling stock, are probably beyond the means of any but a national agency.

The westbound Empire Builder leaves Minneapolis for Seattle, and the North Coast Hiawatha (inset) at Chicago in the 1970s.

CANADIAN RAILWAYS

Although development of railways north of the United States border was relatively slow to get under way, reflecting the sparsity of population and the ready availability of water transport routes, the first railroad was chartered as early as 1832. Built as a short cut between the Richelieu river at St Johns and Laprairie, across the St Lawrence from Montreal, the 14½ mile Champlain and St Lawrence Railroad clipped 90 miles off the river route between Lake Champlain and Montreal, which was then the main artery of communications between New England and the principal city of Lower Canada.

Services began on July 21, 1836, when a Stephenson 'Samson' type locomotive took an hour each way to haul two coaches on a round trip from Laprairie. As an adjunct to the river traffic, the Champlain and St Lawrence in its early years suspended operations when the rivers froze in winter, and did not begin year-round services until 1851, when an extension was completed to Rouses Point, in New York State. This connected with local US lines to give through communications to Boston and New England.

Meanwhile, other short railroads were built to bridge gaps in the river network. The Montreal and Lachine Railroad began operations in November 1848 between Montreal and the head of the Lachine rapids, where the river route to the west started, and in 1850 the small town of Industrie (now Joliette) was provided with a rail link to the St Lawrence. The 12½-mile Carillon and Grenville Railway was built round a stretch of rapids on the Ottawa river in 1854, and the following year the Northern Railway reached Collingwood, on Lake Huron's Georgian Bay, from its starting point at Toronto, on Lake Ontario.

Many similar short railroads were built and operated successfully in the nineteenth century, but a number of more ambitious schemes were hindered by administrative confusion in what were then the disparate colonies of British North America. Some resulted in small but worthwhile sections of the planned lines being built, such as that between Halifax and Truro, in Nova Scotia, completed in 1853. But the most significant was the line from Longeuil, opposite Montreal on the St Lawrence, to Portland, on the coast of Maine. The Canadian section, the St Lawrence and Atlantic, combined with the US Atlantic and St Lawrence in 1853 to enable connection between Montreal and the sea to be maintained when the port was frozen in winter; it also gave rise to the

Opening of the line from Laprairie to St Johns, the first in Canada, on July 21, 1836.

Guarantee Act of 1849, by which the government of Canada first provided assistance for railroad construction.

One new line which was quick to benefit from this provision was the Great Western Railway, which by 1856 linked Niagara Falls and its suspension bridge connection to Buffalo with both Toronto and Windsor, where another bridge link was made with Detroit.

A further source of finance was Great Britain, and in 1852 the Canadian government authorized a British company to build the Grand Trunk Railway. By 1860 the Grand Trunk, with the famous Victoria Bridge at Montreal giving connection with the St Lawrence and Atlantic and a new line to Riviere du Loup, stretched west via Toronto and

Stratford to Sarnia, and then on US soil from Port Huron to Detroit. A 999-year lease of the Atlantic and St Lawrence extended the Grand Trunk to Portland, but this impressive creation of a unified 800 mile route from the Atlantic coast to the Great Lakes was achieved in circumstances that were to have unfortunate consequences.

In 1845 a Royal Commission on railways was given as one of its tasks the establishment of a standard gauge to be adopted, and while this showed commendable foresight, considering the many years during which competing gauges were allowed elsewhere, the selection of the St Lawrence and Atlantic's 5 ft 6 in was not the happiest of choices. The Grand Trunk, the Great

Western – which had planned to use the 4 ft 8½ in standard gauge in anticipation of the crossborder traffic it hoped to attract from the standard gauge US railroads at Detroit and Buffalo – and indeed all Canadian railways more than 75 miles long, were obliged to build to the new provincial gauge, which remained in use for twenty years.

The next great rail project was the Intercolonial Railway, the trunk line between Halifax and Quebec that had first been mooted in 1832. But the settlement of the border dispute with the United States in 1842 placed the

Early communications in Canada were by water: a scene on the St Lawrence Canal in 1781.

ANN AND JANE

J.D.Kelly

intended route across the northern extension of the states of Maine, which blocked the scheme for some years. The desirability of uniting the separate colonies became urgency with the outbreak of the Civil War south of the border and the possibility of Britain and her colonies becoming involved.

In October 1863 Sandford Fleming was appointed to build the railway, and early in 1865 he completed his survey. The route selected ran from the northern end of the Grand Trunk at Riviere du Loup along the St Lawrence before turning southwest through the Matapedia valley to the Bay Chaleur and on to Moncton, where a branch from Saint John joined the main line continuation to Truro and the existing railroad to Halifax.

The provision of a rail link between the maritime provinces and Quebec and Ontario, as Upper and Lower Canada were named, was embodied in the British North America Act of 1867 which confederated the separate provinces into the Dominion of Canada; and as chief engineer of the project Fleming produced a railway built to the highest standard.

In 1873 Prince Edward Island, which had declined to become involved in the federation, objecting to the cost of the Intercolonial Railway, agreed to join, after an ill-fated attempt at providing its own rail system. Its railways were taken over by the government and connected with the mainland system by train ferry.

By the time the Intercolonial was completed, on July 1, 1876, a much greater project was under way. In 1869 the large area to the west was formally handed over by the Hudson's Bay Company, and in 1871 the western colony of

The International Bridge over the Niagara River, built by the Great Western Railway and opened for rail traffic in 1855. This photograph was taken from the river bank in 1859.

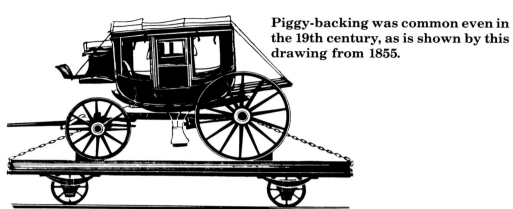

Piggy-backing was common even in the 19th century, as is shown by this drawing from 1855.

The St. Lawrence River and the Grand Trunk Railway's Victoria Bridge at Montreal in 1859, the year in which the bridge was opened.

Scenes on the Great Western Railway of Canada in 1859: a three-tier sleeping car (right), a train crossing the Niagara suspension bridge (far right), and the 4-4-0 locomotive *Essex* from the period when the 5 ft 6 in gauge was in force on Canadian railways.

British Columbia agreed to become part of the confederation. Its agreement, however, was conditional on a railway being built to connect the new western province with the existing eastern provinces, and it was stipulated that work should begin within two years and be completed within ten.

In July 1872 Sandford Fleming set off to begin his survey of the vast and almost uninhabited area. The detailed surveys that began the following year and continued for most of the decade ultimately employed more than 2000 men. The terrain was divided into three regions, the wooded country west of Lake Superior, the prairies, and the mountain ranges in the far west; and the route finally selected by Fleming in 1878 followed the northern shore of Lake Superior, headed across the prairies by way of Edmonton to the Yellowhead Pass, and reached the site of Vancouver on Burrard Inlet via the Thompson and Fraser river valleys.

At the same time, the question of who was to build the railroad had to be settled. In 1872 it was decided that the work should be entrusted to private enterprise, and two companies were

Below:
The Honourable John Ross, first president of the Grand Trunk

Right:
Officials and staff of the Grand Trunk Railway pose with a coal-fired No. 377. Passenger trains no longer stop at Grafton (inset) as their predecessors did in 1858.

GRAND TRUNK RAILWAY.

(T.)
(40.)
No. 480

Good for   First Class   Sept   13   1858.
"   Second "   Full Fares, $ 2 5 8
"   Third "
"   1858.
"   lbs. Extra Baggage
TORONTO To
AMOUNT $ 2 5 8   Agent.

granted charters, the Interoceanic and the Canada Pacific; but in 1873 the government was forced to resign over a political scandal involving attempts to merge the companies.

Although the completion of a line from Emerson, on the US border, gave Winnipeg an indirect connection with eastern Canada over US lines to Chicago, the rest of the decade saw little progress on the transcontinental line. In 1880, however, with agitation south of the border for annexation of the prairies adding urgency to the question, George Stephen was induced to become involved in the formation of a new syndicate to take over the affair. In February 1881 the Canadian Pacific Railway Company was incorporated, with Stephen as president. James J. Hill, subsequent creator of the Great Northern railroad in the United States, was an early member of the board, and although he left over the decision to follow the route north of Lake Superior rather than build via Sault Ste Marie and across the northern United States, Hill made a major contribution to the Canadian Pacific before his departure by employing William Van Horne as general manager.

Horne had served previously with the Illinois Central and the Chicago, Milwaukee and St Paul, leaving the latter to join the new enterprise at the beginning of 1882. With George Stephen, formerly president of the Bank of Montreal, in charge of the company's finances and Van Horne responsible for construction, work was started in 1882. A government grant of 25,000,000 acres of land and the same number of dollars, plus some short sections of rail that had already been laid, formed the foundation for the Canadian Pacific; and despite fantastic difficulty, not only in crossing the Rockies but, even worse, in traversing the nightmare combination of solid rock and rail-swallowing swamp around the top of Lake Superior, the first trains reached Calgary in August 1883.

This more southerly route had been chosen for the Canadian Pacific to counter anxieties over competition from American railroads then under way across the northwestern states. In order to reach Vancouver from Calgary, the line was forced to cross the Rockies via

The use of the completed sections of the Canadian Pacific north of Lake Superior to transport troops to counter the prairie rebellion of 1885 (top left) helped secure government aid for the project. The last spike is driven to complete the route (left) on November 7, 1885, and in June 1886 (top right) the first transcontinental train reaches Port Arthur.

Previous page:
A Canadian Pacific passenger train from Nakusp, British Columbia, arriving at Rosebery on Slocan lake and a rendezvous with the steamer *Slocan*.

The heavily-decorated Ocean to Ocean Special, the first train to arrive at Canadian Pacific's new Vancouver terminus on May 28, 1887.

(Inset) Sandford Fleming, who undertook the first survey for the Intercolonial Railway.

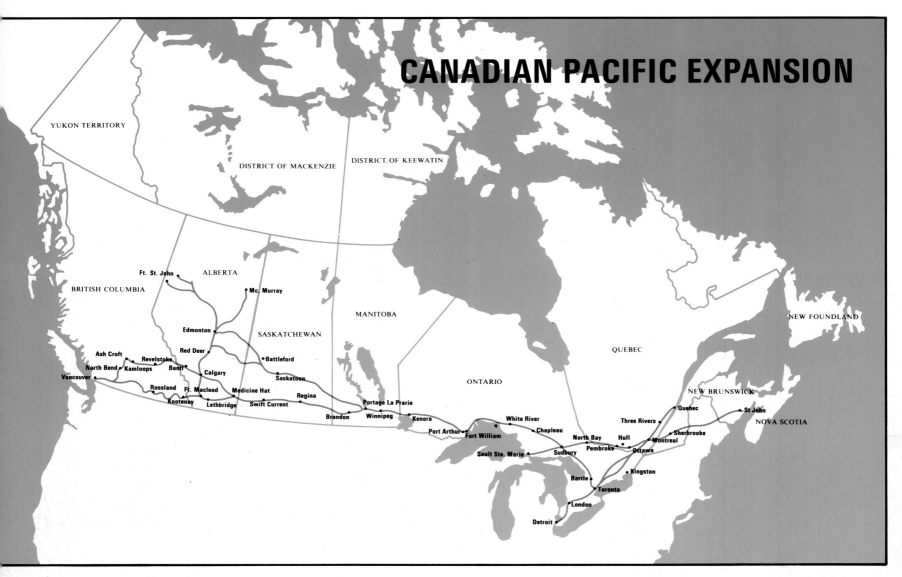

CANADIAN PACIFIC EXPANSION

Kicking Horse Pass, using grades as steep as 4.4 per cent. Continuing difficulties with the mountain and Lake Superior sections were compounded in 1884 by shortages of funds, but in the spring of 1885 the government was persuaded to lend the company assistance after the successful use of the completed sections in conveying government forces to Winnipeg to counter a rebellion in the area. As a result, the ceremonial last spike was driven on November 8, 1885, and by the following June the first scheduled through trains were running from Montreal to Port Moody, a few miles short of Vancouver, which was reached in 1887.

The completion of the first line to the Pacific provided the stimulus for rapid development of the Canadian rail network, spearheaded by the expansion of the Canadian Pacific itself. Rivalry between Montreal and Toronto had caused the government to stipulate a 'neutral' starting point for the CP at the eastern end of Lake Nipissing, on the old canoe route along the Ottawa river. The CP had already bought an existing line along the Ottawa valley to connect it with Montreal, and it soon acquired various other small railroads to extend its operations to Toronto and Quebec, and completed a branch to Sault Ste Marie in 1888. This extension was complemented by traffic agreements with

the Minneapolis and St Paul and the Duluth, South Shore and Atlantic railroads as a protective measure against competition from Jim Hill's spreading northern network. East of the St Lawrence, the system was extended to Saint John, New Brunswick, in 1889 by the direct route across Maine formed from an extension of the South Eastern Railway to Mattawamkeag and a junction with the Maine Central Railroad. The New Brunswick Railway system, which formed the final link to Saint John, was leased by Canadian Pacific the following year.

In the 1890s, two former CP employees, William McKenzie and Donald Mann set up as builders in their own right. In 1896 they began constructing the Lake Manitoba railway up the western side of the lake, gradually extending it to Winnipegosis with the help of Federal land and provincial finance. Changing the name to Canadian Northern Railway in 1899, McKenzie and Mann expanded by takeover and extension, gaining connections to Winnipeg, the US border and Port Arthur on Lake Superior. They continued to build up their system by economical construction and shrewd acquisitions, until by 1905 their network stretched from Edmonton, in Alberta, through Winnepeg to Lake Superior, with further small sections in the vicinity of

The original Canadian Pacific transcontinental route through Kicking Horse Pass.

Montreal and Quebec.

By this time their ambitions had expanded to a transcontinental railroad of their own, and over the next seven years they built extensions along Sandford Fleming's Yellowhead Pass route to Vancouver, and in a wide loop round the top of Lake Superior to Sudbury and Toronto. In 1916 passenger services were inaugurated between Quebec and Vancouver, while an electrified tunnel under Mount Royal gave access to a new terminus in Montreal and in the east the system was extended in Nova Scotia.

At the same time, the British-based Grand Trunk Railway was concentrating on building up its network and improving its connections with the United States. A new bridge at Niagara Falls was opened in 1897, while the Victoria Bridge was given a new steel truss superstructure to accommodate the additional traffic generated by the addition to the Grand Trunk's ranks of the Central Vermont Railway to New London, on the coast of Connecticut.

The resultant stretching of the company's finances led to the recruitment from the Wabash Railroad of Charles Hayes, who reorganized its affairs, linking its operations with those of the

114

Wabash. The influx of immigrants to Canada in the early years of the twentieth century induced Hayes to set about the construction of a third transcontinental railroad, and the Grand Trunk Pacific was established to carry out the work. In 1903 it reached an agreement with the government on a National Transcontinental Railway, under the terms of which the government was to build a line from Moncton, in New Brunswick, more or less straight across Quebec and Ontario to Winnipeg. This was then to be leased to the Grand Trunk Pacific, which would in turn build its own line from the Manitoba capital to the Pacific coast of British Columbia.

Not only was the government line planned to the highest standards of alignment and grading, it was also routed through a vast tract of unsurveyed and virtually uninhabited terrain, while the GTP across the prairies was frequently mere duplication of the existing Canadian Pacific and the Canadian Northern's westward extension. Moreover, the intention to attract traffic in grain way from the waterways onto the new rails for shipment to the Atlantic ports was somewhat betrayed by the first stage of building from Port Arthur, at the head of Lake Superior, and the start of grain traffic to the port in 1910: and at its western end the Grand Trunk Pacific spurned the existing shipping centre of the Puget Sound in favor of an ambitious plan for the entirely new port of Prince Rupert to be established at a site near Port Simpson, 550 miles north of Vancouver at the mouth of the Skeena river.

Still, the new railroad avoided both

A CP Rail mixed freight train negotiates the spiral tunnels on the Kicking Horse Pass section.

The *Dominion*, Canadian Pacific's transcontinental train, headed by a Selkirk 2-10-4 alongside the Bow River in the Rocky Mountains.

Left: Westbound train No. 11 at Calgary Alberta – then the Northwest Territories – in 1884, shortly after the inauguration of services to the city.

Below: D9c class 4-6-0 locomotive No. 579 at the head of the Canadian Pacific's Trans-Canada Limited near Lake Louise, Alberta, in the early 1920s.

Above: A turn-of-the-century scene at Hamilton, Ontario, with a passenger train halted at the Toronto, Buffalo and Lake Huron Railway station.

Left: May 1905: employees of the Toronto, Hamilton and Buffalo Railway, operated jointly by CP and the New York Central until the latter's bankruptcy.

Below: Front and back covers of a pocket time card issued by the Western Division of Canadian Pacific and showing the services in effect from July 3, 1886.

the Kicking Horse Pass route and the muskeg around Lake Superior that had proved such obstacles to the Canadian Pacific; and with steamers ferrying supplies to Prince Rupert and a combined work force that reached 25,000 men, the western section was completed in April 1914, and the National transcontinental line to the east was ready for service the following year.

At this point the Grand Trunk, whose agreement to operate the government-built line required an annual rental of three per cent of construction costs, showed alarm at the final cost of $150,000,000; three times the forecast and with the war in Europe taking its toll of both immigration and investment, it decided that operation of both the Grand Trunk Pacific and the National Transcontinental were beyond its means. At the same time, the Canadian Northern found itself unable to meet the operational and equipment expenses of its transcontiental line.

The Royal Commission appointed in 1916 to investigate the affairs of the two companies recommended that the Grand Trunk, Grand Trunk Pacific and Canadian Northern Railways should be brought under government control. Investigation of their finances revealed a tangled situation that took some years to sort out, but in 1918 the Canadian National Railway Company was formed to carry out the Royal Commission's recommendations.

Canadian National took over the existing publicly-owned railways and the newly-formed Canadian Northern. The

Grand Trunk Pacific was added in 1920, and the parent company followed in 1923. By then, a new board had been formed under Sir Henry Thornton, an American who began his railroad career on the Pennsylvania Railroad, went on to be general superintendent of the Long Island Railroad and until his Canadian appointment was general manager of a British railway, the Great Eastern; in addition to holding this latter post during the First World War, he had acted as his own company's chief engineer and served as Director of Railway Transport in France.

With the benefit of such varied experience, Thornton set about the task of not only uniting a series of separate railway operations, but also coping with their extensive and intricate financial arrangements, having been guaranteed a free hand by the government, provided outstanding commitments were honored. Many of the lines under his control were in need of major improvements in order to bring them up to scratch, but during the ten years of his presidency and chairmanship Canadian National was turned into a sound operational system. As well as

Canadian Pacific passenger services in the early years of the twentieth century: 4-6-0 locomotive No 626, train and crew at the old Toronto Union Station in 1900 (opposite, top); passengers boarding in about 1910 (opposite); and the scene inside a dining car of the 1920s (above).

Construction work on the entrance to the Canadian Pacific's Connaught Tunnel. This tunnel was brought into use in 1916 to eliminate the final stages of the climb to the summit of Rogers Pass, which originally involved 17 miles of grades of over 2%.

Top left: Among the attractions for travellers on Canadian Pacific were the hotels such as the Banff Springs Hotel in Alberta, seen here in the late 1920s.

Above: Golf is the attraction offered in this list of Canadian Pacific hotels, reverse of the Chateau Lake Louise lunch menu for June 7, 1919.

Top: Dining car on the train used by King George VI and Queen Elizabeth for the royal tour of Canada during the spring and early summer of 1939.

Above: Observation car of the train used by the royal party for their tour.

Above: One of the 2800 Class 4-6-4 Hudson locomotives introduced in 1928 and used to haul the transcontinental passenger expresses at an average 33 mph.

Left: Canadian Pacific locomotive No. 209, an Atlantic type 4-4-2.

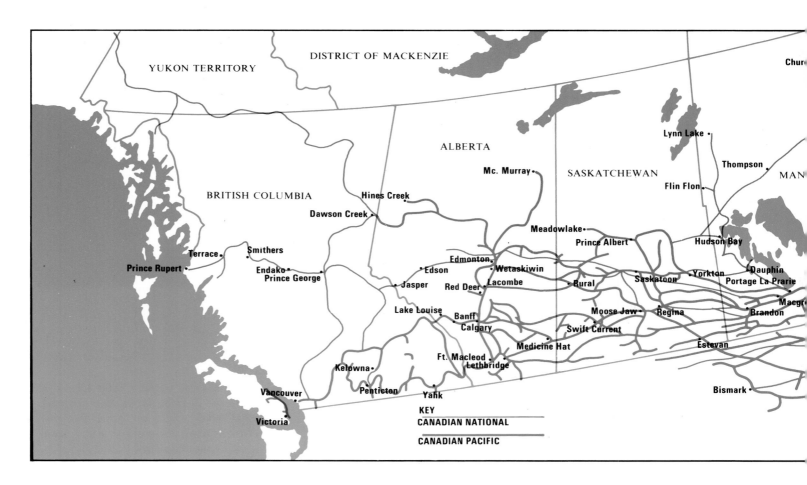

The current network of Canadian National and Canadian Pacific railways main lines.

rationalizing and improving the existing network, Canadian National began the construction of the lines into the Peace River area of northern Alberta, and added the Long Lac cutoff between the old Canadian Northern and Grand Trunk lines, which shortened the distance between North Bay and Winnipeg by 102 miles.

Meanwhile, the Canadian Pacific, after a lean time in the 1890s, had flourished in the years of booming immigration that marked the beginning of the new century. In 1899 a new line through Crows Nest Pass, the southern pass in the Selkirk mountains that had been rejected as a route for the original

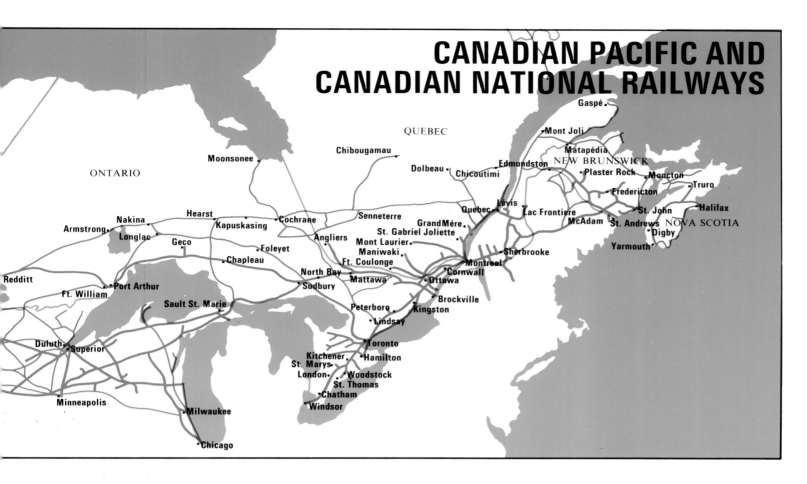

CANADIAN PACIFIC AND CANADIAN NATIONAL RAILWAYS

line to Vancouver because of its proximity to the border, gave access to the important local coal deposits, and the next few years saw considerable activity in the region.

One of the most important achievement was the completion of the famous spiral tunnels in 1909 which significantly reduced the severe grades through the Kicking Horse Pass. The same year saw the completion of the Lethbridge viaduct on the Cross Nest Pass line over the Belly river. More than 5000 ft long, the Lethbridge viaduct is, at 314 ft above the river, the highest railway bridge in Canada. Other routes were opened in the

One of the Canadian Pacific's Royal Hudson 4-6-4s rounds a curve at the head of a fast passenger train.

Massive freight trains now run through the Kicking Horse Pass, part of Canadian Pacific's original transcontinental main line through the Rocky Mountains.

A relatively easy stretch of the Canadian Pacific's route through the Rockies: one of the crews employed by contractor Andrew Onderdonk in the lower Fraser Valley, 1883.

Selkirks through Kettle Valley, and the bringing into service of the five-mile Connaught Tunnel under Mount MacDonald eliminated a 450 ft climb to the top of the Rogers Pass.

At the same time, the Canadian Pacific was busy building up a network of branches in the prairies, and during the prosperous years of the 1920s, when the Canadian National under its new management began to follow suit, there was vigorous competition between the two networks. This was brought to an end, however, by the economic depression of the 1930s, which saw dramatic falls in traffic to barely half its 1928 level. The position was so serious that consideration was even given to a merger of the two networks, but their contrasting natures made this politically impossible.

It was clear that something had to be done, and a Royal Commission appointed at the end of 1931 recommended a

number of steps to improve co-operation between the two systems. There were few tangible results, apart from the pooling of passenger trains over the busiest runs between Montreal and Toronto, where competition had grown so fierce as to produce world-record scheduled runs in the early 1930s.

Canadian 3,500-hp diesel electric locomotive, one of Canadian National's 1957-vintage 6500 series, at the head of the Super Continental near Jasper, Alberta.

Canadian National's Continental Limited at Cisco, British Columbia, where CN and CP tracks cross to opposite banks of the Fraser River.

The gradual easing of the depression towards the end of the decade saw traffic on the increase again, and the Second World War brought record levels of freight movement. The massive war production that was undertaken in Canada stretched the railroads to capacity, especially on the eastern lines to the Atlantic ports of Halifax and Saint John. The single track between Moncton and Halifax, which became the most important of the wartime ports, was especially busy, and in 1941 centralized train control was installed to speed up traffic on this section.

The wartime boom was followed, in Canada as elsewhere, by a severe decline in rail traffic in the postwar years as a result of growing competition from road and air transport: and as on other systems, the accent has been on improving efficiency in all areas of operation.

One of the first moves was towards dieselization. Some experiments with diesel traction had been carried out in the 1930s, and after the interruption caused by the war these were resumed. During the 1950s the two national systems both began a complete switch to the new form of motive power.

Another rationalizing move was the amalgamation in 1961 of the Canadian Pacific's American subsidiaries, the Minneapolis, St Paul and Sault Ste Marie, the Duluth, South Shore and Atlantic, and the Wisconsin Central into the unified Soo Line Railroad, a 4500 mile system spread across the northwestern United States from the Great Lakes to Montana.

The Canadian National also expanded by acquisition of a foreign system in 1949, when Newfoundland finally became part of the Dominion. The railway system on the island was begun in the late nineteenth century, originally with Sandford Fleming as chief engineer. Because of its physical isolation, and for cost reasons, the New-foundland Railway system was built to a gauge of 3 ft 6 in, and though construction started in 1881 the line from Port aux Basques to Saint John's was not completed until 1898. Following the takeover by Canadian National in 1949 some standard gauge track was provided.

Meanwhile, despite the general decline in demand, there were areas where the rail network was being expanded in response to the need for access to undeveloped natural resources, such as the enormous iron ore deposits in the inhospitable region of eastern Quebec and Labrador around Knob Lake, 350 miles north of the St

Canadian Pacific 2-10-4 Selkirk locomotive No 5929 heads a passenger train through the Rockies.

A Canadian Northern freight train passes a row of grain elevators in a typical scene during the railway's brief but spectacular period of expansion in the prairies.

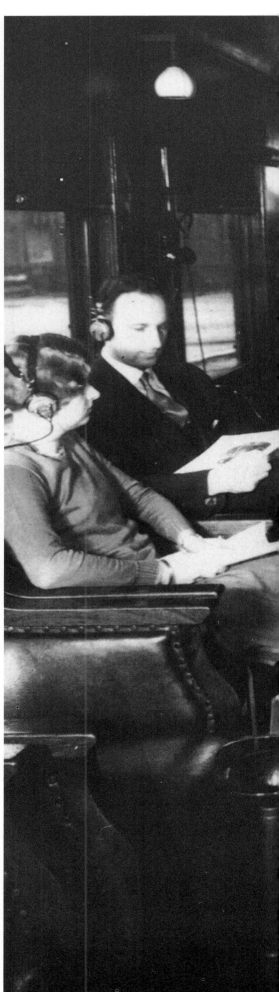

Below: The radio network set up by Sir Henry Thornton to entertain travellers provided the basis for the creation of CBC in the 1930s.

Above: Computer control of train movements were still a world away when this operator was photographed at work in 1942.

Above: Staff of the Canadian National Railways ticket office in Vancouver.

Lawrence estuary. In the late 1940s it was estimated that an annual yield of ten million tons of ore was possible, and with this stimulus construction of the Quebec North Shore and Labrador Railway from Sept-Iles, on the estuary, to Schefferville, was begun in 1950.

The building of the railway required the provision of a series of airstrips so that supplies could be flown in. By 1954 ore trains were in operation, and in 1960 the addition of the Carol Lake branch, incorporating a stretch of fully automatic track supplying the ore-crushing plant, brought the daily total of ore handled to a maximum of over 100,000 tons. West of the Knob Lake Line, the Cartier Railroad, opened in 1962, forms a similar operation between the iron ore fields at Lac Jeannine and Port Cartier.

Left: In old CP colors, the *Dominion* is seen refueling near Field, British Columbia. Locomotives such as this are no longer used.

Above:
The Canadian Pacific's transcontinental *Canadian* crosses the impressive Stoney Creek Bridge in British Columbia.

Below:
A VIA-Rail turbotrain. Passenger services declined rapidly after the Second World War as rail companies found it hard to compete with airlines. The government established VIA-Rail in order to ensure the continuation of a passenger facility.

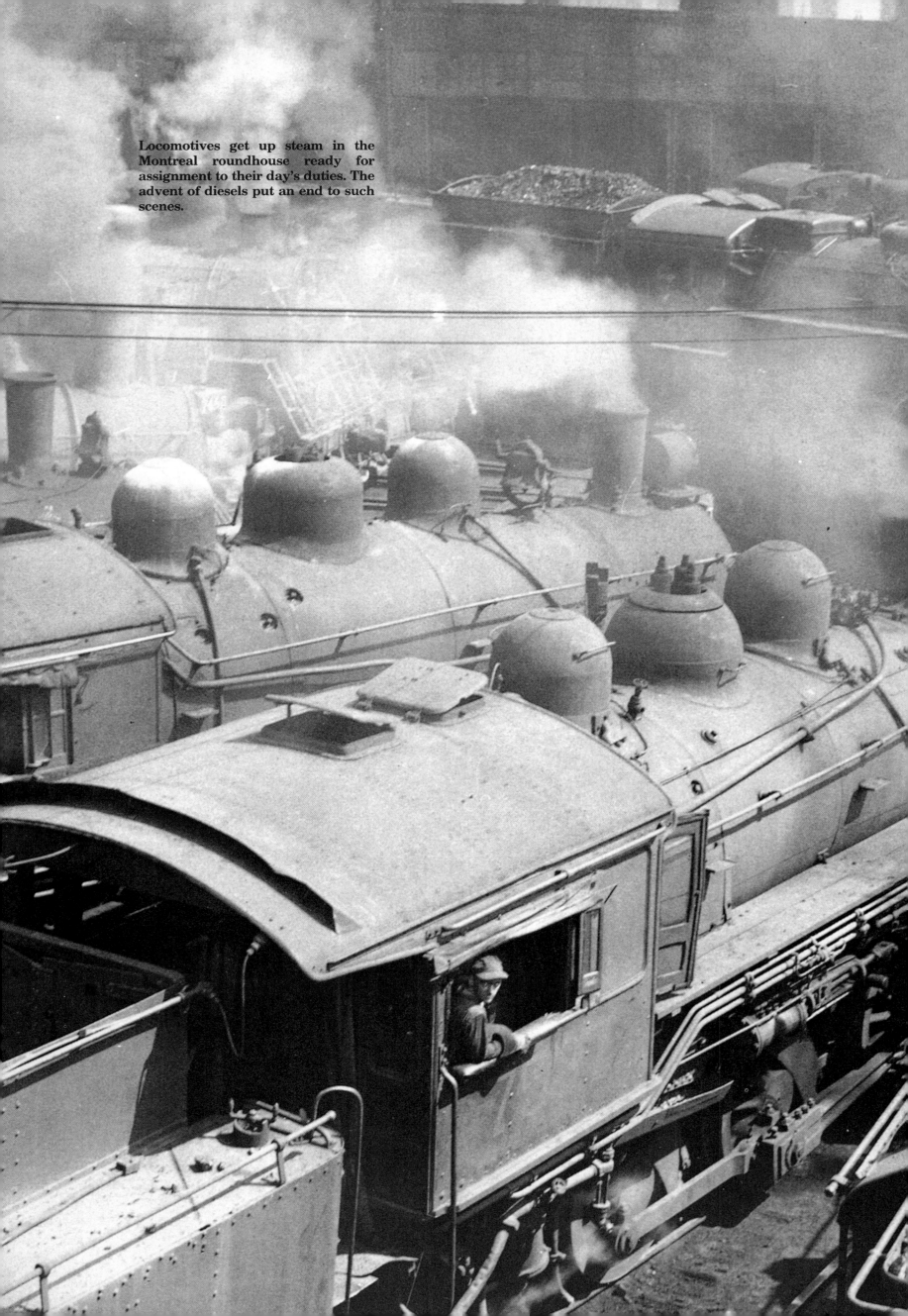

Locomotives get up steam in the Montreal roundhouse ready for assignment to their day's duties. The advent of diesels put an end to such scenes.

The original Pacific Great Eastern line alongside Howe Sound is used by an excursion train hauled by a former Canadian Pacific Royal Hudson.

Other recent lines running north of the main east-west systems include the Hudson Bay Railway, an extension of the original Canadian Northern, which reached Churchill on the bay in 1929. The Ontario Northland Railway, which reaches James Bay, the southern extension of Hudson Bay, was chartered by the province of Ontario in 1902 as the Temiskaming and Northern Ontario, and reached its northern terminus in 1932.

One of the most ambitious of modern developments is that of the British Columbia Railway. The Pacific Great Eastern Railway was chartered in 1912 to build from Squamish up through the lumber country of the Fraser valley to a connection with the Grand Trunk Railway at Prince George. Little progress was made until the provincial government took over the project at the end of the First World War, when construction was resumed. By 1921 344 miles had been built to Quesnel, still some way short of the planned junction at Prince George.

Again work was halted until 1949, when the extension to Prince George was begun. This was completed in 1953, and in 1956 a connecting line from Squamish to North Vancouver was added. Beyond Prince George, the line was extended farther to join the Northern Alberta Railways system at Dawson Creek, and continued north to

Alongside its main task of carrying lumber and coal to the Pacific ports, the British Columbia Railway runs a passenger service to Prince George.

A long line of empty hopper cars
snakes its way around a curve near
Lake Louise in Alberta.

Fort Nelson, which was reached in 1971. At the same time, another branch was begun northwest to Fort St James and on towards Dease Lake. Renamed the British Columbia Railway, in April 1972, this expanding system of nearly 1800 miles is planned to go even farther north into Yukon Territory.

A parallel development in northern Alberta, the Great Slave Lake Railway, was built in 1964–65 from Roma 380 miles north to Hay River, with a branch to the Pine Point lead and zinc mine.

Finally, the northernmost line of all Canada's railways is an old-established private concern built as a result of the Klondyke gold rush of the late 1890s. The 3 ft gauge, 110 mile White Pass and Yukon Route was built between 1898 and 1900 from Skagway (where the prospectors came ashore after their sea journey to the Yukon) to the capital of Yukon Territory at Whitehorse. Having survived the end of the gold boom and served the US Army during the Second World War, it has prospered in recent years with the opening of new mines in the Yukon and the establishment of an integrated container service

for transhipment of the lead-zinc concentrate by ship from Skagway.

The expansion of the Canadian rail network to tap natural resources in remote areas of the country has been accompanied by an impressive modernization of main-line freight services. CP Rail, as Canadian Pacific Railways were renamed in 1971 when the company was reorganized, introduced unit trains in 1967, and has been in the forefront of development of such freight services as containerization, computer-controlled freight yards allied to computerized car-location systems, trailer-on-flat-car 'piggyback' trains, and other innovations.

Passenger services, on the other hand, declined drastically after the

Previous page (inset):
Three of the Cartier Railway's 54 diesel locomotives at the head of a unit iron ore train bound for Port Cartier on the northern shores of the St. Lawrence.

Below:
A unit coal train en route to Roberts Bank port.

Second World War, and by the late 1960s were in danger of disappearing altogether, despite Canadian National's introduction of turbotrains and refurbished streamliners imported from the United States in an attempt to make up in service for its inability to compete with the speed of airlines.

The government's response was the

establishment of the federal VIA-Rail to take over passenger operations. Among the innovations introduced under VIA-Rail are 125 mph tilt-body LRC passenger cars for service on the Montreal-Quebec route. Commuter services in the Toronto region have also been improved by the introduction of bi-level diesel-operated cars.

However, freed of much of the expense of maintaining passenger services, the two national networks are both in a healthy financial state. The Canadian National is one of the most profitable state systems in the world, and CP Rail has contributed, in combination with Soo Line, over a quarter of the parent Canadian Pacific com-

pany's net income, which in recent years has exceeded half a billion dollars.

Dinner is served in the dining car of the Canadian, towards the end of Canadian Pacific's transcontinental passenger operation, now the responsibility of VIA-Rail.

BUILDING THE RAILROADS

The first railroads in the United States were among the first anywhere in the world, and from the outset they were the longest that had been planned. Apart from the resulting fact that basic construction techniques had to be evolved more or less by trial and error, the American builders faced some special problems of their own. Until the establishment of an indigenous iron industry, rails had to be imported, usually from England; heavy engineering, too, was in its infancy, though inventive individuals were not slow to appear with designs for locomotives and other equipment which rapidly came to assume a distinctively American form. Most immediately, however, as soon as the coastal settlements were left behind, the builders had to contend with largely unknown territory, so that the first requirement was to survey the terrain to be crossed.

The surveying work was carried out in a series of stages. First of all, a visual reconnaissance by the engineer-in-chief would establish the general direction to be followed. Then would come instrument surveying, with a lead flagman to mark out the approximate route being followed by the transitman, a team to record the distances and angles that were involved, and the leveler, who measured the elevations and inclines of the selected routes. At the same time, other teams would be engaged in clearing away trees and undergrowth, while a topographer might be employed to make a visual record of the landscape, including hills and rivers that could have a bearing on the ultimate choice.

Of course, this orderly process would be adapted to the circumstances of the particular project under consideration; and when it came to building the transcontinental railroads, the enterprise took on an entirely new aspect.

During the 1850s, when realization of the new dream was becoming a practical possibility, a series of surveys were carried out by the Corps of Engineers of the U.S. Army. After nearly a year, they produced thirteen illustrated volumes of reports on the country they had examined, though the detailed information thus presented had more to say about the specific geography of the Far West than about the practical route for a railroad.

The route actually followed was that explored by Theodore Judah and his employers of the Southern Pacific. Yet even this was subject to alteration depending on the willingness or otherwise of the towns along the way to make a contribution to the road's construction costs. And while the route of the Union Pacific from the east was generally that of the old Mormon Trail to Utah, roads that were passable with ox-teams and horsedrawn wagons were not necessarily suitable for railroads.

One of the main obstacles to the Union Pacific's westward progress was the Black Hills spur of the Rockies between Cheyenne and Laramie in southern Wyoming. Grenville Dodge, who had led the Indian campaigns of 1865–66 in the area before being appointed chief engineer of the U.P., gathered detailed reports on the region, as well as exploring it personally during that period, but had little success in finding a suitable gap from the east until a chance encounter with some Indians proved to be the breakthrough he was seeking.

During one trek with a handful of men, Dodge was making his way south along the crest of the range from the Cheyenne Pass while the body of his troops, then returning from the Powder River expedition, continued along the trail at the foot of the mountains. Finding themselves cut off from the main force by a band of Indians, Dodge and

USMRR train crosses a newly repaired bridge on the Orange and Alexandria Railroad during the Civil War.

his party managed to fight their way down from the crest and chanced on a ridge which formed an unbroken line down to the plains below. It was the railroad's ideal route into the mountains. Accordingly, the Union Pacific crossed the Black Hills by the pass which Dodge named after his old commander, General Sherman; at over 8000 ft above sea level, it was the highest point thus far reached by an American railroad.

Some 20 years later, the Canadian transcontinental railroad also faced formidable natural barriers, in country even less well known than the Great Plains and Rocky Mountains south of the 49th parallel. On the coast of British Columbia there were two potential termini for the new railroad, the Burrard and the Bute inlets from the Georgian sea. The former was on the mouth of the Fraser river, which forms a natural entry to the Coastal mountain range and had been used as such during the

gold rush of 1858, while the latter, though less familiar, provided a possible site for a bridge to Vancouver Island and the provincial capital of Victoria.

Inland, while the course of the Fraser turns north, the Thompson river joins it from the east at Lytton. Up the Thompson lay Kamloops Lake, and beyond this was Eagle Pass, discovered by an early surveyor, Walter Moberly, following the flight of a pair of eagles he disturbed from their nest. But the Selkirk and Rocky ranges still had to be crossed to continue the journey to the east. The Yellowhead Pass had been used by gold prospectors from the east in 1858, and was favored by Sandford Fleming, who had been appointed engineer-in-chief of the Pacific railroad: Moberly had recommended the Howse Pass, reached from Eagle Pass by following a northward sweep of the Columbia river. Far to the north, other surveys had located the Pine River Pass, reached via the Fraser valley.

The first government contracts for railroad construction in British Columbia, issued in 1880, called for a line running from Burrard Inlet up the old gold route to Kamloops, and in the following year the Canadian Pacific syndicate was formed to undertake the main transcontinental line. All the routes previously considered had involved long detours to the north, with the Yellowhead offering the easiest grades, but James J. Hill, one of the original Canadian Pacific directors, was not satisfied and ordered still more surveys south from Howse Pass.

Of two other likely routes, the southern Kootenay Pass lay too close to the U.S. border for comfort: the possibility of war with the United States was always a consideration in those days. Alternatively, the routes north of Howse Pass not only involved considerable extra distance, but would leave the southern prairies dangerously exposed to infiltration by railroads being built in the northwestern states, not to mention the annexation that was being demanded by many American politicians at the time. In any case, Hill seems to have decided in advance that the Bow River route through Kicking Horse Pass should be followed, going so far as to offer the new surveyor, Major A. B. Rogers, a bonus of $5000 for discovering a usable Kicking Horse route. Rogers duly found his route, through the pass that still bears his name, though he sadly underestimated the severity of the grades involved.

Even when luck, politics and commercial considerations had played their

Steel truss bridge and tunnel on a mountain section of the Canadian Pacific Railway.

part in determining the general direction to be followed, there was still the precise work of measurement to be done. In the case of Fleming's original surveys for the transcontinental line, no fewer than 2000 men were involved, and of the 46,000 miles reconnoitred on foot, a quarter were subject to the detailed measuring and recording process of the instrument survey.

So – reverting to the standard procedure for locating the line – the engineer-in-chief, with the benefit of the data collected by the instrument party, would then be in a position to

make the final selection of the route to be followed. At this point, virgin territory might be selected as most likely to provide the easiest possible course; alternatively, the presence of established towns or the location of physical features such as mountain passes or bridging points on rivers might be a deciding factor; or, again, where a specific feature such as a mine in a mountainous area, was the eventual destination, the railroad would have to follow whatever route could be found.

No matter what the circumstances, the choice of route was critical, since a

The difficulties of building the first transcontinental railroad were at their greatest in the mountain sections, where keeping the grades within reasonable limits involved a great deal of cutting, filling, tunneling and bridging. Opposite: Tipping earth to form an embankment in Heath's Ravine on the Central Pacific's route through the Sierra Nevada, 1865. Left: Excavating a cutting by stages to the west of Weber Canyon, Utah, nearing the end of the Union Pacific's westward progress in the fall of 1868. Below: Laying tracks on the prepared roadbed of the Prescott and Eastern Railroad through Arizona Territory in 1898.

poor track could always be improved, whereas a mistake in location might mean abandoning the line and starting all over again. The main elements to be taken into account were the sharpness of curves and the steepness of grades. Generally speaking, American railroads permitted much sharper curves than their European counterparts, with curves under 300 ft in radius being relatively common, while in Europe 1000 ft was generally the minimum radius allowed on main lines. This was one of the reasons for the swiveling pilot truck and equalized driving wheels suspension of the American Standard locomotive that was adopted universally in the early years of the railroads. The penalty for increasing the sharpness of curves is inevitably a reduction in permissible speeds.

Gradients allowed less room for maneuver. The low degree of friction between metal rail and metal wheel that make the railroad such an economical form of transport – a 40-ton railcar set rolling at 60 mph on level track will travel for five miles before coming to a stop, five times as far as a motor truck in comparable conditions on a highway – imposes limits on the grades a

locomotive can negotiate before its wheels start to slip; and even a slight increase in the grade will cause a dramatic reduction in the weight of train that can be hauled by a locomotive.

On the other hand, building a straight, level track will almost certainly involve much more labor in cutting through hills and filling in hollows. Such work was made considerably easier when the first steam shovels were introduced, and the development of sophisticated modern earth-moving equipment steadily expanded the potentialities in comparison with manual operations. But additional cutting and filling, by whatever means, increases the expense of construction, so that the art of railroad location has always been to achieve the best balance between construction costs and eventual operating convenience.

In fact, this basic compromise became a distinctive feature of American railroads during the nineteenth century. The accepted principle was to select the right route, build the road as quickly and economically as possible, bypassing obstacles even at the expense of making a longer or slower line, and then, once

The American Standard locomotive, typified by No 119 (above) and the restored *Jupiter* (opposite) at Promontory was evolved to meet the demands of twisting track. The Promontory section was by-passed in 1904, and in 1967 the Southern Pacific opened its new line through the Cajon Pass in California (right).

the trains were running and the revenue was coming in, use the proceeds to improve the track and carry out such major works as might prove desirable.

One of the best known examples of this process in operation eliminated the historic meeting place of the original Union Pacific and Central Pacific lines at Promontory, in Utah. In 1904 the Southern Pacific, which by then had absorbed the Central Pacific, laid a new line 132 miles long across the Great Salt Lake, not only saving 44 miles in distance over the old route but also avoiding many severe grades and sharp curves. More recently, in 1967, the Southern Pacific eliminated another bottleneck in its operations by means of a new line from Palmdale, California, to the classification yard at Colton.

Above and right: Construction work on the entrance to the Canadian Pacific's Connaught Tunnel. This tunnel was brought into use in 1916 to eliminate the final stages of the climb to the summit of Rogers Pass, which originally involved 17 miles of grades of over 2%. The Connaught Tunnel, double tracked and five miles long, carries the main line 552 ft below the summit of the pass, and as well as shortening the distance by more than four miles enabled more than six full circles of curvature to be dispensed with, along with the miles of snow sheds that were needed to protect the track from avalanches. The Great Northern Railway's Cascade Tunnel (opposite, top), some 7.8 miles long, is the longest in North America, and replaced an earlier 2.6-mile tunnel. Electric operation of the earlier route was extended with the construction of the new tunnel, completed in 1929, to cover a 71-mile section of the route between Appleyard and Skykomish.

Previously, freight from the northwest bound for the southern sections of the railroad had to pass through Los Angeles on the original San Joaquin Valley line. To eradicate consequent delays, a new line was built from Palmdale through the Cajon Pass to Colton, the whole 78 miles of new main line together with 12 miles of associated sidings being constructed, with the aid of the most modern equipment available, in only fifteen months.

Another notable cutoff was constructed on the Denver and Rio Grande Western to shorten the distance between Denver and the west via Salt Lake City. Originally, the route involved a lengthy detour to the south via Pueblo, but the completion of the 6.2-mile Moffat Tunnel between Bond and Dotsero in 1928 enabled the Dotsero cutoff to be brought into operation, reducing the distance by some 65 miles.

A year after the opening of the Moffat Tunnel, the Cascade Tunnel on the Great Northern line through the Cascade mountain range in the state of Washington became the longest in

North America. It was actually the second line improvement on this section of the Great Northern, a 2.6-mile tunnel having been completed in 1900 to avoid the original switchbacks through the mountains. Heavy approach grades were still needed, however, and with the competition of the Milwaukee Road on the route to Seattle the Great Northern began a further stage of improvement. Not only was the 7.8-mile Cascade Tunnel built, but a 71-mile section of track was electrified, and a 10-mile reduction in the overall distance was accompanied by the elimination of several miles of snowsheds, older tunnels and grades in excess of 2 per cent.

Perhaps the most spectacular of all such improvements, however, are those carried out on the Canadian Pacific main line over Kicking Horse Pass. From the east, seven miles of grades in excess of 4 per cent down into the Columbia valley were followed, after a relatively level stretch, by another spell of 2.2 per cent grades up to Rogers Pass. In steam days this involved using as

many as three locomotives to propel a mere eight cars over the passes, and the dangers of the descent going west were matched by the difficulties in working the eastbound trains back up. Avalanches were an additional hazard in winter, and the miles of loops involved in reaching the heights were another drawback.

The first stage in improving this situation was the boring of the famous spiral tunnels under Field Hill. Switchbacks, which extended the principle of the zigzag up a mountainside, whereby grades are made easier at the expense of additional distance by adding loops at the ends of the straight sections, were an early solution to the problem of taking railroads up hills. The Field Hill tunnels virtually extended this practice inside the mountain: one, 3206-ft long, turns through 234 degrees and is followed by another, 2890 ft in length, with a further 232 degrees of turn, and together they produce a drop of 93 ft.

The second stage was the completion

The Connaught Tunnel requires constant ventilation, provided by the fan house at the western entrance (right). Modern track uses continuously welded rails, like those laid on the B & O (below).

of the five-mile Connaught Tunnel in 1916, which eliminated turns amounting to more than six full circles, as well as five miles of snowsheds, and lowered the summit of the line by 540 ft. Although this left some heavy grades to be worked, the task was made easier with the introduction of diesel power and its facility for multiple operation.

In the 1970s, however, with predictions of a 60 per cent increase in traffic during the 1980s pointing to mounting pressure on the Rogers Pass section, C.P. Rail began planning a new grade improvement. This will involve some 21 miles of new track, incorporating a nine-mile tunnel that will be the longest in North America and which is expected to take four years to complete.

When the railroads were first built, such schemes were rarely considered, and the next steps after deciding on the location were to make working plans, secure rights of way and prepare the project for letting to the many subcontractors who were usually involved. Grading was carried out first, and ideally the cutting and filling were balanced so that material dug away to run the line through rising ground could be used to form the embankments which carried it across depressions. Culverts at the bottom of the embankments

would be included to allow the passage of any watercourses. On level ground, to keep the roadbed above the surface so as to improve drainage and minimize interference from drifting snow, ditches dug alongside would provide the material for the raised bed.

Next came the crossties for supporting the rails. In the early days various systems were tried, including piles sunk in the ground and stone sills laid along the surface, but wooden ties quickly came to be the accepted method. As techniques improved, it became customary to treat the wooden ties chemically to prolong their lives, usually with creosote applied under great heat and pressure. A system of steel ties was developed by the Carnegie Steel company, and used for a time on the Bessemer and Lake Erie Railroad early in the twentieth century. In recent years reinforced concrete ties have gained favor, although less than half of one per cent of the total of over 25,000,000 ties laid annually are of anything except wood.

With the ties in place, it was time to lay the rails. Again, there has been great improvement in the standard of rail employed. At first, iron rails weighing only 30 lb per yard were the standard, but over the years the weight was

Left: A track gang positions 440-yard sections of rail ready for welding on the Santa Fe main line.

Below left: A 780-ft timber trestle built by United States Military Railroad engineers at Whiteside, Tennessee.

Below: Temporary and permanent bridges under construction along Central Pacific lines of the transcontinental railroad.

increased, and from the 1870s rails of rolled steel began to be used. Current practice is to use rails of 132 lb per yard and weights of up to 155 lb have been adopted by some railroads. Whereas the earliest procedure was to use only four spikes per rail, this number was increased to give greater support as the trains grew heavier. Recently, welded rail has come to be recognized as the ideal, the gaps that previously occurred every 13 yards being eradicated to give a smoother ride at high speeds, though its use is generally confined to the busiest main lines.

The actual process of tracklaying has been automated, with impressive results. Machines are used to lift the old rails and remove old ties, insert new ties and pack new ballast around them.

Such operations are expensive: in 1977 the Rock Island line was spending $5,000,000 on rehabilitating 134 miles of its double track between Joliet and Rock Island itself, the road having deteriorated badly since the 1950s, when the effects of a general declines in traffic were accentuated by heavy competition on its main lines. The consequence of such deterioration can be even more costly – reductions in permissible speeds and operating efficiency, leading inevitably to further erosion of business.

In the past, before the introduction of such specialized machinery, laying new track necessitated the employment of large numbers of men, though with a high degree of organization some impressive results were achieved. In 1887

the St Paul, Minneapolis and Manitoba system was extended 545 miles through Dakota and Montana between April and October. Some 10,000 men were involved, and a considerable amount of work remained to be done before the road was complete, but while that was being done the line was already earning. Twenty years later, the Milwaukee Road was built for 2300 miles across Montana, Idaho and Washington to Seattle in only three years.

Maintenance of the track, once laid, is of paramount importance. Ideally, the line on busy sections will be inspected twice a day for any misalignment or other fault. One of the main reasons for the Pennsylvania Railroad's preeminence towards the end of the last century was its comprehensive

program of track maintenance, which was reinforced by annual inspections of the whole road, with prizes awarded to the supervisors and foremen in charge of the best-kept sections.

Whatever the efforts of the locating engineer to keep the track on level ground, building railroads soon involved the building of bridges to carry them across rivers, ravines and valleys which were too deep for embankments to be practical: and as with other aspects of the railroads in America, bridges soon developed distinctive features.

Stone arches, of the type commonly found in Europe, were used where stone was available and a permanent structure desirable. The approaches to the Harlem Valley bridge, for example,

were carried on 60-ft granite spans, and the Pennsylvania Railroad's depot in Philadelphia was reached over a series of brick arches, each spanning one street. But the sheer number and size of rivers and other obstacles that had to be crossed, and the high-quality stone and skilled labor that such structures demanded, ruled them out as a normal solution.

The obvious substitute for stone was wood, and the wooden trestle quickly became a standard feature of the North American railroad. The Baltimore and Ohio, in its progress across Maryland, reached Harper's Ferry in 1834, and was held up at this point until the first railroad bridge was opened two years later. A remarkable feature of this bridge was its incorporation of a

junction with the branch line to Washington in the middle of the river, though floods which washed away the bridge at regular intervals soon put a stop to the arrangement, and a metal bridge was erected in its place in 1852.

Ideally, weathered timber at least two years old was needed for sound construction, but as the railroads spread out across the west there was a great

Four diesels head a unit tanker train over the Canadian Pacific's Lethbridge viaduct, which carries the line at a height of 314ft over the Oldman River, Alberta. In the Canadian mountain sections avalanches were a major hazard, and miles of snow sheds were needed to protect the track (bottom).

temptation to use fresh wood, which naturally shrinks and warps with the passage of time. An ingenious solution to this problem was the use of the Howe truss, which featured adjusting screws at the joints to compensate for shrinkage and distortion of the timbers.

The primary advantage of the timber trestle was that it could be erected by unskilled workmen using materials readily available, and for the first few decades of railroad construction it was the standard form of bridge. A great drawback, however, was the need for constant maintenance, with the wooden members needing to be replaced at regular intervals as they rotted, and from the 1870s iron came to be used instead.

Nevertheless, the wooden trestle was a vital part of the railroads' growth, and some of the longest bridges ever built were of this type. Longest of all was the 20-mile trestle across the Great Salt Lake which formed part of the Lucin cutoff on the Southern Pacific's bypassing of the old Promontory route. Completed in 1904, the Salt Lake bridge was gradually replaced by an embankment formed of earth tipped over the sides, and this was the fate of many of the early timber trestles in the west.

More spectacular than the Salt Lake trestle was the Great Trestle on the old Colorado Midland Railway's line in the Rockies. Over 1000ft long, the Great Trestle formed part of a system of loops by which the Colorado Midland reached the Ivanhoe Pass, and carried the road on a curve. This structure was abandoned in 1900 after snow had rendered the line unusable for several weeks.

A related type of timber construction found commonly on mountain railroads were the snowsheds built to protect the line from blockage by drifting snow and destruction by avalanches. The scale of the problem is indicated by the amounts of snow involved, up to 250,000 cubic yards weighing over 100,000 tons often being encountered in a single slide. Canadian Pacific engineers even calculated that the air currents set up by the mountains of sliding snow could split a 2-ft tree trunk. Consequently, snowsheds were a vital part of railroad building, and the Central Pacific, which encountered such severe weather in its passage across the Sierra Nevada, at one time had 60 miles of sheds protecting its road.

When wood came to be replaced generally by metal in the 1870s, an unintentional spur to the builders' ingenuity was provided by the perpetuation of the old system of contracting for construction by the foot. Given the relative prices of the materials involved, the contractors were forced to devise construction methods that used the least possible amount of iron.

The basic element of most bridges

was the truss, which is effectively a girder incorporating a framework of individual members. At first, trusses were built up of plates in the form of a box, and this method was used by the English engineeer Robert Stephenson for his famous Victoria bridge over the St Lawrence at Montreal. The undoubted strength of such structures was only obtained at the expense of constant maintenance – the Victoria bridge included no less than 30 acres of metal

which had to be painted at regular intervals – and a telling comment on the more pragmatic construction methods used by North American engineers was provided by Stephenson himself, in his reported comment to the architect of the Niagara suspension bridge, 'If your bridge succeeds, mine is a magnificent blunder.' Completed in 1855, the Niagara Falls bridge did succeed, and the plate form of construction was never used widely in North

America. In general, however, the flexibility of suspension bridges, overcome in the Niagara model by forming the span of two floors trussed together, has prevented their widespread adoption for railroad use.

The need for economy in construction of iron bridges encouraged the use of metal pins in preformed holes rather than rivets for connecting the members, which, as mentioned, were kept to the minimum. Where very wide rivers had to be crossed, a series of trusses would be supported on masonry or metal-framed piers. The foundations for the piers in a river might be built by the use of a coffer dam, from which the water could be pumped, or by sinking wooden piles in the river bed.

Often the piers would have as much of their height under the water as above the surface. In the case of the bridge over the Ohio river at Cairo, built by the Illinois Central in the late 1890s, the engineers had to allow for a difference between high- and low-water marks of as much as 60 ft, while the St Louis bridge over the Mississippi had piers whose underwater depth was twice the height of the superstructure above the water.

Where piers are not used for support, increasing the length of the span means a corresponding increase in the depth of the truss. The longest single girder is found on the Burlington Northern's Metropolis bridge over the Ohio at Paducah, Kentucky. The span of 720 ft requires a truss 110 ft deep. Conversely, as long as piers can be provided, there is practically no limit to the number of consecutive girders which can be linked to form the bridge, as exemplified by the Southern Pacific's Huey P. Long bridge which crosses the Mississippi at New Orleans, the 4.4-mile total length including a longest single span of 790 ft.

When the provision of supports for the bridge becomes impossible, one solution is the cantilever system, which uses self-supporting structures built out from the ends to support a smaller girder in the center. Cantilevers are used for the biggest river crossings, and the longest-span railroad bridge of all, the Canadian National's Quebec bridge over the St Lawrence, is a cantilever. The Quebec bridge had an unfortunate start in life, with a design fault leading to the collapse of one of the incomplete cantilevers in 1907, and after work was resumed in 1910 the central span was dropped in the river during the first attempt to raise it into position in 1916. The span was finally fixed in place in 1917.

Other cantilever bridges have been built in Canada, including the Lachine bridge over the St Lawrence at Montreal and the Niagara cantilever; but the first bridge of this type in North America was built over the Kentucky River at Cincinnati, where a canyon 1200 ft wide and 275 ft deep was regularly subject to surges of 55 ft in the river. Two 177-ft iron piers were built on masonry foundations in the river itself, and three sets of cantilevers were used to bridge the gaps, each span being 375 ft long and carried 276 ft above the river bed.

Finally, the availability of steel, and more recently the use of concrete, has allowed arched bridges to be built without the use of brick or stone. An early example of this type was the St Louis bridge over the Mississippi, where quicksand in the river bed and icefloes and debris in the river itself precluded the use of intermediate piers.

The Santa Fe's bridge over the Mississippi at Fort Madison, Iowa, incorporates a lifting span of 525 ft in its 3347 ft overall length to allow ships to pass.

STEAM LOCOMOTIVES

By the middle of the nineteenth century, the American Standard type of locomotive had assumed a form that was to remain in almost universal use for another fifty years. The 4–4–0 wheel arrangement was, of course, first adopted at an early stage, but it was in the early 1850s that Thomas Rogers of the Paterson, New Jersey, firm of Rogers, Ketchum and Grosvenor began to produce the engines that embodied the typical form that was to be so widely imitated.

The most distinctive feature of the Rogers design was the lengthened wheelbase which allowed the cylinders to be mounted in a horizontal position at the sides of the smokebox, this being carried on the four-wheel pilot truck that had proved so vital in enabling locomotives to cope with the irregularities of early track. The equalizing beams carrying the driving wheels were also a standard feature by this stage, and other characteristics of the Rogers locomotive and its imitators was the tapered boiler surrounding the large firebox at the rear.

Other external features of American locomotives derived directly from their operating environment. Large cabs for engineer and fireman were essential for their protection in the extremes of climate that were encountered; big chimneys with spark-arresters were used to prevent fires in the woods and prairies through which they passed; bells, headlights and cow-catchers were necessary to protect the train and to warn against interlopers on the track; and the big sandbox on top of the boiler enabled the engineer to cope with slipping wheels on remote stretches of line where no assistance could be expected.

Another external characteristic which, however, had no practical reason behind it, was the elaborate ornamentation widely displayed during this period. Bright colors, burnished copper and brass trim, even flags and pictures painted on side panels, were often sported by the early locomotives. The practice died out partly as a result of the ending of the system whereby each crew was allotted its own engine and held responsible for its appearance as well as its mechanical order.

Internally, the American 4–4–0, like all steam locomotives, was based on the principles developed by George Stephenson and embodied in his famous *Rocket* in 1829. The hot gases from a firebox were carried through a system of tubes inside a boiler to a smokebox; the water heated by the tubes formed steam, which was collected and fed into cylinders where, acting on a piston, it drove the wheels by means of a connecting rod. The motion of the wheels was in turn transmitted to the valves admitting the steam to the cylinders, allowing the spent steam to escape from the cylinder. The exhaust steam was then fed into the smokebox to create the draft on the fire and so keep the whole process repeating itself.

During the 1850s and 1860s the 4–4–0 was generally used to haul both passenger and freight trains, neither of which attained any great speeds, but during the 1870s the appearance of the

Wootten firebox began to produce changes. The Wootten was designed to burn the powdery residue from anthracite coal that otherwise had been wasted, and its wide, shallow form demanded some reconsideration of the wheel arrangement.

One method tried was known as the camelback or Mother Hubbard: to avoid an excessively long wheelbase, the engineer's cab was built on top of the boiler, leaving the stoker to feed the firebox from a platform on the front of the tender. The cab on top of the boiler had earlier been used by Ross Winans of Baltimore, and in a series of locomotives for the Baltimore and Ohio Railroad, but then it had been adopted for the purpose of giving the engineer a better view forward. Combined with the Wootten firebox, the camelback arrangement was used by a number of railroads and in several different wheel configurations.

Wootten himself was general manager of the Philadelphia and Reading Railroad at the time, so it was

natural that the Reading should be among the principal users of the type. It was originally applied to 4–6–0 freight engines with small driving wheels, but for the Atlantic City route, where the Reading was in direct competition with the Pennsylvania Railroad, Wootten developed a 2–4–2 fast passenger engine, with the two small trailing wheels supporting the firebox. As well as his own design of firebox, Wootten incorporated another innovation that was the work of Samuel Vauclain of the Baldwin locomotive works.

Vauclain's system of compound working was one of a variety of methods for using the partially expanded steam from one cylinder to work another cylinder, usually of greater diameter to allow for the lower pressure of steam. The distinctive feature of Vauclain's system was that both cylinders drove the same crosshead, thus removing some of the complications.

The Reading 2–4–2s proved rather unstable at the high speeds for which they were designed, and in 1896 Woot-

ten produced a much more significant design using the 4–4–2 wheel arrangement that has become known from its origins as the Atlantic type. The new engines proved capable of covering the 55½ miles between Camden and Atlantic City in a flat 60 minutes, and in special circumstances of turning in an overall speed of 71.6 mph.

The Pennsylvania also adopted the type for its competing services. The Pennsylvania Atlantics reached their highest development in the guise of the E6 class, first built in 1910, which included another refinement in the form of superheating. This was an invention of a German engineer, Wilhelm Schmidt, and involved collecting the steam in the normal way, then leading

Wood-burning American 4–4–0s at the United States Military Railroad depot at City Point, Virginia, in 1864. The Baldwin 4–4–0 (inset), built for the Wilmington and Weldon Railroad in 1859, displays typically lavish ornamentation.

Baltimore and Ohio locomotives of the Ross Winans 'camelback' type at Martinsburg, Virginia, in 1858.

Inset: The reconstructed Union Pacific locomotive *Jupiter*, a product of the Rogers factory.

180

The 4–4–2 Atlantic was a popular type of passenger locomotive. The two examples shown opposite are a Canadian Pacific Vauclain compound (top), a design dating from 1899, and the Erie Railroad's No 537 near Rutherford, New Jersey, in 1929. The Pennsylvania Railroad K4 Pacific carries test equipment on the smokebox, while the later New York Central 4–6–4 Hudson (below) featured a streamlined casing.

it through elements inside the firetubes so that it was superheated to much greater temperatures and pressures before being admitted to the cylinders. With the addition of superheating in 1910, the E6 Atlantics developed 2400 hp, which for their weight of 110 tons made them among the most powerful locomotives ever built. They remained in use until after the Second World War.

The Pennsylvania Atlantics did not use Wootten fireboxes, having adopted the square-topped Belpaire type for the bituminous coal to which it had easier access than the Reading. The latter persevered with the Wootten, however, and in 1915 added a four-wheel trailing truck to produce a 4–4–4 type. Apart from some high-speed machines built for special services with lightweight trains during the 1930s, this was the last development of the four-coupled passenger engine, the four-wheel trailing truck reaching its true potential in other applications. For mainline passenger service the next type of major importance was the 4–6–2 Pacific.

A slightly earlier type, the 2–6–2 Prairie, had, like the 2–4–2 that preceded the Atlantic, proved unstable at high speeds, though the examples built during the 1900s were among the biggest passenger engines in the world at the time. The first Pacifics were built for the Missouri Pacific Railroad in 1902, thus providing the derivation of their generic name. Again, it was the Pennsylvania which produced the most impressive examples of this engine type, and again the new wheel configuration was combined with other

innovations to reach its highest peak of development.

The Pennsylvania's first Pacifics were the K2 class of 1907, and these used the conventional arrangement of cylinders outside the wheels of the leading truck, controlled by a Stephenson-type link motion carried between the wheels. These were replaced by another type of link motion, named after its Belgian inventor, Egide Walschaert, which operated outside the wheels and used more rugged piston valves. By 1914 the original K2 had been developed into the K4 with the addition of the Walschaerts gear. Although only 15 per cent heavier than their predecessors, the K4s developed 33 per cent more tractive effort, and were particularly useful on the Pennsylvania's heavily graded line between New York and Chicago. The addition of mechanical stokers in the 1920s allowed them to indulge to the full their appetite for fuel, which the stokers had labored hard to satisfy, and as the weight of trains increased they were provided with tenders carrying 24,400 gallons of water and 25 tons of fuel.

On the New York-Chicago run the Pennsylvania's great rival, the New York Central, had a longer but rather easier route, running alongside the Hudson river and Erie Canal to the shores of the Great Lakes, rather than following the Pennsylvania on the direct route across the mountains. The N.Y.C. had also developed a series of Pacifics, starting with the first models in 1905, to take advantage of the easier route by running heavier trains. A series of N.Y.C. Pacifics culminated in the K5 class of 1925, and an indication of the work required from them is given by the 15,000 gallons of water they carried in their tenders.

However, the K5 class were fast approaching the limits of the Pacific's capacity, and the demand for yet heavier locomotives was met in 1927 with the introduction of the first 4–6–4, known as the Hudson, from the location of the Central's main line out of New York. The four-wheel trailing truck was adopted to allow a bigger grate to be used, and a development of the Walschaerts valve gear, the Baker, was used on later models. Another feature of the Hudsons, which had earlier been fitted to the New York Central Pacifics, was the inclusion of a small booster engine on the trailing truck to give extra power when starting.

The original J1 class Hudsons were developed over the years, their ultimate form being reached in the streamlined J3s which achieved fame hauling the prestige Twentieth Century Limited between New York and Chicago in the late 1930s. But the New York Central had a requirement for still greater power, and this was supplied in the form of the 4–8–4 Niagara type, developed from a series of 4–8–2 freight engines, the Mohawks, by way of the L3 class 4–8–2s which had proved capable of speeds in excess of 80 mph even with the relatively small wheels commonly used on freight machines.

Of course, the above account ignores the many hundreds of different types of passenger engines used by other railroads. The Milwaukee, for example, had followed a similar progression, starting with a series of 4–6–0 types in the 1890s. Both these and the succeeding Atlantic designs employed the Vauclain compound system, and in 1907 another type of Atlantic was produced with the balanced system of compounding. The latter also used two high-pressure and two low-pressure cylinders, but instead of having them in pairs one above the other outside the leading truck wheels, the balanced system mounted the low-pressure pair inside the frames. From this position they drove the axle of the leading pair of driving wheels, which was cranked for the purpose, while the high-pressure cylinders drove the leading coupled wheels in the normal way.

Because of the additional complication, this system was never very popular on American railroads, and the more common Vauclain type was used

again on the Milwaukee's last Atlantics in 1908. In 1910 the first class of Pacifics, the F3s, were introduced, to be followed by the F4 class in the next two years, and then the superheated F5 class: ultimately all 160 engines of the three classes were fitted with superheaters.

The Milwaukee, after the completion of its route to Tacoma and Seattle, had to cater for the contrasting demands of this long transcontinental route which, even with its electrified sections, was subject to severe weather, as well as such shorter but more competitive routes as those to Milwaukee, St Paul and Omaha. Until the late 1920s the Pacifics covered both types, but in 1929 a new class of locomotive was introduced in the form of the 4–6–4. The new engines proved exceptionally fast, and on the 86-mile Chicago-Milwaukee route in July 1934 a special high-speed run produced the remarkable speeds of 92.3 mph average over a 65.6-mile section, with a maximum of 103.5 mph.

For the long hauls on the Pacific route, a more powerful type, the S1 4–8–4s, was introduced, the first of which was produced by Baldwin in 1930. With a tractive force of over 62,000 lb, compared with the 45,820 lb of the F6 class 4–6–4s, the S1s were

capable of hauling the heaviest passenger trains.

During the 1930s the Milwaukee introduced their celebrated streamlined Hiawatha services, and for the Chicago-Minneapolis run, with a train of six cars, the American Locomotive Company (Alco) produced the A class 4–4–2 design in 1935. These proved capable of sustaining speeds of well over 100 mph, but as the popularity of the trains caused their size to be increased to nine and then 12 cars, the F7 4–6–4s, first built in 1938, replaced them. The new engines were able to take the heavier trains at maximum speeds of over 120 mph, and worked one of the fastest-ever steam-hauled scheduled runs in the world, the 81-mph Sparta-Portage section of the Minneapolis-Milwaukee route.

Elsewhere, among the outstanding engines of the late 1930s were the Santa Fe's 3771 class 4–8–4s, which handled the services over the 1791 miles between Kansas City and Los Angeles. Not only were these locomotives capable of completing the through journey in 26 hours, but after only a few hours they would be ready to make the return trip.

Derelict streamlined Hudson built for the Milwaukee Road.

By this stage, the need for minimum servicing and maintenance was becoming paramount, as the locomotives had been developed to a peak of speed and power where track limitation rather than locomotive ability was the governing factor in the schedules. It was against the background of increasing competition from new diesel locomotives, one of whose attractions was their greater availability, that the New York Central produced its ultimate development of the Niagara type.

The aim in designing the Niagaras was a 6000-hp engine with a weight to horsepower ratio no higher than that of the 4–6–4s. In pursuit of this end, a new design of boiler was adopted which omitted the steam dome to allow increased diameter; at the same time the firebox, steam passages and superheater elements were made bigger, carbon steel was employed where appropriate, and roller bearings were adopted. Furthermore, to permit a full evaluation of the design, driving wheels of two diameters, 75 in and 79 in, were supplied.

After their appearance in 1945 the S1 Niagaras were employed on the New York-Chicago run, regularly working

New York Central 4–8–4 Niagara at Albany, New York, in April 1952.

through the 930 miles from Harmon, where they took over from the electric locomotives that brought the trains out of Grand Central Station, to Chicago. Detailed studies of their performance, compared with that of a group of diesels, were carried out, and it was found that the six Niagaras attained an availability rate of nearly 76 per cent and a utilization rate of over 69 per cent. This amounted to a yearly average milage of 260,000 miles, while the equivalent figure for the diesels, which cost more than twice as much, was 330,000 miles.

Unfortunately, the carbon-silicon steel used for the boiler shells as a weight-saving measure began to develop cracks; faced with the cost of providing new boilers, the management inevitably turned to diesels for their subsequent motive power requirements. Within a few years the same course was followed by every other railroad, although there were various attempts to prolong the use of steam.

While passenger engines were being developed to their ultimate peak, parallel evolution of their freight counterparts was occurring. As early as 1842 Matthew Baldwin had designed a specialized 0–8–0 freight locomotive for the Georgia Central Railway, and while the mechanical complications of this design prevented its adoption by

more than a few railroads, larger numbers of smaller wheels were the obvious answer to the freight requirement of increased power at low speeds.

One railroad which had a particular need for increased power was the Central Pacific, with its steep climb from Sacramento up into the Sierra Nevada, and in 1882 A. J. Stevens produced a successful 4–8–0 design, 20 of which were built for the line. The following year he extended the idea to produce the 4–10–0 *El Gobernador*, but this 65-ton monster proved too much for the track at that time, and had to remain content with being the biggest locomotive in the world rather than a working engine.

In the later stages of the nineteenth century, 2–6–0 Mogul and 2–8–0 Consolidation engines became the standard types for freight operations, with the latter proving more popular. Among the most powerful at the turn of the century were a pair of 2–8–0s built for the iron ore-carrying Bessemer and Lake Erie Railroad by the Pittsburgh Locomotive Works in 1900. Weighing over 250,000 lb and developing a tractive effort of nearly 64,000 lb, these engines were built specially for working the steeply graded line between the railroad's docks at Conneaut and its yard at Albion: other 2–8–0s from the same

builder for service on easier parts of the route weighed a more modest 179,000 lb and were capable of a tractive effort of 38,400 lb.

The principal advantage of the eight-coupled layout was to concentrate weight on the driving wheels and as a result improve adhesion. An indication of the popularity of the type in the early years of the twentieth century was the government's orders, totalling 680, for locomotives of the 2–8–0 wheel arrangement for military service in France during the First World War. By early 1918 no fewer than 30 were being completed every day, though by then bigger types were being adopted for regular use.

Since freight locomotives were not called on to match the high speeds required in passenger service, two-wheel leading trucks were normally used, although the Pennsylvania Railroad, for example, produced the first of a long series of 4–8–2s for fast freight duties in 1918. Culmination of the series was the M1a class of 1930, which weighed 342 tons, including the tender, and produced a tractive effort of 64,550 lb.

The more common freight equivalent of the Pacific passenger engine was the 2–8–2, or Mikado, and while the 9500 or so engines built amounted to less than half the total of nearly 22,000 2–8–0s, no other type came close in terms of numbers. The Santa Fe went one better in 1903 with the production of the first 2–10–2, which used the trailing truck to give greater flexibility on the Santa Fe's mountain divisions, with their heavy grades and sharp curves.

A natural progression from the two-wheel trailing truck was to four wheels at the back supporting a firebox of increased size, and in the mid-1920s both eight-coupled and ten-coupled freight engines appeared with this arrangement. The 2–10–4 was known in the United States as the Texas type, the first being built for the Texas and Pacific Railroad in 1925, while in Canada their use in the mountain regions of the west from 1929 led to their being called Selkirks. Use of the 2–8–4 was pioneered by the New York Central, again in 1925, which gave rise to their common name of Berkshire, after the mountains of western Massachusetts.

Among the biggest of non-articulated freight locomotives were the 4–10–2 and 4–12–2 types built by Alco for the Union Pacific from 1926. The four-wheel pilot trucks allowed the use of three cylinders, thus maximizing the power that could be obtained without resorting to articulation. Weighing 350 tons, the 90 4–12–2s which were built delivered a tractive effort of 96,600 lb and were capable of working 3800-ton trains at average speeds of 35 mph.

The biggest steam locomotives of all, however, were of the articulated type. The system of articulation used on American railroads was first developed by Anatole Mallet in France toward the end of the nineteenth century, and involved the use of a single boiler to supply two sets of cylinders. The steam was used first by a pair of high-pressure cylinders and then fed to a low-pressure pair, but the distinguishing feature of the Mallet system as against other compound systems was the use of two sets of driving wheels on separate chassis, the leading chassis being arranged so that it could turn and swivel and thus negotiate curves satisfactorily.

The first Mallet built in North America was delivered by Alco to the Baltimore and Ohio Railroad in 1904, and within a few years Mallets were very popular for heavy freight duties. As the number of driving wheels was increased from 12 to 16 and even 20,

leading and trailing trucks were added to improve riding qualities and later to support an enlarged firebox. The most popular configuration was the 2–6–6–2, while the biggest of the Mallets were the Union Pacific's 4–8–8–4 Big Boys of 1941. The latter were the biggest steam locomotives ever built, weighing 354 tons. Although not the most powerful of all locomotives, the Big Boys were built for speed and efficiency and, like their predecessors on the Union Pacific, the 4–6–6–4 Challengers, were capable of hauling express freight trains at speeds of up to 80 mph.

The Big Boys came into their own on the Union Pacific's route through the mountains between Ogden and Cheyenne, running fruit trains between Ogden and Green river, where the Challengers took over. Both these Union Pacific types, like later Mallets on other U.S. railroads, dispensed with

the compound arrangement when the low-pressure cylinders grew so big that they could no longer be accommodated, and the valves were no longer adequate to deal with the volume of steam.

Among the many varieties of Mallet were some unusual designs. In 1914 the Erie took delivery of a 2–8–8–8–2 Triplex Mallet, a type developed by the Baldwin concern which mounted a second set of low-pressure cylinders on the tender, for use as a helper. Although the Erie subsequently bought another two engines of this type, the addition of extra cylinders without extra steam-generating capacity prevented the triplex from becoming a success, while a 2–8–8–8–4 with a larger boiler and slightly smaller cylinders, built for the Virginian Railroad, suffered from the same deficiencies in steaming. No more successful were the Santa Fe's 2–10–10–2s, which were rebuilds of earlier machines and featured jointed boilers.

The Virginian, on the other hand, after its disappointment with the triplex type, bought ten 2–10–10–2 Mallets which proved eminently suitable for their job of helping 6000-ton coal trains up an 11-mile section of 2 per cent grades in the Alleghenies.

Another notable user of Mallets was the Denver and Rio Grande Western on its difficult main lines in the Rockies, while the Southern Pacific developed a cab-first design for its mountain section in the Sierra Nevada between California and Nevada. The use of oil for fuel enabled these 4–8–8–2s, of which 195 were built between 1928 and 1944, to run backwards, in effect, with the tender trailing and the engineer thus provided with the best possible view forward.

As well as being the biggest steam locomotives built in North America, engines of the Mallet type were also among the last. After the Second World

A Santa Fe 3800 class 2–10–4, one of a long series of ten-coupled express freight engines used by the railroad. The Baltimore and Ohio started a new trend with its 0–6–6–0 Mallet compound No 2400 of 1904 (inset).

War, when American railroads were turning in increasing numbers toward diesel power, the Norfolk and Western Railway, whose main operation was the transport of coal from the mining areas of Kentucky and West Virginia, made a determined effort to improve its locomotives to the point where they could compete, in terms of operating efficiency and availability, with the new diesels.

In its own design offices and its own locomotive works at Roanoke, the Norfolk and Western produced three new models. The J class 4–8–4, first built in 1941, was designed to haul the prestige passenger services at 100 mph and

more, while the A class 2–6–6–4 and Y class 2–8–8–2 articulated types, dating from 1936 and 1948 respectively, were used for freight work, the A class at speeds up to 70 mph and the Y6 class developing maximum power at lower speeds. The real advance with these and the Y6b type, the ultimate development of the Mallet, was the rationalizing of maintenance facilities to the point where less than an hour was required for a complete inspection, refueling and lubrication between runs. Moreover, the Y6b enabled maintenance costs to be reduced by an impressive 37 per cent compared with their predecessors of the Y5 class.

However, even the Norfolk and Western was forced to give way to the advance of the diesel, and although the Y6b remained in production until as late as 1952, by 1957 the N. & W. had placed orders for 75 diesels. Its last steam locomotive, and the last for any mainline railroad in the United States, was an 0–8–0 switcher produced in 1953; but the problems of keeping a steam fleet going when everyone else had turned to diesels finally forced the Norfolk and Western to end steam services in 1960, the last run being made by a Y6b on April 4.

Of course, there were many other varieties of steam locomotive apart from the mainline freight and passenger machines. Some were actually at-

tempts to extend the life of steam, such as the steam turbines with which a few railroads experimented around the time of the Second World War.

One line of turbine development was represented by the Pennsylvania Railroad's geared turbine 6–8–6 of 1944, which actually saw service but was too far outside the mainstream of development to have a lasting impact. Turbines were also used to generate electricity to power motors on the driving axles, and turbo-electric engines that were built included examples for the Union Pacific in 1938, the Chesapeake and Ohio in 1947 and the Norfolk and Western in 1952; but the interruption of the Second World War prevented Union Pacific from taking the experiment any further, while the later types simply appeared too late to make any great difference.

An earlier design of locomotive which used geared transmission was designed for the specific purpose of operating on the makeshift railroads built in logging country. This was the Shay, named after the engineer who built the first example in 1880. Engines of this type remained in production until 1945, and actually formed the foundations of the Lima Locomotive Works' rise to its position as one of the main locomotive builders in the United States, along with Baldwin and the American Locomotive Company (Alco).

Among the last steam locomotives built for service on American main lines were the Norfolk and Western J class 4–8–4s (above). The Union Pacific was noted for the size of its locomotives: the 4–8–4 (opposite, top) preserved at Cheyenne, and the 4–6–6–4 at North Platte, Nebraska (opposite) date from the late 1930s.

Another type of logging engine, the chain-drive Robb, was developed in Canada, built in 1903 to run on timber tracks and featuring a tilted boiler; and other transmission systems were used on the Hiesler and Climax logging types. The former had a V arrangement of the cylinders and was driven by a central shaft and universal couplings; the latter employed a combination of chains and gears.

Apart from such specialized forms of locomotive, there were legions of little 0–6–0 and 0–8–0 switching engines used for making up trains in the classification yards. Often these would be machines past their prime which had been relegated to the yards from the main lines, but many were purpose built for the bigger railroads. It was also in the yards that the earliest forerunners of the new form of motive power that was to displace the fascinating variety of steam made their appearance.

The 90 4–12–2s built by Alco for UP in the late 1920s were the longest non-articulated locomotives ever built. Inset: A N&W Y6b class 2–8–8–2 is assembled in the Roanoke yard in 1949.

DIESEL AND ELECTRIC POWER

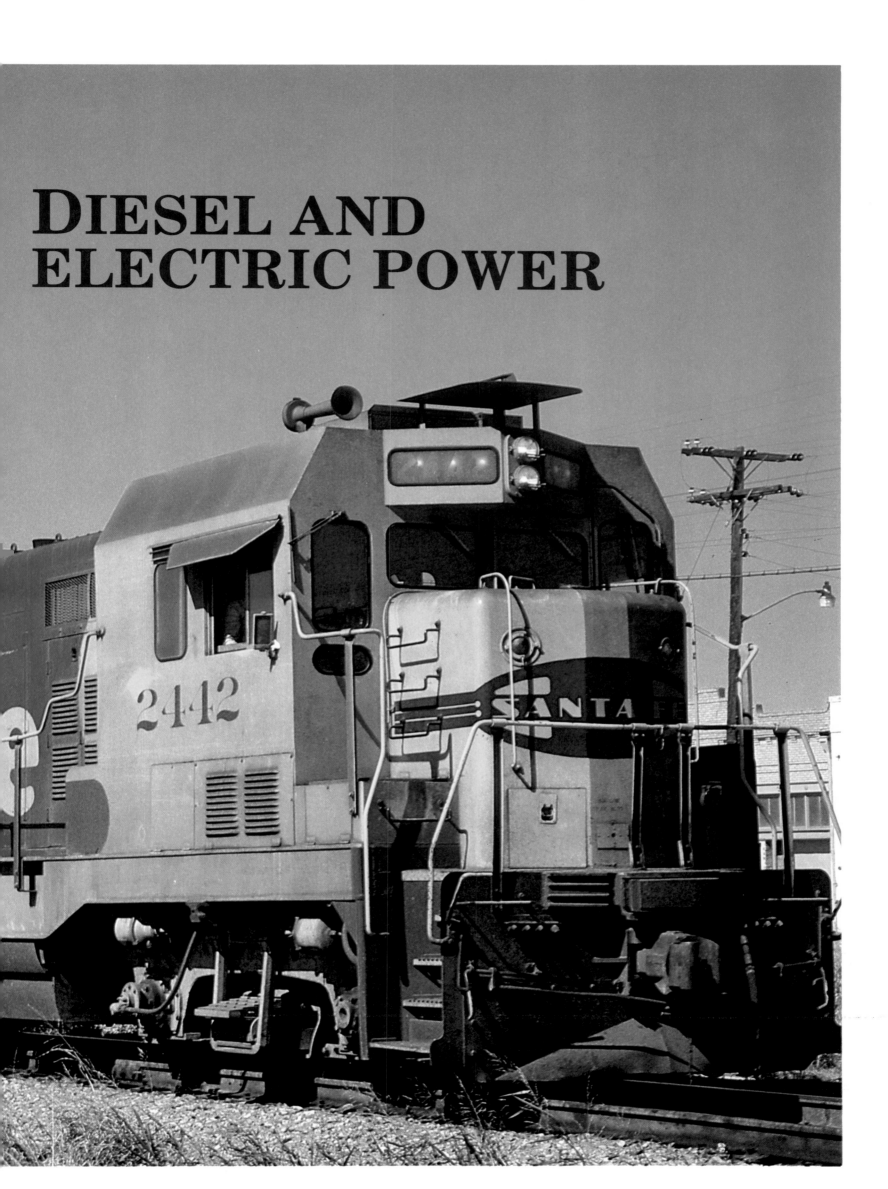

Despite a variety of undoubted advantages over any other method of operation, there was never any real likelihood of electric traction replacing steam on American railroads. The operational benefits can only be realized once the power supply has been provided, and at the time when many main lines in Europe were being electrified, early in the present century, the U.S. network was still growing toward its final total of a quarter of a million miles. The cost of equipping even a fraction of the total with the necessary power supply could not be contemplated when the cost of building the railroads themselves had driven so many companies out of business.

On the other hand, the quietness and absence of pollution associated with electric power made it very attractive in some applications, while the electric locomotive's ability to increase its power output to well over its nominal rating for short periods have enabled trains to be operated in some places where expense or other types of problem might well have made the venture either practically or economically impossible. Its third common application has been in areas where the volume of traffic has been great enough – or the cost of electricity low enough – to make the savings in operating expenses outweigh the initial high equipment expenses, or where automated operation has been desirable on cost or other grounds.

A number of scientists and engineers during the nineteenth century conducted experiments aimed at using electricity to propel a vehicle. As early as the 1880s an electrified tramline was built in Toronto, but the first mainline electrification was carried out in Baltimore in 1895 after the Baltimore and Ohio Railroad was ordered by the city authorities to stop using steam locomotives inside the city. A seven-mile section of track, including the mile-long tunnel under the Patapsco, was fitted with an overhead supply system for 650-volt DC current to enable 1080-hp locomotives to haul trains to the city center.

New York was another city which acted early to eliminate steam traction from its central districts. Steam locomotives were banned from Manhattan Island after 1908, and by that time the New York Central had electrified its approaches to Grand Central Station from Harmon, some 20 miles away, while the New York, New Haven and Hartford line, first to Stamford, Connecticut, and then to New Haven, was converted by 1907.

The most ambitious electrification

Early electric operation on the Baltimore and Ohio, the first mainline electrification in the USA.

scheme in the New York area was carried out by the Pennsylvania Railroad following its acquisition of the Long Island Railroad in 1900. The Long Island line itself was electrified in 1905, and the Pennsylvania's system of tunnels, by which it established its new terminus at Pennsylvania Station, included a through connection with the Long Island system.

The Pennsylvania extended its electrification scheme to the Philadelphia suburban lines from 1915, and by 1933 electric trains were running between Philadelphia and New York. Further work brought the electric service to Washington in 1935, completing a system that included 364 route miles and a total of 1405 miles of track.

Tunnels were other obvious candidates for electrification. The St Clair River Tunnel between Port Huron and Sarnia on the Grand Trunk Railway of Canada's cross-border operation into Michigan was equipped with electric traction in 1908, and the following year the Great Northern's Cascade Tunnel and its approaches followed suit. The Boston and Maine's Hoosac Tunnel was electrified in 1911, and the Mount Royal Tunnel to the Canadian National station in the center of Montreal was operated by electric locomotives as soon as it was completed a few years later.

The 1920s brought further electrification schemes in the new Cascade Tunnel, the 7.8-mile tunnel itself forming part of a system that embraced a total of 72 miles of track, in the Michigan Central's tunnel at Detroit, and on the Illinois Central's suburban lines in Chicago.

Electric locomotives also came into their own on sections of route where steam operation was proving excessively difficult or expensive. The outstanding example was the Milwaukee Road's total of 656 miles of main line in the Rocky and Bitter Root Mountain sections, while the Norfolk and Western and Virginian railroads also used electricity to overcome some severe operating problems.

The Norfolk and Western electrified a 30-mile section between Bluefield and Vivian, where steam locomotives were being pushed to operate the 4000-ton coal trains over 2 per cent grades and through the Elkhorn Tunnel, the initial scheme of 1915 being extended to Williamson in 1926. The line was subsequently rebuilt with easier grades and a new tunnel, and the electric working abandoned. The neighboring Virginian Railroad had similar problems on its route between Mullens and Roanoke, and in the mid-1920s it replaced its big Mallets on this stretch with powerful electric locomotives that could handle coal trains of up to 16,000 tons.

The trouble with such piecemeal

development of electrification schemes was that each operator tended to choose its own system, so that research and development suffered; and the long life of electric locomotives further reduced the incentive for any concerted effort at

The use of electric traction in North America was restricted generally to routes where steam operation was either difficult or inconvenient. The former category included several mountain areas in the northwestern United States, where both the Great Northern and Milwaukee railroads had substantial electrified sections. The GN's 41-mile scheme (left and opposite) was brought into operation in 1929, and used 11,000-volt alternating current to power Baldwin-Westinghouse locomotives. City centres were also prime candidates for electrification: steam locomotives were banned from Manhattan Island at an early stage, and the Pennsylvania Railroad's construction of its New York terminal, carried out between 1903 and 1910 (below) was accompanied by electrified tunnels under the North and East Rivers. Ultimately the Pennsylvania extended electrification north to New Haven, east to Harrisburg and south to Washington DC, the NY-Washington route being operated by 4260-hp GG-1 locomotives (opposite, below).

rationalization. One of the results can be seen in the problems experienced by Amtrak in its plans to renew the electrified route between Washington and New York and extend an integrated operation to Boston. The Pennsylvania uses a 12,000-volt 25-cycle AC system on the New York-Washington route, the line to New Haven has been renewed and extended to Boston using 25,000-volt supply, while in New York itself the Metropolitan Transportation Authority lines supply 12,500-volt current at 60 cycles. Without the resources to renew the supply system on the remainder of the New York-Washington sector, Amtrak is faced with the need for locomotives able to operate on all three types of current.

The cost of providing the supply system has also prevented Canadian Pacific from proceeding with a plan to electrify its lines in the mountain regions in the west of the country. The increased power and traction offered by electric locomotives would solve a lot of Canadian Pacific's problems in the mountains, as well as proving cheaper in terms of fuel cost, but the expense involved would be prohibitive in present economic circumstances.

Some modern industrial lines have been built using electric traction to allow automation. The Carol Lake iron ore mines in northeastern Quebec use a 6-mile track to ferry ore to the crushing plant, while the 15-mile Muskingum Electric Railroad in Ohio and the 78-mile Black Mesa and Lake Powell are other examples, the latter using 6000-hp locomotives to haul 8000-ton coal trains which supply the generating plant on Lake Powell.

However, the appearance of diesel traction has tended to remove the needs that were met originally by some of these electrification schemes. The Milwaukee's electric sections became an inconvenience when diesels proved able to operate satisfactorily over the whole route in the northwest, and a number of other electric operations, such as that on the Norfolk and Western, were abandoned when the original grades were eased as a result of rebuilding.

In fact, the new form of motive power that completely replaced steam and also eliminated a number of the electric operations effectively overcame the principal drawback to wholesale electrification – the enormous initial cost of installing the power supply system – by combining the flexibility of electric motors with their own generating plant on the same vehicle.

The original Diesel engine was patented by its German inventor in 1892. It was another 20 years before a successful method was found to overcome its main handicap as far as railroad application was concerned, namely how to use the power generated.

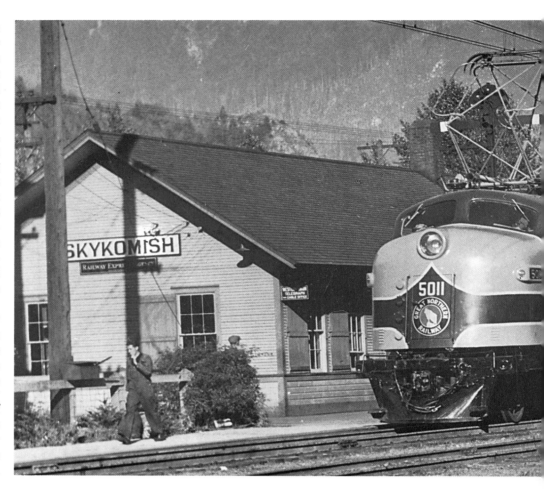

Various transmission systems have been developed, but the most common, and the universal method on American railroads, was to use the diesel engine to generate electricity, this in turn being utilized to drive axle-mounted electric motors.

In the United States, General Electric produced a 300-hp Bo-Bo – that is, two pairs of axles, each with its own motor – in 1924, and this engine and its derivatives were eventually adopted by many railroads for switching duties. For their power, these early machines were exceptionally heavy: the original 300-hp switcher weighed 60 tons. A similar power-to-weight ratio on a mainline engine would have made it unacceptably massive even if it had been feasible to design such an enlarged version. They were also much more expensive than equivalent steam engines, though this factor was offset by the considerable reduction in fuel costs that they made possible.

Among the many experimental developments of the 1920s and 1930s, one line of research was to prove most significant. This was begun by the Electromotive and Winston Engine companies, which in 1930 became a division of General Motors, and centered on the production of a lightweight powerplant which materialized in the form of the 201A. Offering a dramatically reduced weight-to-power ratio of only 20 lb per horsepower, the 201A found its first application in the famous Zephyr streamlined passenger train built for the Burlington Route in 1934.

On May 26, 1934, the Zephyr put on a spectacular demonstration of the diesel's capabilities when a special run took it from Denver to Chicago, 1015 miles, nonstop in just over 13 hours. The three-car Zephyr, however, was a special lightweight train powered by a single 600-hp unit, and a more sig-

nificant breakthrough came the following year when two of the new engines were mounted in a prototype road locomotive. The eight-cylinder engines used on the Zephyr became 12-cylinder models of 900 hp each, 1800 hp for the pair, and when two of the new vehicles

An electrically hauled Great Northern train at Skykomish, on the Cascade electrified section.

were coupled together the resulting 3600 hp at last began to compete with the already established forms of steam

Below: A Pennsylvania Railroad electric GGI locomotive hauls the 18-car Congressional.

locomotive.

The first sales of the new locomotives were made to the Baltimore and Ohio and Santa Fe railroads, and Electromotive proceeded to develop the 1800-hp E1 into the 2000-hp E6 of 1938. Standardizing this basic design, they produced it in both cab and booster versions, normal operating practice being to use two cab units with a booster in between, thus producing a 6000-hp locomotive that could be driven from either end.

Given the versatility of the new units, their reduced fuel costs and maintenance requirements, and consequent greater availability, the railroads soon began to find them extremely attractive compared with their existing steam locomotives; and the consider-ably higher cost was offset both by projected operational savings and readily available finance for their purchase. Steam engines designed to meet the particular needs of an individual road would not necessarily find a ready market on resale, but the standardized diesels could be used anywhere, and were thus excellent security for loans.

Over the next 25 years a total of nearly 1300 E-series locomotives were sold to railroads throughout the country, and many survived to serve Amtrak in the 1970s.

The next stage in diesel development was the production of a more powerful locomotive suitable for freight services, and by adapting the 567 engine used in the E6, Electromotive came up with the 16-cylinder, 1350-hp that was to power it. Four units, two cab and two booster, combined to form a 5400-hp locomotive. Tests with a special demonstration model revealed fuel costs half those for equivalent steam power, and a further advantage was its ability to be used as separate 2700-hp combinations. Again, the new locomotive proved an immediate success, and its FT and F series developments brought eventual sales approaching 7000 units.

During the Second World War, Electromotive was largely insulated from competition by a directive of the War Production Board which stipulated that manufacture of road diesels should be left to the General Motors subsidiary, while other firms concentrated on smaller types.

Among such other firms was the American Locomotive Company, which had begun production of a 2000-hp units in 1940. Previously, Alco, in collaboration with General Electric, had built large numbers of switchers, and during the war they were restricted to diesel units of 1000 hp or less. One outcome of this restriction was their production of a general-purpose type which became known as the road-switcher, being basically a switching engine but with provision for extra fuel and heating equipment to enable it to be used for mainline freight or passenger work.

By the time the war was over, it was generally accepted that the operational and other advantages of the diesel were conclusive compared with steam power. In fact, by 1948 demand for new diesels was far greater than the manufacturers could meet. By this time Alco were back in business with 1500-hp road-switchers and 2000-hp passenger locomotives, while Baldwin and Fairbanks-Morse also began production of commercial diesel locomotives. However, Electromotive remained the dominant supplier, and by the late 1960s all the above competitors had given up.

In the meantime, General Electric, having ended its partnership with Alco in 1953, began to produce its own road-switchers. By this time, the multi-purpose road-switcher had been accepted as the logical form for utilizing the diesel's inherent versatility, and another step forward was the abandoning of the cab bodies, in which the first commercial machines were shrouded, in favor of the hood unit.

Basically, the hood type of diesel has a casing which covers the machinery but does not extend to the full width of the locomotive, allowing a full-width cab to give adequate views for driving in both directions. The resulting flexibility of operation was reflected in Electromotive's designation of GP, for general purpose, which was applied to subsequent road-switchers. Over 6000 of the 1500-hp GP7 and 1750-hp GP9

The Burlington Route's Pioneer Zephyr, which made a sensational non-stop run between Denver and Chicago in 1934 to advertise the new diesel's capabilities, and (inset) the later Denver Zephyr streamliner.

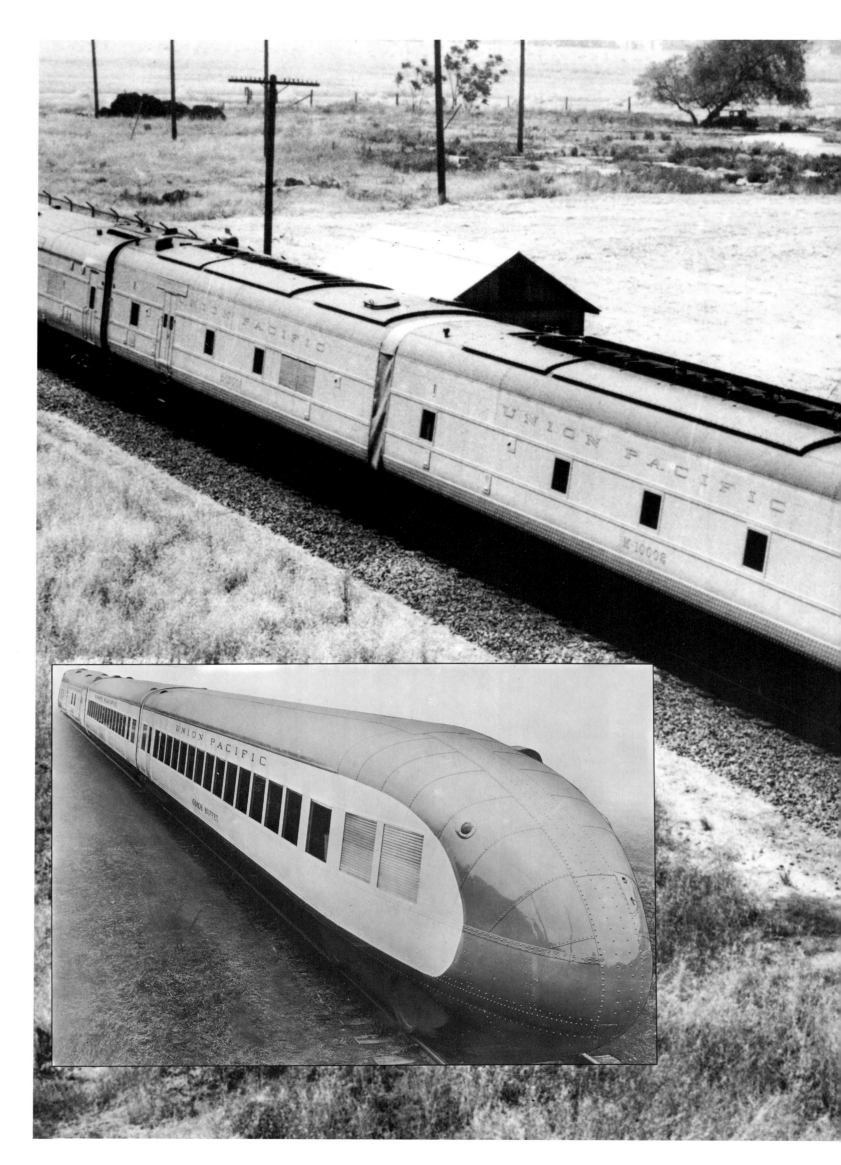

The Union Pacific streamliner City
of Los Angeles on its inaugural run
in May 1936, and (inset) the tail of the
railroad's original oil-engined
streamliner, later named City of
Salina, the Pullman-built M-1000.

The introduction of diesel power, enabling multiple locomotive units to be built up from standard components, permitted a great deal of flexibility in the provision of motive power. Opposite: The Baltimore and Ohio was an early customer for the products of the Electromotive Division of General Motors. Here a cab and booster head the railroad's Columbian Express in 1949. Opposite, bottom: Cab and booster of 3000 hp each at the head of a Pennsylvania Railroad freight train. Right: Two cab and three booster units make up the motive power to take the Santa Fe streamliner The Chief through Navajo Indian country en route for California. Below: Six Electromotive SD40-2 hood units of 3000 hp each head a joint Burlington Northern-Santa Fe coal train at Cleburne, Texas, in May 1980. The hood units dispense with the cab type casing thus allowing the engineer an adequate view in both directions to allow still greater flexibility and ease of operations.

were sold during the 1950s. More powerful models subsequently produced include the 2000-hp GP20 and GP38 and 3000-hp GP40, while cab versions have also been built.

In general, 3000 hp has become recognized as the maximum useful power for a single unit. Much bigger models have been built, such as the 5000-hp types supplied to Union Pacific in the early 1960s, but in view of the diesel's ability to form multiple units adaptable to virtually any power requirement, the concentration of so much power in a single locomotive makes little economic sense. Nevertheless, Union Pacific went even bigger in 1969 with the 6600-hp DDA40X, which amounted to two standard units combined in a common case, buying no less than 47 of this type in the following two years.

The most recent ranges of diesels, however, accept 3500 hp as being the largest desirable size. Both Electromotive and General Electric produce units in this range, notably the former organization's four-axle GP50 for fast freight services and six-axle SD50 for heavier duties, and the latter's 3000-hp C30 and 3600-hp C36.

The production of passenger locomotives, meanwhile, has slumped along with the demand for passenger services.

One of the problems facing Amtrak on its formation was the replacement of the ageing fleet of diesels which it inherited, along with its other rolling stock, from the railroads who took the opportunity to hand over their passenger operations.

Among these were 286 of the old E- and F-series diesels, the Pennsylvania's fleet of 40 GG-1 electric locomotives, dating from the 1930s, and the modern

Budd Metroliners. The problem of old stock was compounded by the condition of much of the track over which it was forced to run: Amtrak was established to operate the services, and had no authority over the maintenance of track, which remained the responsibility of the railroads who owned it.

The first replacement for the diesels was in the form of new Electromotive 3000-hp SPD40F cab versions of the

standard SD40. Unfortunately, all attempts to run these six-axle units at high speeds on poorly maintained track led to a number of derailments and consequent speed limitations. The solution was an expensive rebuilding process to convert them into four-axle models, with further examples ordered from the manufacturers under the designation F40PH.

On the electrified main line between

Opposite, top: Atchison, Topeka and Santa Fe 2300-hp GP39-2 road switcher. The GP – general purpose – designation was introduced by Electromotive for hood diesels with B-B axle arrangements: the equivalent designation for special duty types with six axles was SD. Opposite: A pair of Missouri Pacific road switchers at the head of a chemical unit train. Above: The Union Pacific maintained its record of using the most powerful of all locomotives with the 6600-hp DDA40X Centennial type, 47 of which were produced by Electromotive starting in 1969, the hundredth anniversary of the completion of the transcontinental railroad. The Centennial effectively combines two standard locomotives in a single body, but the concentration of so much power within a single unit has proved economically dubious, when one fault can put the equivalent of two units out of action. Right: Chicago and Northwestern diesels await work in the yard.

Opposite, top: Cab and twin booster units head a train of VIA-Rail, operators of Canadian passenger services. Above: VIA-Rail LRC (light, rapid, comfortable) set with diesel-alternator power car and tilt-body passenger cars. Left: Amtrak Metroliner on the electrified northeast corridor route between Washington and New York.

New York and Washington, in the absence of any suitable contemporary designs of electric locomotives, Amtrak resorted to an adaptation of the General Electric freight engines built for the Black Mesa and Lake Powell coal line. Again, these proved disappointing, and no better results were obtained from the subsequent purpose-built General Electric E60s, which were limited to a maximum speed of 85 mph. The final solution came from Sweden in the form

of ASEA Type Rc4 locomotives to be built by Budd and General Electric, using electrical equipment supplied by the Swedish firm.

Finally, on its New York-Boston route, Amtrak inherited three of the Turbotrains built by United Aircraft under the federal High Speed Ground Transportation program of the late 1960s. The advanced technology on which these trains were based, however, proved unequal to high-speed railroad operation, and rising oil prices during the 1970s finally led to their abandonment on economic grounds. Canadian National had experienced similar trouble with its turbotrains, which were introduced on the Montreal-Toronto route in 1969. These have periodically disappeared from service, most seriously in 1979 following the destruction of three cars of one of the nine-car trains, when a fire was caused by a fractured oil pipe spraying

oil over the turbine in the power car.

Again, Amtrak turned to a European design for the Turbotrains' replacements. A two-year trial of French RTGs on the route between Chicago and St Louis resulted in Amtrak buying six sets from the French builders and arranging for the construction of a further seven by Rohr of California.

The total number of locomotives in service with U.S. railroads declined steadily from 1929, firstly as a result of the depression of the 1930s and more recently because of the increased efficiency of the diesel. Since the mid-1960s about 28,000 locomotives, more than 99 per cent of them diesels, have operated the railroads of the United States, with replacements running at between 1000 and 1500 per year, though in 1976 new orders slumped to under 500. Against that, the most recent figures indicate an increase of over 500 locomotives in service during 1980.

Above: The Swedish ASEA Type Rc4 electric locomotive adopted for the northeast corridor route as the AEM-7. Right: Amtrak Turboliner, based on a French design, for the Boston-New York express passenger services.

PASSENGER SERVICES

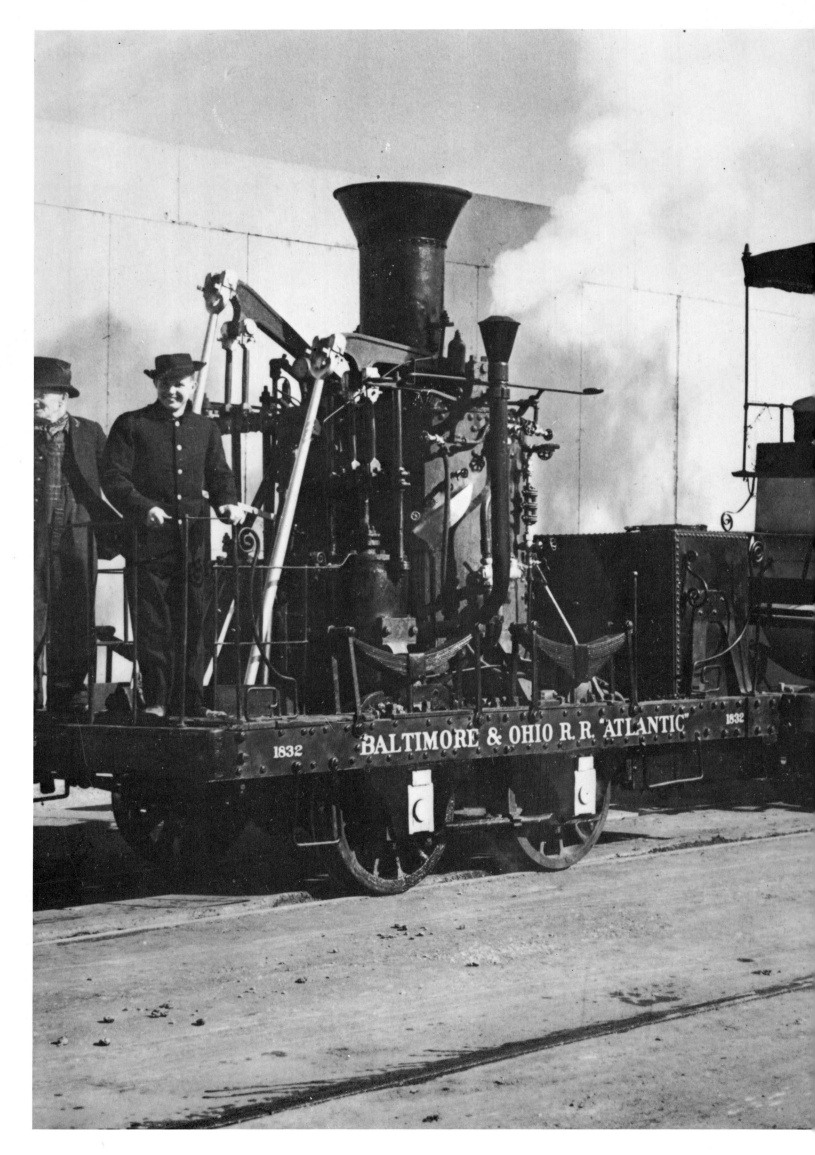

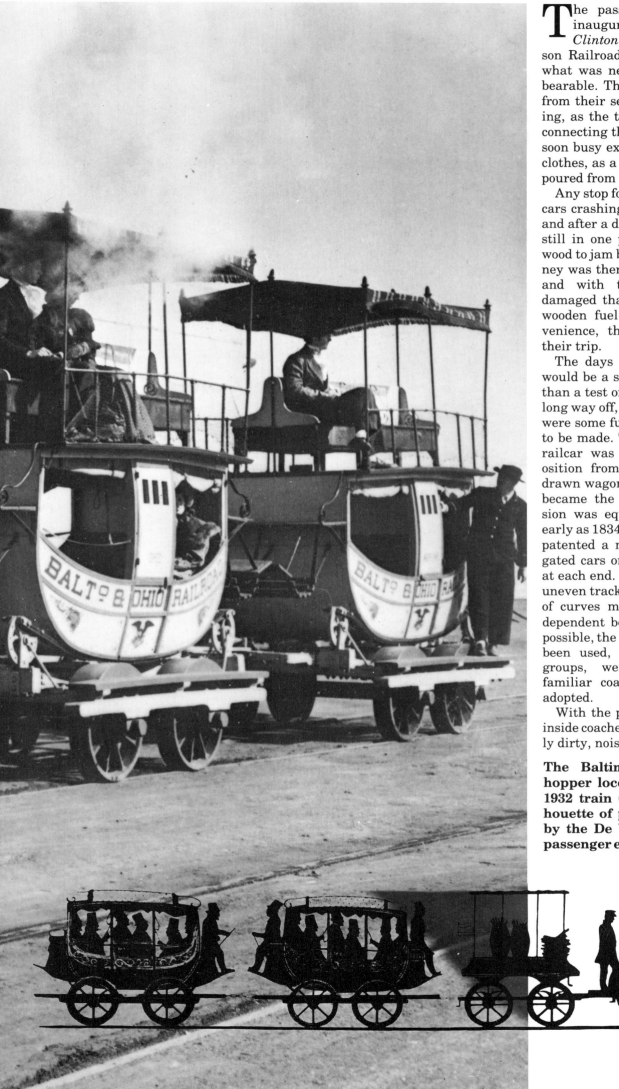

The passengers who braved the inaugural service of the *De Witt Clinton* on the Mohawk and Hudson Railroad in 1831 soon discovered what was needed to make rail travel bearable. Those who were not thrown from their seats by the shock of starting, as the three-foot lengths of chain connecting the cars snapped taut, were soon busy extinguishing their burning clothes, as a stream of glowing embers poured from the smokestack.

Any stop for water sent the unbraked cars crashing into the braking engine, and after a drenching those passengers still in one piece fashioned buffers of wood to jam between the cars. The journey was then resumed more smoothly, and with their clothing so badly damaged that the fiery rain from the wooden fuel was now a mere inconvenience, they eventually completed their trip.

The days when a journey by train would be a source of enjoyment rather than a test of endurance were clearly a long way off, but in the meantime there were some fundamental improvements to be made. Travel on the outside of a railcar was clearly a different proposition from the outside of a horse-drawn wagon, and inside seats quickly became the rule. Stagecoach suspension was equally inadequate, and as early as 1834 Ross Winans of Baltimore patented a method of mounting elongated cars on short, four-wheel bogies at each end. This improved running on uneven track and made the negotiation of curves much easier. Once the independent bogies made longer frames possible, the stagecoach bodies that had been used, first singly and then in groups, were discarded, and the familiar coach layout was generally adopted.

With the passengers safely enclosed inside coaches, rail travel became merely dirty, noisy, uncomfortable and dan-

The Baltimore and Ohio grasshopper locomotive *Atlantic* with a 1932 train (left), and (below) a silhouette of part of the train hauled by the De Witt Clinton on its first passenger excursion in August 1831.

gerous. Riding quality, however, was further improved by the development of cast-iron wheels that could be made more regular than early hand-crafted examples. Spark-arresters helped to limit the damage done by stray embers, but there was always the danger of sprung rails penetrating the coach floor; and in the case of a derailment there was a strong likelihood of a fire caused by the kerosene lamps and wood stoves used to provide light and heat.

Added to the physical discomfort and danger were many inconveniences. For many years it was impossible to obtain through tickets covering more than one railroad, there were no baggage handling facilities, and no refreshments were served on board. As the railroads expanded, however, competition appeared, public expectation rose and the government began to take an interest in the safety of passengers. Gradually, things changed for the better.

Particularly during the 1870s and 1880s, much was done to eliminate the unnecessary hazards of rail travel. Improvement of the actual roads, with the use of heavier steel track, and the recognition of the need for regular maintenance, reduced the danger from sprung rails and derailments. The introduction of the Westinghouse vacuum brake and the Janney automatic coupler made starting and stopping more predictable. The suppression of stoves and kerosene lamps, to be replaced by steam heating from the engine and gas or electric lighting, reduced the frequency of fires. Improved signaling and the spread of the telegraph also did much to reduce the accident rate.

Perhaps the advance that was most appreciated by passengers, however, was the enormous improvement in the design of the cars and their internal fittings, and in this context the name of George Pullman became a byword for the highest standards in comfort.

Pullman was not the first to design and build a sleeping car for overnight accommodation during a journey. The first recorded sleeping car was actually used as early as the mid-1830s on the Cumberland Valley Railroad in Pennsylvania, where stagecoach passengers arriving at Chambersburg late at night took an overnight train to Harrisburg for a connecting service to Philadel-

Cross section (above) and interior view (right) of George Pullman's first sleeping car, Old No 9, which was produced in 1858 and was the first step towards the later cars for which Pullman became famous.

Immigrants could not afford to pay fares that would bring them some comfort, so were given minimum facilities (below).

phia. But crude berths without bedding were the rule, and in 1853 Pullman found himself on one such sleeper traveling between Buffalo and Westfield.

Apart from the obvious hardness of the wooden berths, the most serious drawback, in his view, was that they were permanently fixed to the side of the car, so that it could not be used for daytime travel. Being a carpenter, Pullman set about finding a better solution, and in 1858 he converted two old sleeping cars of the Chicago and Alton Railroad. Neither these nor several subsequent conversions made much impression, but they gave Pullman a chance to experiment, and after a short visit to the Colorado goldfields he returned to Chicago resolved to build

nothing less than the best car ever.

This car, the *Pioneer*, was indeed a splendid contrivance, but it had the disadvantage of being much too big for the Chicago and Alton's structures; consequently, its carpets, brocade upholstery, polished wood, silvered oil lamps and gilded mirrors, assembled at a cost of $20,000, compared with the normal price of $4000, remained objects of wonder rather than practical use.

In 1865, however, the body of the assassinated President Lincoln arrived in Chicago on its way to Springfield; and since the *Pioneer* was the obvious conveyance for the journey, the line was modified to accommodate its passage. Later, the line between Detroit and Galena was similarly altered so that

General Grant could travel home in the new car, which was then placed in regular service on the Chicago and Alton. Pullman himself formed the Pullman Car Company in 1867 and his products soon became synonymous with luxury rail travel.

Although the first cars produced by the new company were sleepers, the range was soon expanded. Hotel cars, combining sleeping accommodation with a kitchen and portable tables, were built for the Great Western Railway of Canada in 1867, and in 1888 the first dining car was built for the Chicago and Alton. Luxury day coaches known as Palace Cars followed, and it was soon apparent that connection between the individual cars was desirable.

The result, in 1887, was Pullman's

patented vestibuled car, which used steel springs to hold a steel-framed diaphragm over the platform at the end of one car against a similar arrangement on its neighbor. This enabled passengers to cross in safety from car to car, and also made a major contribution to safety, by helping to suppress the tendency of the platforms to ride over each other and increase the damage caused in crashes.

Thanks to the vestibuled car, the limited train, with its combination of sleeping, dining, smoking, library, bathroom and barber facilities, became fashionable; and on the long trips to the west coast passengers queued to pay the supplementary charge for Pullman service.

Nor did Pullman simply build the cars and leave them to others to operate. Each car was provided with its own attendant, punctiliously schooled in the minutiae of caring for passengers, his conduct governed by a rule book that detailed every aspect of his job. This arrangement persisted until 1947, when an antitrust suit forced the company to choose between building and operating cars. Unfortunately, the company chose to keep on building, and gave up their operation to a new consortium formed by a group of railroads. Uncertainty over the future of American passenger travel subsequently led to the company's decision to abandon the construction of the cars themselves.

Pullman's enterprise inspired a host

Early travellers on the transcontinental railroads met with contrasting conditions depending on their status and the fare they were able to afford. Immigrants were carried in what became known as Zulu cars (opposite, top), which provided the minimum of sleeping accommodation and were designed to be easily hosed out at the end of the journey. The introduction of the first Pullman cars on the Union Pacific (opposite) enabled wealthier travellers to enjoy a degree of comfort, and the provision of dining cars (above) proved a welcome addition to the facilities. Railroad presidents and other VIPs were able to make use of private cars equipped to the highest standards of luxury, and a special class of passenger was the royal party which accompanied the Prince of Wales on his visit to Canada in 1860. Although most of his journey was made by river, a special car was produced especially for his short rail journey (right) by the Buffalo and Lake Huron

of imitators. Many railroads built their own cars, while other organizations, such as the Woodruff and Wagner companies, were formed as specialist builders and operators. But the name of Pullman retained its magic, and over the years new designs were produced to meet changing requirements.

In 1907 the first all-steel Pullman was produced. By this time the accommodation included curtained seating sections which could be converted to incorporate berths at night, a ladies' drawing room at one end of the car, and a gentlemen's smoking compartment at the other end. Air-conditioning was added in the late 1920s, and in the 1930s the roomette was introduced, replacing the curtained alcoves with individual compartments that combined day seating, folding berths and toilet facilities. At first 18 roomettes were contained in each car, but by staggering the position of the floors and arranging for one bed to slide underneath the higher floor and the bed in the next compartment to fold against the wall, 24 individual roomettes were packed into a single car.

Matching this improvement in accommodation was an acceleration in the speed of services. In the late nineteenth century 40-mph trains boasted names like Thunderbolt or Cannonball, but long-distance travelers were still forced inevitably to make frequent changes.

Even in New York, many train journeys began with a ferry across the Hudson, since only the New York Central, with its Grand Central Station, had a terminus in the city, and the only other railroad to operate from it was the New York, New Haven and Hartford.

This latter situation, at least, was remedied in 1910 when the Pennsylvania Railroad opened its own station on Manhattan Island. One consequence of this move was to intensify com-

Above: the Union Pacific M-10000T.

petition on the route to Chicago, which in the 1890s had been covered by as many as 44 through trains daily.

Wide variation in routes led to wide variation in timings, and before the First World War, the railroads concerned agreed a standard timing of 28 hours for the journey. Since the distances involved ranged from the Pennsylvania's 902.7 miles to the Erie's 995.6 miles, it was further agreed that a supplementary charge of one dollar should be levied for each hour by which the standard time was reduced.

The leaders on the Chicago run were the Pennsylvania and the New York Central, who ran their prestige trains, the Broadway Limited and the Twentieth Century Limited, between the two cities in 18 hours, though after the war this was raised to 20 hours. Given the additional charges for the Pullman service on these trains, there was a sub-

Following several early prototypes, Pullman's real breakthrough came with the construction of the *Pioneer* (left) for the Chicago and Alton Railroad. Originally rejected as too big for the line structures, the car was used to carry the body of President Lincoln back to Springfield in 1865, the line being widened to accommodate it, and the publicity attracted on that occasion was the first step towards the Pullman car's general acceptance. Most travel continued to be in standard day coaches such as those on the typical mid-century train below.

Above: Tail observation platform of the Great Northern's Oriental Limited at the turn of the century.

Right: The Centennial club car produced in the style of the 1890s for use on the Atchison, Topeka and Santa Fe's Kansas City Chief.

stantial price differential between the slower services and their more famous counterparts.

During the 1920s the accent was on service, the last word in luxury being matched by the opulence of the catering; but as the private automobile began to make its presence felt, speed was the vital factor enabling the railroads to compete in an area where they had previously enjoyed a virtual monopoly. This trend was epitomized by the introduction of the streamliners in the 1930s, for the publicity value of their spectacular appearance was a valuable weapon in the fight against the falling traffic that stemmed from the combination of economic depression and the growth of private transport.

The first streamliner was introduced by the Union Pacific, using Pullman-built aluminum cars and an early diesel engine. In 1934 this train, which went into service after a demonstration tour as the City of Salina, recorded speeds of up to 110 mph with only a 400-hp engine, so promising to combine impressive economy with a speed of ser-

vice and appearance that would help lure passengers back onto the rails.

It was considered essential that the new services should bear names that would appeal to the public's imagination. The Chicago, Burlington and Quincy was one of the first railroads to operate streamliners, setting a number of trends with its Zephyr, introduced in 1934. The first Zephyr was a three-car train built by the Budd company of Philadelphia and using one of the early 600-hp Electromotive diesel engines. The first service established was between Lincoln, Nebraska, and Kansas City by way of Omaha, and passenger reaction was sufficiently encouraging for the services soon to be extended to other cities.

Nevertheless, not all the new streamliners were diesel powered. In 1935 the Milwaukee Road began operating its Hiawathas with magnificent speed-shrouded steam locomotives. The Hiawatha service was initially restricted to the highly competitive route between Chicago and Minneapolis and St Paul, but was also extended to include runs north to the shore of Lake Superior, and west to Omaha, Sioux Falls and across the continent via the Olympian Hiawatha to Spokane.

Among other western long-distance streamliners were such famous trains as the Santa Fe's Super Chief, introduced in 1937 with diesel power and

To match the image of the stream-lined trains of the 1930s new types of Pullman car were produced. The Duplex car of 1936 (left) included two double and 14 single sleeping compartments, and like the Roomette car of the following year (below left), which had 18 individual bedrooms, featured air-conditioning and separate heating and ventilation controls for each compartment.

had run through services between Montreal and Vancouver. In 1955, Canadian Pacific introduced its own domecar train for the aptly named Canadian service.

Declining traffic affected the Canadian services, as it did every other service in later years. In 1965 Canadian National's Dominion transcontinental service was withdrawn, and in 1978, with the formation of the national VIA-Rail passenger service operation, the surviving Canadian and Canadian National's Super Continental were combined over a long portion of the transcontinental route between Sudbury and Winnipeg.

Left: A pair of the Burlington Route's Zephyr streamliners at Chicago in the late 1930s.

Pullman coaches for the marathon Chicago–Los Angeles route. Another streamliner between these two cities was the Union Pacific's City of Los Angeles, while the City of Portland and City of San Francisco served their respective cities.

One exception to the general rule of streamliners aiming for highest speeds plus finest accommodation came after the Second World War, by which time trains were facing new competition from the airlines on the longer routes. Having pioneered the high-speed concept in the 1930s, the Burlington, in 1949, introduced the domeliner, in the form of the California Zephyr. Coaches for the California service included domed observation cars specially built by Budd and intended to offer an extra ingredient to the journey by making the most of the magnificent scenery of the Far West.

The Burlington's lead was followed by a number of railroads, among them the Canadian Pacific. In Canada, of course, the transcontinental railroads really were transcontinental, and since the 1880s Canadian Pacific, with later competition from Canadian National,

In the United States, the arrival of Amtrak heralded the end of many of the famous old names. The Rio Grande persisted with its Rio Grande Zephyr between Denver and Salt Lake City, and Southern Railways kept its Southern Crescent in service between Washington and New Orleans, with a through sleeping car service, after a night spent in the stationary sleeper, to Los Angeles; but there was not enough demand to keep many of the other services in operation.

Some of the services, however, were given new names. One of the most renowned of the old streamliners was the Southern Pacific's Coast Daylight between Los Angeles and San Francisco, nowadays replaced by the Coast Starlight, which extends along almost the whole Pacific coastline from Seattle to Los Angeles. The Hiawatha also lives on as the North Coast Hiawatha, but the vast majority of the railroads today are devoted exclusively to freight. Passenger trains are operated over only a fraction of the total track.

Moreover, timings of the modern services are substantially down on those operated during the 1950s or 1930s, though any attempt to compete with the airlines in terms of speed would be pointless over the longer routes. The main reason for the deterioration of schedules is the dilapidated state of much of the track, which simply does not permit high-speed trains.

One specialized service has been established in recent years by offering a facility that no other form of transport can match. This is the Auto-Train Cor-

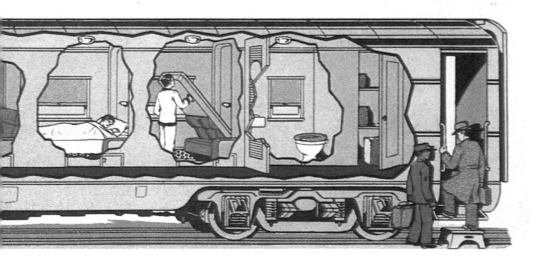

Above: Interior of the tail observation car on CP's Canadian.

Left: Interior of the Silver Tureen, dining car of the Burlington Route's Twin Cities Zephyr.

Below: The Skytop Lounge car at the tail of a Milwaukee Road Hiawatha at Columbus in 1950.

Above: A streamlined Hudson of the New York Central with a royal train northbound at Paskill, New York.

Below: The full-length dining car of the Twentieth Century Limited introduced in 1948. With seats for 60 passengers and piped music, this car was unusual in not also containing the kitchen.

Below: Interior of a bedroom on the Chicago, Burlington and Quincy's California Zephyr streamliner.

Below: Interior of a lounge car on the Baltimore and Ohio Railroad's Columbian in 1957. Far left: Inside the dome car of the Columbian in 1949. Opposite: The cocktail lounge of the Atchison, Topeka and Santa Fe's Super Chief. Opposite, bottom: Dome cars enabled two levels of accommodation to be combined, with facilities such as this elegant Union Pacific dining room on the lower deck.

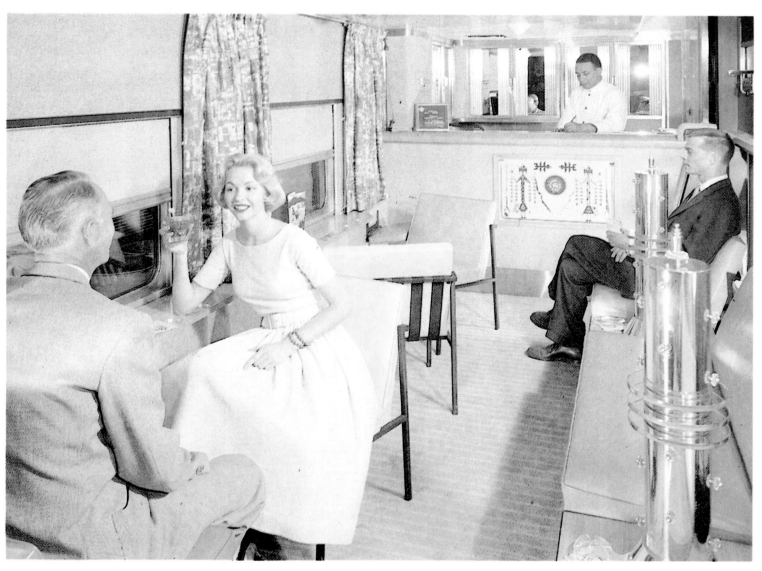

poration, formed in 1969 after studies by the Ford Motor Company and federal agencies had agreed that there was a potential profit to be made from an automobile ferry service, giving passengers the comfort of long-distance train transport plus the convenience of taking their automobiles with them.

Auto-Train, having purchased sleeping cars and day coaches from a variety of railroads who had no further use for them, together with auto-carrying cars from Canadian National and new locomotives from General Electric, began operations in 1971 over the tracks of the Seaboard Coast Line and the Richmond, Fredericksburg and Potomac Railroad between Lorton, Virginia, and Sanford, Florida. The popularity of the holiday route to Florida enabled Auto-Train to show a

Left: The lower level kitchen in the dining car of an Amtrak Superliner.

Opposite and below: CP's Canadian eastbound in the Rockies.

The Autotrain Corporation's vacation specials to Florida, shown here, enable passengers to combine the comfort of rail travel with the convenience of the automobile.

healthy operating profit by the mid-1970s. Although a second service between Louisville and Sanford, operated in conjunction with Amtrak, was discontinued in 1977, another innovation was introduced together with Eastern Airlines, enabling tourists to fly to Florida and have their automobiles delivered by train.

While the prestige services inevitably attract the most attention in any review of rail travel, these have always represented only a part of the railroads' passenger operations. During the late nineteenth century, for example, there were large numbers of special immigrant trains, used to transport settlers from Europe to the new land in the west. Several of the transcontinental lines, especially those operating in the northwest, employed large numbers of agents in Europe who would advertise the attractions of the new country and arrange passage for those who were persuaded to seek their futures there.

Inevitably, conditions on many of the trains that met the new arrivals were little better than primitive. Sleeping cars were designed with wooden benches along the sides for bunks, and internally they were kept as spartan as possible so that they could be hosed down quickly at the conclusion of their journeys.

At the other end of the scale were the lavish private saloons used by the wealthiest travelers. Built to individual

Above: One of the Budd Metroliner electric trains used by Amtrak on the northeast corridor route between New York and Washington.

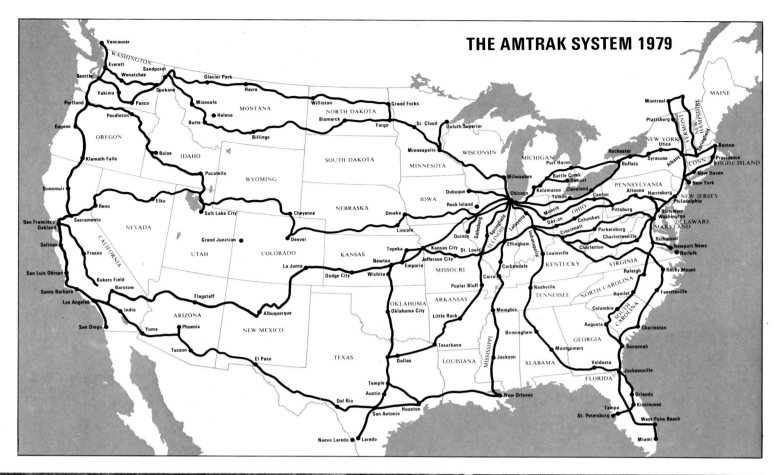

THE AMTRAK SYSTEM 1979

The Amtrak North Coast Hiawatha, successor to the old Milwaukee Road service, with inset views of the Amtrak passenger depot at Richmond, Virginia, passengers boarding the Coast Starlight, and the interior of the Southwest Limited.

times that amount.

Finally, there was one type of passenger that the railroads positively discouraged, since he paid no fare and preferred to avoid passenger trains altogether. The innumerable hobos who roamed the railroads became an integral part of the scene, as they followed the harvests in search of seasonal work. In fact, while some railroads discouraged free rides to the point of brakemen throwing them off moving trains, others, especially in the early days of settlement in the Far West, accepted them, knowing that without migrant laborers the crops that constituted their freight traffic would rot in the fields.

Left: The Frontier Shack tap car on the Union Pacific's City of Denver. Below. Missouri Pacific lounge car of 1936. Opposite: The Little Nugget saloon car of the Union Pacific's City of Los Angeles. Opposite, bottom: Skytop lounge on the Olympian Hiawatha.

specifications, the only limit on what they might offer was the size of the coach and the depth of the customer's purse. The Pullman company alone built some 450 coaches for private customers before the great crash of 1929 put an end to such extravagance, with prices ranging from $50,000 to seven

FREIGHT TRANSPORT

Before steam locomotives were ever thought of, railways were used to ease the handling of heavy loads. In quarries and mines they found their first application, and in the United States it was the prospect of gathering the harvests of the west that first encouraged the builders of railroads to lay their tracks from the east coast toward the great rivers of the interior.

At first, it was the intention of those builders to operate their railroads in the same way as toll roads or canals: they would provide the tracks, and anyone prepared to pay the fee would be allowed to haul their own vehicles over them. This system was soon realized to be impractical, however, and the operators assumed responsibility for all aspects of transport.

This involved the provision of suitable vehicles, the motive power to get them to their destination, depots where goods could be delivered, loaded, unloaded and collected, and a system of recording the movement of the cargoes in their care. From these basic elements all the characteristics of modern freight operations have been developed.

At first, the motive power was the same for any kind of train, but increasing sophistication led to the production of faster locomotives for passenger services, while the accent in freight movement was placed on power, speed being only a secondary consideration. Consequently, freight locomotives tended to have larger numbers of smal-

Above: An early iron ore train crosses a lake. Right: A local mine railroad above tracks of the Fremont, Elkhorn and Missouri Valley and Chicago, Burlington and Quincy railroads in South Dakota.

ler wheels to increase the traction on the rails and, as we have seen, during the twentieth century they assumed massive proportions.

The object was usually to move the maximum possible amount of freight in each train, and in this respect the appearance of the diesel proved an extremely significant development. As long as all the motive power was concentrated at one end of the train, which was generally the case with steam locomotives, there was a practical limit on the load that could be sustained by the couplings. But when diesels made possible the remote control of a number of power units, slave locomotives could be positioned at intervals to spread the load and balance the power exerted.

An earlier breakthrough in controlling long trains was the production of the quick-acting airbrake. Originally, cars were provided with individual brakes that had to be applied by a brakeman climbing along the top of the cars to reach the wheels by which they were adjusted, and the hazards of this occupation were reflected in the heavy casualties sustained.

The obvious need was for a brake that could be applied simultaneously to every car in the train from the locomotive, and by the 1870s the first Westinghouse airbrakes were proving their worth in passenger service. Their drawbacks in freight service were demonstrated with trains of fifty or more cars, when the time taken to transmit the braking force could lead to severe shocks in the rear cars. By the mid-1880s, however, a new quick-acting version of the Westinghouse brake was perfected, which enabled very long trains to be stopped without excessive delays in transmission or the resultant shock effects.

The adoption of a universal method of braking was especially important because the growth of through traffic had led to the cars of the various railroads being distributed throughout the network. To keep track of car movements the railroads maintained car-accounting departments whose task it was to keep records of car movements. Daily charges were levied for the use of cars by 'foreign' railroads, so it was vital both to have an accurate account of the location of the railroad's own cars, for which other users were charged a rental, and to ensure the return of

Trailer-on-flat-car, or piggyback, services enable highway trailers to be transported over the bulk of their journey by rail. Opposite, top: Three of these special Southern Pacific flat cars are carried on only four sets of wheels. Opposite bottom: Baltimore and Ohio piggyback loading. Left: Burlington Northern piggyback train.

empty cars as quickly as possible.

The modern equivalent of the old car-accounting department can be found in such computerized arrangements as the Southern Pacific's Total Operations Processing System. Based in the company's head office in San Francisco, the TOPS information bank is constantly updated with details of every aspect of the railroad's activities, so that, within seconds, any of the 120,000 or so cars anywhere on its 13,500 miles of line can be identified and precisely located. The railroad is thus enabled to monitor the efficiency of its train movements and to provide customers with accurate information on the progress of their shipments.

Freight cars themselves have become steadily more specialized over the years. The basic types that evolved in the early days were flat, box and coal cars, large numbers of which are still in use, but even within those categories there has been constant improvement and refinement. In addition, there are refrigerated cars for perishable fruit and other produce, and a whole range of specially designed cars from triple-deck automobile carriers to tank wagons for bulk liquids.

One of the most important trends has been toward the use of standard containers: and additional efficiency has been provided by the trailer-on-flat-car, or piggyback system, whereby highway trailers are loaded complete onto a flat car to minimize transfer time between road and rail at transhipment points. In recent years, piggyback traffic has been the biggest growth area in railroad freight, and in the number of cars loaded annually has come to be second only to coal.

Coal has long been established as the biggest single type of freight carried by the railroads, with more than five million cars being loaded every year. A high degree of automation has been applied to coal traffic, as exemplified by the Norfolk and Western's coal movements from the Kentucky and West Virginia coalfields, both to domestic customers, especially in the industrial cities south of the Great Lakes, and via its port facilities at Lamberts Point on Chesapeake Bay to export customers.

In handling over two million tons of coal a month at Lamberts Point, the Norfolk and Western employs a range of sophisticated equipment, from infrared thawing sheds to defrost the coal that is often frozen solid after its journey from the mountain mining districts, to radar speed measuring, automatic weight recording and blending, and rotary dumpers that tilt the whole car through 165 degrees to empty the coal and are able to handle up to 252 cars per hour.

Another impressive coal operation is carried out in even more arduous conditions by C.P. Rail. From the Crowsnest Pass area of the Rockies near the U.S. border ten trains ferry eight million tons of coal a year to the new port of Roberts Bank, near Vancouver, for export to Japan. Continuous loading and rotary dumping are needed to maintain the flow of coal, but the most difficult aspect of the work is actually moving the trains from the mountains to the coast.

The trains are worked as permanent-

Coal continues to form the bulk of the railroads' freight. Above and opposite, top: Burlington Northern unit coal trains. Continuous loading at a silo at Gillette, Wyoming, enables 110 cars to be loaded in only two hours, while the 105 cars of the train headed by four 3000-hp diesels near Decker, Montana, carry 10,000 tons of coal. Opposite: Slave locomotives on a Santa Fe coal train near Kansas City.

ly coupled unit trains, with 95 cars each carrying some 115 tons of coal for a total train load of over 11,000 tons. At some stages of its journey, as many as 11 3000-hp locomotives are used on each train, making it necessary to install a computer on board to control the locomotives, ensuring that load and traction are balanced to avoid broken couplings and drawbars caused by the concertina action of the cars in motion.

Unit trains are especially welcome to railroads, since they avoid the need for making up trains of cars from different shippers to different destinations. This has been a necessity since the first railroads began to intersect; and to overcome the delays in transhipment of loads from the cars of one railroad to the cars of another, fast freight lines were established during the nineteenth century. Formed either by agreement between groups of railroads or by independent companies, these lines would contract with shippers to supervise the through working of consignments between different railroads.

After the First World War, the handling of individual cars and the making up of trains was rendered much more efficient by the automation of the classification yards where the work was carried out. One of the first modern yards was the Illinois Central Railroad's Markham Yard, a few miles south of Chicago. The principal device

which made large-scale automation possible was the remotely controlled retarder, used in combination with power-operated switches and a hump to enable all the yard's activities to be controlled from a central tower.

In the early days, all movement of cars in the yards had to be done by switching the engines individually, propelling them into the siding where their train was being made up. This slow and tedious business was simplified con- siderably in the 1880s by the introduc- tion of humps, or artificial mounds, over which all the cars could be pushed in turn and allowed to coast under the in- fluence of gravity, with the appropriate switch setting, to their allotted sidings. Power-operated switches were a further step in speeding up the process, but it was the provision of retarders – beams alongside the rails which gripped the wheels of a passing car to brake it – that enabled control of all the various opera- tions in the yard to be exercised from a single position.

When Markham Yard opened in 1926, the northbound classification sec- tion alone was equipped with as many as 121 retarders and 69 pairs of switches feeding 67 tracks, and five control towers were needed to supervise all the movements. More recent yards have been equipped with computerized control systems that enable all the operations to be brought under fully

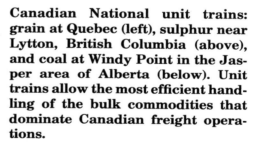

Canadian National unit trains: grain at Quebec (left), sulphur near Lytton, British Columbia (above), and coal at Windy Point in the Jas- per area of Alberta (below). Unit trains allow the most efficient hand- ling of the bulk commodities that dominate Canadian freight opera- tions.

centralized control. An outstanding example of this is provided by C.P. Rail's Alyth Yard at Calgary, where the entire operation, apart from the uncoupling of the cars as they pass over the hump, is controlled by computer.

To enable single cars to be directed to the correct siding, a system of automatic car identification has been adopted whereby a label on the side of the car read by a photoelectric scanner identifies the type of car, the owner, and its individual number. It is this system, extended onto the main line by other scanners at strategic points, that enables central computers like the Southern Pacific's TOPS to provide instant reports on the location and progress of any car.

The application of braking force by the retarder has to be finely calculated to take account of a number of variable factors. The type of car, the presence or absence of a load, its degree of freedom in running, the strength and direction of the wind, and the route to the individual siding will all affect the amount of braking needed to ensure that it neither stops short of the cars already in the siding (which will vary constantly in number), nor reaches them at too high a speed, which may result in damage.

It was this large number of variables, and the consequent need for the cars to be kept under observation throughout the entire shunting operation, that necessitated the provision of multiple control towers; and it is the computer's ability to assess them all automatically and apply the correct degree of braking that has enabled the process to be streamlined so effectively. The application of such a high degree of automation enables Alyth Yard alone to deal with 3000 car movements a day, and to accommodate a total of 5200 standing cars.

Many other refinements are made possible by comprehensive automation of yard facilities. Where a line concentrates on handling a single commodity in massive quantities, as with the Norfolk and Western coal traffic to

Lamberts Point or the neighboring Chessie System's port of Newport News, it becomes economic to install the most specialized equipment possible. The Norfolk and Western's coal, for example, is divided into nearly a thousand different classes, and the blends specified by different customers are produced by an automated blending system. Coal falling from bins onto conveyor belts is controlled in both speed and ratio to produce the exact combination of sizes or grades required. Then the actual loading of the ships is carried out by massive loading towers which deposit the coal in the ships' holds by means of 120 ft extending booms.

In the normal classification yards where mixed traffic of every type is handled, there are general procedures such as the automatic weighing of the cars passing over the hump. At the same time, a more sophisticated arrangement enables not only the car's gross weight but also its distribution on the wheelbase to be assessed, so that imbalance of a load, with potential dan-

Opposite: Control tower, hump and tracks of the Santa Fe's classification yard at Barstow, California. Below: Car retarders used to control the speed of cars in the Canadian Pacific's Alyth classification yard.

gers in high-speed running, can be remedied before the car is attached to its train.

One of the most significant contributions big freight yards can make to operating efficiency is in compiling unit trains, in which all cars are bound for the same destination. This was the principle behind the Santa Fe's construction of its enormous yard at Barstow, California. At Barstow, all traffic previously assembled at various yards throughout California is concentrated before making the journey east, so that cars for a particular destination will accumulate in greater numbers in a shorter time, enabling unit trains to be made up with less delay to the individual consignments. In the reverse direction, there is a big classification yard at Kansas City for the Santa Fe's westbound freight, but intermediate traffic is run to Barstow in mixed freights and then made up into trains for the various destination points in California.

Once the train has been made up and has left the yard, its progress and movements need to be controlled not only to ensure efficient delivery of the freight, but also to ensure the safety of all the traffic on the road. The system that developed in the nineteenth century, after the introduction of the telegraph,

was that of train orders. A central dispatcher, communicating by telegraph with station operators, would transmit instructions governing the movements of all trains on the line. These were then written down and handed to the engineer and conductor of every train to which they applied.

In this way, engineers would be given their instructions, warned of other traffic on the line, advised of the priority accorded to the various trains, and so on. This system is still used in many parts of the country, being particularly important on long stretches of single track, where trains in both directions need to pass each other safely. Consequently, the engineer might be told to proceed as far as a particular passing point, where a loop in the track would allow him to pull off the main line, and wait there before continuing until another train had passed.

The engineer of the other train, meanwhile, would have been authorized to proceed, while at the same time being warned of the presence of the first train and told where to expect to find it waiting in its loop. Naturally, if the sidelined train was not in its appointed place, the train with the right of way would be expected to stop and telegraph the dispatcher, using a portable telegraph machine that could be tapped into the

line at the side of the track, to report on the situation and receive further instructions. So vital a part did the telegraph play in the operation of the railroads, that it was a fundamental rule that no train should leave a depot without a telegrapher aboard.

As the years passed, block signaling was introduced on heavily used sections of track such as station approaches, so that all trains would be controlled by semaphore or color light signals from a central control which would also incorporate the control levers for setting the switches. A refinement of this system was the introduction of an interlocking arrangement between signals and switches. This connected all the controls in a mechanical arrangement that ensured no signal could be set unless the individual switches were in the appropriate position for the instruction given; conflicting settings of the various switches, which might allow two trains to converge on the same track, were physically impossible.

The vast extent of the railroad network, however, made the use of such systems impractical on most lines, and the modern form of traffic regulation is centralized train control. C.T.C. was first introduced in the 1920s, and placed the whole section of line under the direct control of the dispatcher. Points and signals were set personally by the dispatcher via electrical circuits, while a control panel would indicate the location of the trains on the section concerned. The inherent time lag in transmission of the command signals has been reduced by the substitution of electronic systems for the old electromechanical methods, and the control panels themselves have been expanded to the point where colored lights can give a continuous representation of the trains' movements.

The installation of radios in the engineers' cabs provides an additional means of control, and instant communication with the control center, while cab signals have also been introduced to give a continuous survey of the line ahead, rather than the periodic indications obtained from the intermittent trackside signals.

One example of the ability of C.T.C. to bring operational control of a railroad together at a central point is provided by the Illinois Central Gulf's headquarters in Chicago, from which the whole of the 9600-mile system is monitored. Not only are the control panels for the C.T.C. sections, which form the majority of the lines, located there, but the control center also includes terminals for the hot box detectors, which monitor passing trains to detect overheating axle boxes so that prompt remedial action can be taken.

Such centralization of control systems reflects the overall pattern of railroad operation in the United States, which, since the earliest days, has seen a gradual trend toward merger and consolidation. Now that the railroads involved are generally so much bigger, the effects of mergers are such as to create gigantic combined systems. Two of the most recent have seen the merger of the Chessie and Family Lines systems to form the C.S.X. Corporation, with responsibility for 26,600 miles of railroad, while the Burlington Northern and Frisco systems also completed a merger, bringing a combined total of 27,300 miles under the same management. The pattern is expected to continue, with more giant systems

The yard controller of the Burlington Northern classification yard at Pasco, Washington.

created from combinations such as that of the Norfolk and Western with Southern Railways.

The Norfolk and Western itself is the product of a series of mergers. In 1959 it combined with the neighboring Virginian Railway, and in 1964 it absorbed the Wabash and Nickel Plate, along with three smaller lines. The effect of the first merger was to consolidate its position as a leading coal carrier, while the second extended its activities into such areas as automobile parts, as well as expanding its area of operations into the Kansas and Nebraska grain producing areas, adding a main line into Canada and giving it access to many important cities.

The pattern of mergers is likely to be accelerated by the Staggers Rail Act, which became law in October 1980. As well as amending the conditions under which the I.C.C. is able to approve merger proposals, the Staggers Act relaxed the conditions for abandonments of lines, and, perhaps most significantly from the railroads' viewpoint, removed many of the regulations governing freight rates. The intention was, apparently, to 'strip away needless and costly regulation in favor of marketplace forces wherever possible,' as President Carter expressed it; or, in the

words of Association of American Railroads president William H. Dempsey, to lay 'the foundations for a new era of railroad growth and prosperity by granting railroads greater opportunity to respond to the disciplines and opportunities of the marketplace.'

Meanwhile, U.S. railroads continue to carry over nine hundred billion ton-miles of freight each year, representing, in the most recent figures available, roughly one and a half million tons of freight carried, on average, some 600 miles. Coal was by far the single most important type of freight, accounting for just over a quarter of the total of 22,598,000 cars loaded in 1980. Of course, the pattern of freight is subject to market forces, reflecting both short- and long-term fluctuations in demand, but in 1980 over a million cars were loaded with metallic ores, grain, chemicals and related products, forest products, pulp, paper and associated products.

One of the most important growth areas in freight transport in recent years has been in piggyback container traffic, which in 1980 amounted to 1,661,110 cars carrying over 3,000,000 trailers and containers. Such figures, as previously mentioned, make container traffic second only to coal in terms of the

The control panel and operator in the tower of the Canadian Pacific classification yard at Alyth.

number of cars loaded; and to exploit such growth railroads have introduced a number of innovatory services in an attempt to increase their share of this form of traffic, which is only a fraction of that conveyed by road, especially over distances of under a thousand miles. The latter category comprises 90 per cent of the total, but the railroads' share is less than 2 per cent.

The obvious area for improvement is in speed of conveyance, and one railroad that has made concerted efforts to offer a service to compete with road transport in this area is the Illinois Central Gulf. The I.C.G.'s highspeed container service, known as Slingshot, runs between Chicago and St Louis, and is timed to cover the 298-mile journey in a competitive seven hours.

Another move toward the economical handling of containers is the Santa Fe's Ten-Pack. The Ten-Pack uses specially designed container cars with only a skeleton bed to support the trailer's undercarriage, the cars being unusually low to reduce wind resistance. The reductions in weight and wind resistance enable substantial fuel savings to

be made on runs of 100-car sets between Chicago and Los Angeles.

Yet another stage in the integration of road and rail carriage of containers is represented by the roadrailer. An initial vogue for trailers with dual running gear to enable them to run on either rails or the highway faded in the face of operational problems during the early 1960s. A recent revival of the concept by the Chessie, however, has seen the production of a roadrailer whose running gear can be changed between the different modes in under three minutes, and which have been run on rails at over 100 mph in tests with 75-car trains.

Meanwhile, as piggyback and container traffic have boomed, some traditional areas of traffic have virtually disappeared. One of the railroads' greatest contributions to the myth of the old West was its part in establishing the trade in cattle from Texas, and with it the legend of the cowboys who drove the stock north along the Chisholm Trail to the cattle towns of Abilene, Dodge City and other points in Kansas. From the western trail ends, the railroads brought the cattle north to Chicago and Kansas City, and later the settlement of the northwest added new beef-producing areas which depended on the railroads to get the animals to the customers.

Speed in transporting live cargo was

The old type of freight train, represented (above) by an example of the Missouri Pacific Railroad, was a slow and inefficient method of conveying goods. Frequent sorting, as cars to and from various points were added and detached prevented rapid shipment, and the introduction of unit trains, such as the diesel-hauled Missouri Pacific grain train (left) was aimed at eliminating delays by using permanently coupled consists to convey bulk goods between centralized loading and unloading points. For small quantities of merchandise, containers allow efficient handling, and piggyback services, with complete highway trailers carried on flat cars, has taken the process one stage further by minimizing the transshipment time. The Illinois Central Gulf's Slingshot service between Chicago and St Louis (opposite, top) makes maximum use of the facility, while centralized control of sorting yards, as in the Santa Fe's Barstow yard (opposite), further streamlines the process.

an obvious necessity, and some of the fastest livestock trains were run by the Chicago, Burlington and Quincy. Average speeds approaching 50 mph were attained with some of the livestock services, and the journey from Denver to Chicago in the early 1960s was scheduled at under 30 hours. At that time the Burlington was using double-deck stock cars and even experimented with special containers for livestock that could be mounted on ordinary flat cars in an attempt to avoid the expense of maintaining specialized cars for what was a largely seasonal trade.

The changing pattern of the beef trade, however, has seen the meat packing plants move out to the ranges, and the stock train has become a thing of the past.

Another traditional area of railroad activity which has now been superseded by more rapid air transport is the carriage of mail. The use of railroads as mail carriers dates back to 1838, when all railroads were designated by Congress as postal routes. Even before this, however, they had been used for carrying mail, and one postmaster-general had proposed that government locomotives, with right of way over other traffic, should be placed in service.

The first provision for mail on board trains was a simple lockable compartment, but in the 1860s a more ambitious scheme was suggested. With the completion of the railroad to St Joseph, and the establishment of the Pony Express service from that city to California, a local mail clerk proposed that the mail should be sorted on board the train to save time at the departure point. Accordingly, in August 1864, the system of mail handling developed in Britain and already in use in Canada was introduced on the Hannibal and St Joseph Railroad.

Subsequently, the provision of post office cars attached to trains became a standard feature of American railroads. The mail car was usually attached to the fastest trains, and always at the head end. Inside, teams of clerks would sort the mail for the various points on the route, and as demand increased, solid mail trains would be run.

Mail trains and stock trains, along with the mixed train of local passenger and freight cars, have passed into the history of the railroads, leaving the tracks to the occasional passenger train and the new types of freight, with multiple diesel power hauling 100,000

The Santa Fe's Ten-Pak piggyback system uses special cars to carry the highway trailers, and the reductions in weight and wind resistance enable substantial fuel savings to be made on long-distance runs with the light, low-slung trains.

255

loaded cars, and almost as many empties, every day. Painted in the vivid colors of their owners, sorted at huge yards, scanned by electronic eyes, their every movement recorded on a distant computer, the almost two million freight cars on North American railroads carry more than ever before; and if they carry a smaller proportion of total freight, that is a reflection of the growth in production that they made possible.

The transport of automobiles between factories and regional distributors forms a substantial part of the railroads' freight business, and triple-deck cars are used for the purpose. The vulnerability of new automobiles to damage in transit led to the development of enclosed cars for the most valuable models, the Santa Fe enclosed transporter being named Safe-Pak. Examples are shown in the view of the autoveyor yard at Amarillo, Texas (above), and the loading process is illustrated (opposite). Opposite, top: imported autos are loaded on autoveyor cars at Long Beach, California. Right: Interior of a Union Pacific mail storage car of 1949.

THE GREAT STEAM LOCOMOTIVES

List of abbreviations

cm	centimetres
cw	hundredweight
ft	feet
in	inches
gal	gallons
kg	kilograms
kg/cm^2	kilograms per square centimetre
km	kilometre
km/h	kilometres per hour
lb	pounds
lit	litres
m	metres
m^2	square metres
ml	mile
mm	millimetres
mph	miles per hour
psi	pounds per square inch

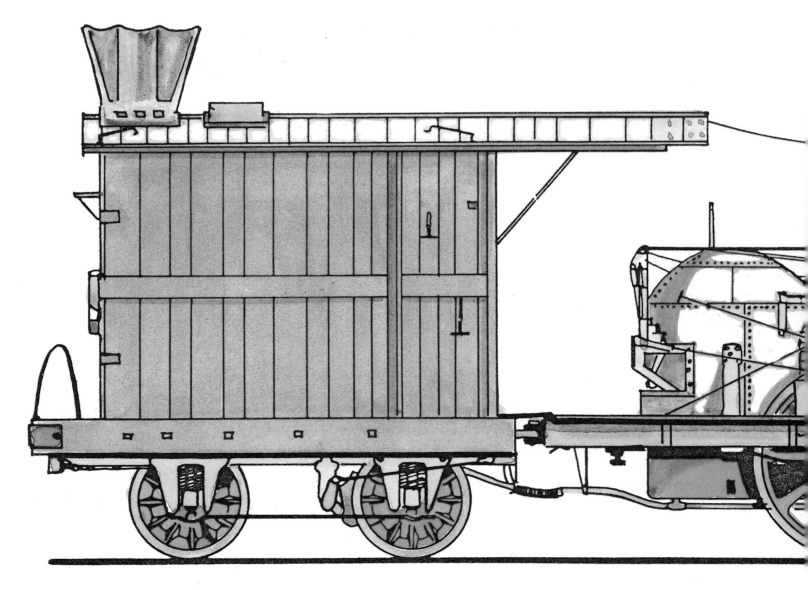

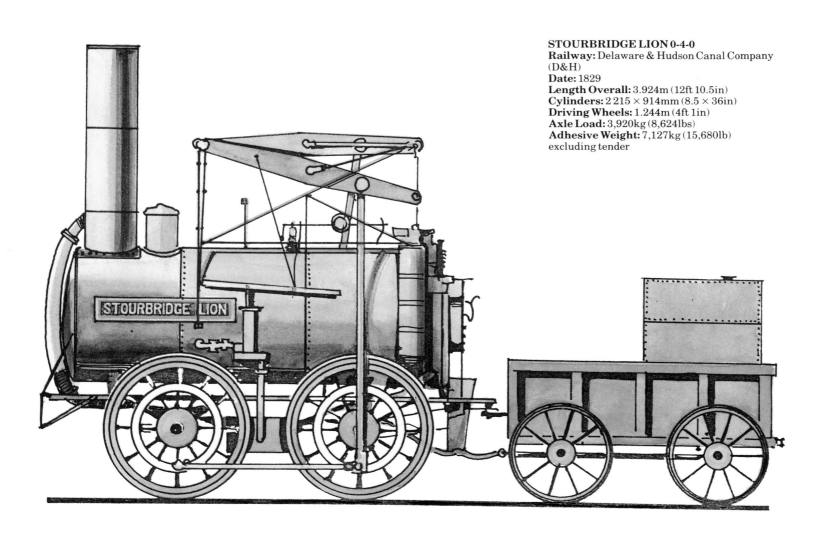

STOURBRIDGE LION 0-4-0
Railway: Delaware & Hudson Canal Company (D&H)
Date: 1829
Length Overall: 3.924m (12ft 10.5in)
Cylinders: 2 215 × 914mm (8.5 × 36in)
Driving Wheels: 1.244m (4ft 1in)
Axle Load: 3,920kg (8,624lbs)
Adhesive Weight: 7,127kg (15,680lb) excluding tender

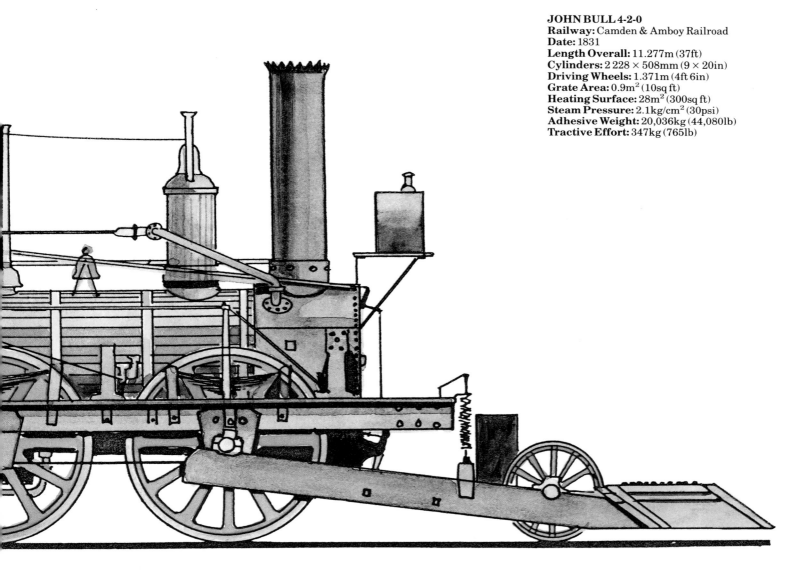

JOHN BULL 4-2-0
Railway: Camden & Amboy Railroad
Date: 1831
Length Overall: 11.277m (37ft)
Cylinders: 2 228 × 508mm (9 × 20in)
Driving Wheels: 1.371m (4ft 6in)
Grate Area: 0.9m² (10sq ft)
Heating Surface: 28m² (300sq ft)
Steam Pressure: 2.1kg/cm² (30psi)
Adhesive Weight: 20,036kg (44,080lb)
Tractive Effort: 347kg (765lb)

LAFAYETTE 4-2-0
Railway: Baltimore & Ohio Railroad (B&O)
Date: 1837
Length Overall: 9.25m (30ft 4in)
Total Weight: 20,000kg (44,000lb)
Cylinders: 2 268 × 457mm (10.5 × 18in)
Driving Wheels: 1.22m (4ft)
Axle Load: 5,909kg (13,000lb)

Fuel: 1,000kg (2,200lb)
Grate Area: 0.8m² (8.6sq ft)
Water: 2,045lit (450gal) (540 US gal)
Heating Surface: 36.6m² (394sq ft)
Steam Pressure: 4.2kg/cm² (60psi)
Adhesive Weight: 13,636kg (30,000lb)
Tractive Effort: 957kg (2,162lb)

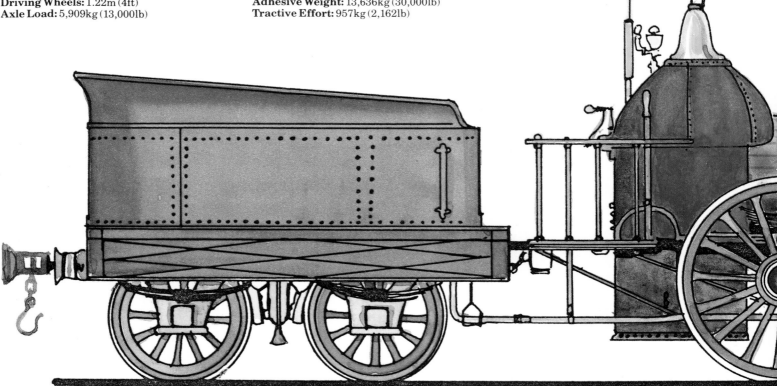

MUD-DIGGER 0-8-0
Railway: Baltimore & Ohio Railroad (B&O)
Date: 1844
Length Overall: 6.045m (19ft 10in)
excluding tender
Total Weight: 21,363kg (47,000lb)
excluding tender
Cylinders: 2 432 × 610mm (1.7 × 24in)
Driving Wheels: 0.838m (2ft 9in)
Axle Load: 5,875kg (12,925lb)
Adhesive Weight: 21,363kg (47,000lb)

Above
JOHN STEVENS 6-2-0
Railway: Camden & Amboy Railroad
Date: 1849
Length Overall: 9.042m (29ft 8in)
excluding tender
Total Weight: 22,727kg (50,000lb)
excluding tender
Cylinders: 2 330 × 863mm (13 × 34in)
Driving Wheels: 2.438m (8ft)
Grate Area: 11.4m² (15.2sq ft)

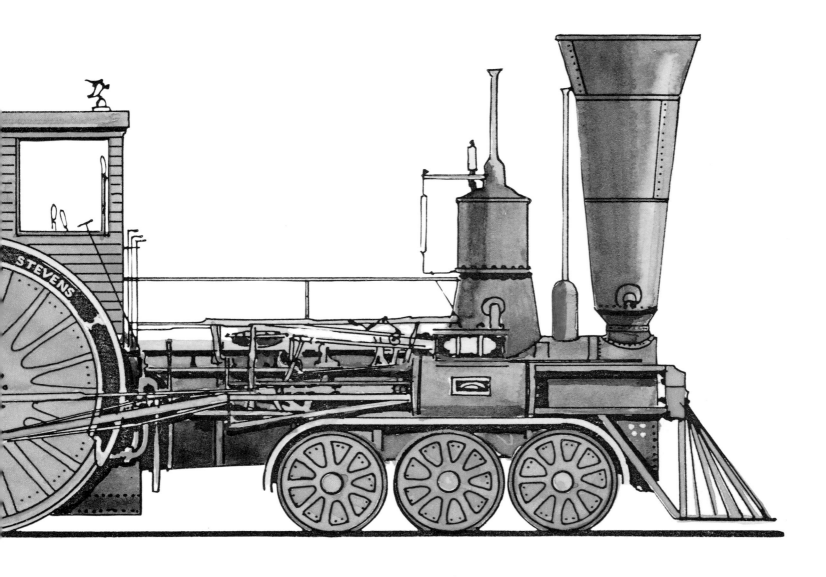

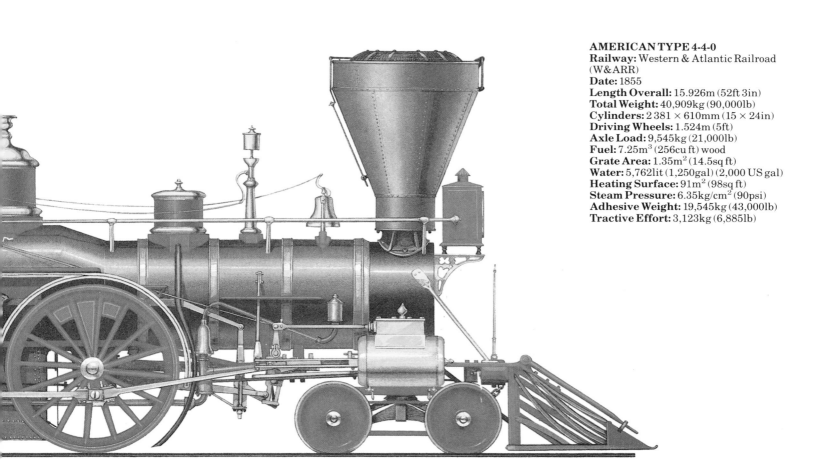

AMERICAN TYPE 4-4-0
Railway: Western & Atlantic Railroad
(W&ARR)
Date: 1855
Length Overall: 15.926m (52ft 3in)
Total Weight: 40,909kg (90,000lb)
Cylinders: 2 381 × 610mm (15 × 24in)
Driving Wheels: 1.524m (5ft)
Axle Load: 9,545kg (21,000lb)
Fuel: 7.25m³ (256cu ft) wood
Grate Area: 1.35m² (14.5sq ft)
Water: 5,762lit (1,250gal) (2,000 US gal)
Heating Surface: 91m² (98sq ft)
Steam Pressure: 6.35kg/cm² (90psi)
Adhesive Weight: 19,545kg (43,000lb)
Tractive Effort: 3,123kg (6,885lb)

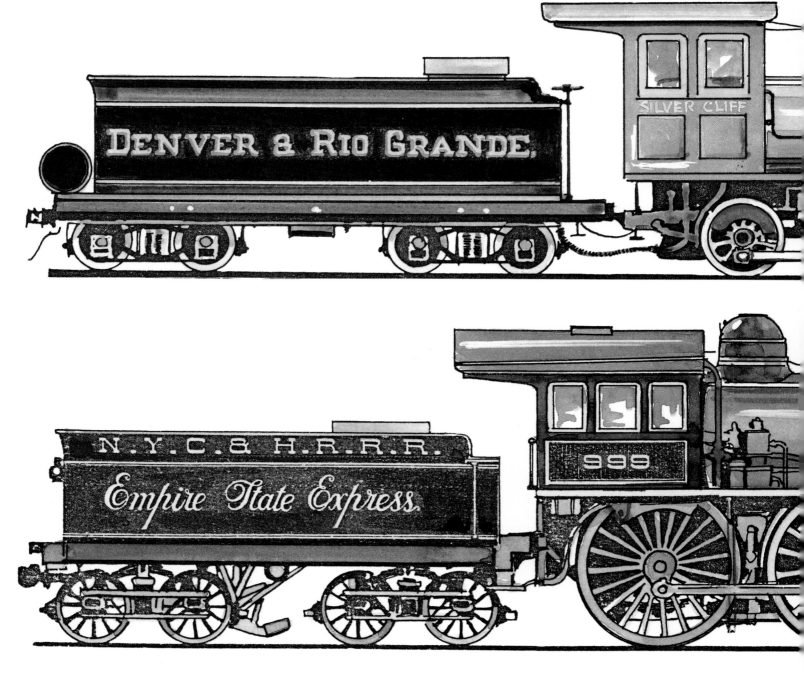

CONSOLIDATION 2-8-0
Railway: Lehigh Valley & Mahoney Railroad (L&MRR)
Date: 1866
Length Overall: 10.312m (33ft 10in) excluding tender
Total Weight: 45,454kg (100,000lb) excluding tender
Cylinders: 2 508 × 609mm (20 × 24in)
Driving Wheels: 1.219m (4ft)
Axle Load: 11,000kg (24,200lb)
Grate Area: 2.6m² (27.6sq ft)
Heating Surface: 119m² (1,281sq ft)
Steam Pressure: 9.1kg/cm² (130psi)
Adhesive Weight: 40,000kg (88,000lb)
Tractive Effort: 9,556kg (21,061lb)

C-16-60 2-8-0
Railway: Denver & Rio Grande Railroad (D&RG)
Date: 1882
Length Overall: 17.189m (56ft 4.75in)
Total Weight: 50,727kg (111,600lb)
Cylinders: 2 381 × 508mm (15 × 20in)
Driving Wheels: 0.939mm (3ft 1in)
Axle Load: 6,280kg (13,818lb)
Fuel: 5,454kg (12,000lb)
Grate Area: 1.3m² (14sq ft)
Water: 9,464lit (2,083gal) (2,500 US gal)
Heating Surface: 77m² (834sq ft)
Steam Pressure: 11.3kg/cm² (160psi)
Adhesive Weight: 22,841kg (50,250lb)
Tractive Effort: 7,623kg (16,800lb)

NO. 999 4-4-0
Railway: New York Central & Hudson River Railroad (NYC&HRRR)
Date: 1893
Length Overall: 17.63m (57ft 10in)
Total Weight: 38,181kg (84,000lb)
Cylinders: 2 483 × 610mm (19 × 24in)
Driving Wheels: 2.184m (7ft 2in)
Axle Load: 19,091kg (42,000lb)
Fuel: 7,000kg (15,400lb)
Grate Area: 2.85m² (30.7sq ft)
Water: 13.393lit (2,950gal)(3,500 US gal)
Heating Surface: 179m² (1,927sq ft)
Steam Pressure: 12.6kg/cm² (190psi)
Adhesive Weight: 38,181kg (84,000lb)
Tractive Effort: 7,382kg (16,270lb)

NO. 382 4-6-0
Railway: Illinois Central Railroad (ICRR)
Date: 1896
Length Overall: 18.364m (60ft 3in)
Total Weight: 93,431kg (205,550lb)
Cylinders: 2 495 × 660mm (19.5 × 26in)
Driving Wheels: 1.752m (5ft 9in)
Axle Load: 16,783kg (36,923lb)

Fuel: 8,181kg (18,000lb)
Grate Area: 2.9m² (31.5sq ft)
Water: 18,928lit (4,166gal) (5,000 US gal)
Heating Surface: 176m² (1,892sq ft)
Steam Pressure: 12.7kg/cm² (180psi)
Adhesive Weight: 45,772kg (100,700lb)
Tractive Effort: 9,950kg (21,930lb)

LYN 2-4-2T
Railway: Lynton & Barnstaple Railway (L&B)
Date: 1898
Length Overall: 7.162m (23ft 6in)
Total Weight: 2,400kg (5,280lb)
Cylinders: 2 254 × 406mm (10 × 16in)
Driving Wheels: 0.838m (2ft 9in)
Axle Load: 7,127kg (15,680lb)
Grate Area: 0.7m² (7.7sq ft)
Water: 3,030lit (667gal) (800 US gal)
Heating Surface: 35m² (379sq ft)
Steam Pressure: 12.7kg/cm² (180psi)
Adhesive Weight: 14,254kg (31,360lb)
Tractive Effort: 3,364kg (7,415lb)

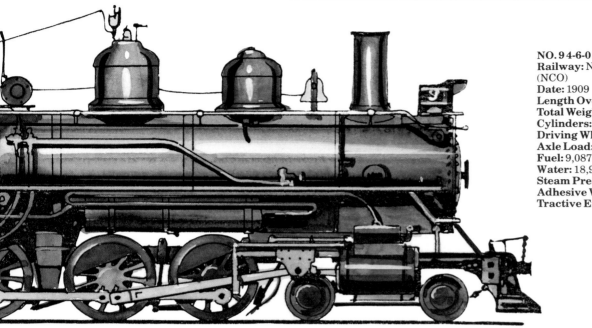

NO. 9 4-6-0
Railway: Nevada-California-Oregon Railroad (NCO)
Date: 1909
Length Overall: 16.433m (53ft 11in)
Total Weight: 75,068kg (165,150lb)
Cylinders: 2 406 × 508mm (16 × 10in)
Driving Wheels: 1.117m (3ft 8in)
Axle Load: 10,893kg (23,966lb)
Fuel: 9,087lit (2,000gal)(2,400 US gal) oil
Water: 18,931lit (4,167 gal) (5,000 US gal)
Steam Pressure: 12.7kg/cm² (180psi)
Adhesive Weight: 29,709kg (65,360lb)
Tractive Effort: 8,076kg (17,800lb)

Above
CLASS H4 4-6-2
Railway: Great Northern Railway (GNR)
Date: 1909
Length Overall: 20.498m (67ft 3in)
Total Weight: 174,431kg (383,750lb)
Cylinders: 2 597 × 762mm (23.5 × 30in)
Driving Wheels: 1.854m (6ft 1in)
Axle Load: 25,181kg (55,400lb)
Fuel: 12,727kg (28,000lb)
Grate Area: 4.95m² (53.3sq ft)
Water: 30,291lit (6,667 gal) (8,000 US gal)
Heating Surface: 295m² (3,177sq ft)
Superheater: 57.6m² (620sq ft)
Steam Pressure: 14.75kg/cm² (210psi)
Adhesive Weight: 68,727kg (151,200lb)
Tractive Effort: 16,193kg (35,690lb)

Left
NO. 7 2-4-4T
Railway: Brighton & Saco River Railroad (B&SR)
Date: 1913
Length Overall: 10.65m (34ft 7.75in)
Total Weight: 31,681kg (69,700lb)
Cylinders: 2 304 × 406mm (12 × 16in)
Driving Wheels: 0.889m (2ft 11in)
Axle Load: 9,700kg (21,340lb)
Fuel: 1,363kg (3,000lb)
Water: 3,786lit (833gal)(1,000 US gal)
Steam Pressure: 12.7kg/cm² (180psi)
Adhesive Weight: 17,636kg (38,800lb)
Tractive Effort: 4,570kg (10,072lb)

K4 CLASS 4-6-2
Railway: Pennsylvania Railroad (PRR)
Date: 1914
Length Overall: 25.451m (83ft 6in)
Total Weight: 242,272kg (533,000lb)
Cylinders: 2 686 × 711mm (27 × 28in)
Driving Wheels: 2.032m (6ft 8in)
Axle Load: 32,727kg (72,000lb)

Fuel: 16,363kg (36,000lb)
Grate Area: 6.5m² (70sq ft)
Water: 45,400lit (10,000gal) (12,000 US gal)
Heating Surface: 375m² (4,040sq ft)
Superheater: 88m² (943sq ft)
Steam Pressure: 14.4kg/cm² (205psi)
Adhesive Weight: 95,454kg (210,000lb)
Tractive Effort: 20,170kg (44,460lb)

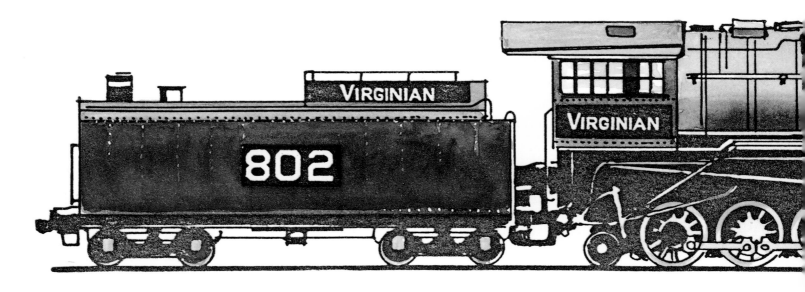

Above
800 2-10-10-2
Railway: Virginian Railroad (VGN)
Date: 1918
Length Overall: 30.368m (99ft 8in)
Total Weight: 408,181kg (898,000lb)
Cylinders: HP: 2 762 × 872mm (30 × 32in);
LP: 2 1,219 × 812mm (48 × 32in)
Driving Wheels: 1.422mm (4ft 8in)

Axle Load: 28,045kg (61,700lb)
Fuel: 10,909kg (24,000lb)
Grate Area: 10.1m^2 (108.7sq ft)
Water: 49,070lit (10,800gal) (13,000 US gal)
Heating Surface: 799m^2 (8,605sq ft)
Superheater: 197m^2 (2,120sq ft)
Steam Pressure: 15.1kg/cm^2 (215psi)
Adhesive Weight: 280,454kg (617,000lb)
Tractive Effort: 80,127kg (176,600lb)

Left
NO. 24 2-6-2
Railway: Sandy River & Rangeley Lakes
Railroad (SRRL)
Date: 1919
Length Overall: 13.589m (44ft 7in)
Total Weight: 41,363kg (91,000lb)
Cylinders: 2 304 × 406mm (12 × 16in)
Driving Wheels: 0.838m (2ft 11in)
Axle Load: 2,454kg (5,400lb)
Fuel: 2,727kg (6,000lb)
Water: 7,572lit (1,667gal) (2,000 US gal)
Steam Pressure: 12.0kg/cm^2 (170psi)
Adhesive Weight: 19,091kg (42,000lb)
Tractive Effort: 4,576kg (10,085lb)

9000 4-12-2
Railway: Union Pacific Railroad (UP)
Date: 1926
Length Overall: 31.267m (102ft 7in)
Total Weight: 35,545kg (782,000lb)
Cylinders: 2 685 × 812mm (27 × 32in);
1 685 × 787mm (27 × 31in)

Driving Wheels: 1.70m (5ft 7in)
Axle Load: 27,272kg (60,000lb)
Fuel: 19,090kg (42,000lb)
Grate Area: 10m² (108sq ft)
Water: 56,750lit (12,500gal) (15,000 US gal)
Heating Surface: 544m² (5,853sq ft)

Superheater: 238m² (2,560sq ft)
Steam Pressure: 15.5kg/cm² (220psi)
Adhesive Weight: 16,136kg (355,000lb)
Tractive Effort: 43,852kg (96,650lb)

K-36 2-8-2
Railway: Denver & Rio Grande Western
Railroad (D&RGW)
Date: 1925
Length Overall: 20.802m (68ft 3in)
Total Weight: 130,227kg (286,500lb)
Cylinders: 2 508 × 609mm (20 × 24in)
Driving Wheels: 1.117m (3ft 8in)
Axle Load: 17,980kg (39,558lb)
Fuel: 7,272kg (16,000lb)
Grate Area: 3.7m² (40sq ft)

Water: 18,931lit (4,166gal) (5,000 US gal)
Heating Surface: 196m² (2,107sq ft)
Superheater: 53m² (575sq ft)

Steam Pressure: 13.7kg/cm² (195psi)
Adhesive Weight: 65,386kg (143,850lb)
Tractive Effort: 16,425kg (36,200lb)

CLASS Ps-4 4-6-2
Railway: Southern Railway (SR)
Date: 1926
Length Overall: 28.038m (91ft 11.9in)
Total Weight: 255,454kg (562,000lb)
Cylinders: 2 686 × 711mm (27 × 28in)
Driving Wheels: 1.854m (6ft 1in)
Axle Load: 27,727kg (61,000lb)

Fuel: 14,545kg (32,000lb)
Grate Area: 6.55m² (70.5sq ft)
Water: 52,664lit (11,600gal) (14,000 US gal)
Heating Surface: 343m² (3,689sq ft)
Superheater: 92.3m² (993sq ft)
Steam Pressure: 14.1kg/cm² (200psi)
Adhesive Weight: 82,727kg (182,000lb)
Tractive Effort: 21,590kg (47,500lb)

A-6 4-4-2
Railway: Southern Pacific (SP)
Date: 1927
Length Overall: 23.99m (78ft 8.5in)
Total Weight: 211,772kg (465,900lb)

Cylinders: 2 558 × 711mm (22 × 28in)
Driving Wheels: 2.057m (6ft 9in)
Axle Load: 15,000kg (33,000lb)
Fuel: 11,123lit (2,450gal)(2,940 US gal) oil
Grate Area: 4.6m² (49.5sq ft)

Water: 34,050lit (7,500 gal) (9,000 US gal)
Steam Pressure: 14.8kg/cm² (210psi)
Adhesive Weight: 28,181kg (62,000lb)
Tractive Effort: 18,768kg (41,360lb)

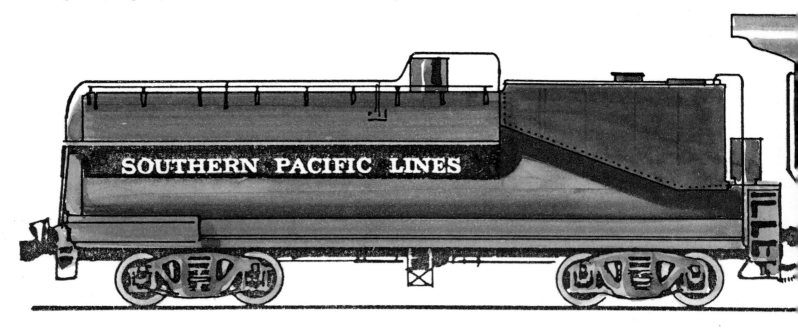

AC-4 Cab Forward 4-8-8-2
Railway: Southern Pacific (SP)
Date: 1928
Length Overall: 38.075m (124ft 11in)
Total Weight: 477,818kg (1,051,200lb)
Cylinders: 4.609 × .812m (2ft 0in × 2ft 8in)
Driving Wheels: 1.61m (5ft 3.5in)
Axle Load: 31,800kg (69,960lb)

Fuel: 23,076lit (5,083 gal) (6,100 US gal) oil
Grate Area: 12.9m² (139sq ft)
Water: 83,232lit (18,333 gal) (22,000 US gal)
Heating Surface: 601m² (6,470sq ft)
Superheater: 243m² (2,616sq ft)
Steam Pressure: 17.6kg/cm² (250psi)
Adhesive Weight: 241,682kg (531,700lb)
Tractive Effort: 56,397kg (124,300lb)

CLASS A 4-4-2
Railway: Chicago, Milwaukee, St Paul & Pacific
Railroad (CMStP&P)
Date: 1935
Length Overall: 27.026m (88ft 8in)
Total Weight: 244,091kg (537,000lb)
Cylinders: 2 483 × 711mm (19 × 28in)
Driving Wheels: 2 134m (7ft)
Axle Load: 32,955kg (72,500lb)

Fuel: 14,982lit (3,300 gal) (4,000 US gal) oil
Grate Area: 6.4m² (69sq ft)
Water: 49,032lit (10,800 gal) (13,000 US gal)
Heating Surface: 301.5m² (3,245sq ft)
Superheater: 96m² (1,029sq ft)
Steam Pressure: 21kg/cm² (300psi)
Adhesive Weight: 65,682kg (144,500lb)
Tractive Effort: 13,920kg (30,685lb)

CLASS J3a 4-6-4
Railway: New York Central Railroad (NYC)
Date: 1937
Length Overall: 32.342m (106ft 1in)
Total Weight: 354,545kg (780,000lb)
Cylinders: 2 572 × 737mm (22.5 × 29in)
Driving Wheels: 2.007m (6ft 7in)

Axle Load: 30,681kg (67,500lb)
Fuel: 41,818kg (92,000lb)
Grate Area: 7.6m² (82sq ft)
Water: 68,100lit (15,000gal) (18,000 US gal)
Heating Surface: 389m² (4,187sq ft)

Superheater: 162.1m² (1,745sq ft)
Steam Pressure: 18.6kg/cm² (265psi)
Adhesive Weight: 91,590kg (201,500lb)
Tractive Effort: 19,000kg (41,860lb)

ROYAL HUDSON CLASS 4-6-4
Railway: Canadian Pacific Railway (CPR)
Date: 1937
Length Overall: 27.686m (90ft 10in)
Total Weight: 299,545kg (659,000lb)
Cylinders: 2 559 × 762mm (22 × 30in)
Driving Wheels: 1.905m (6ft 3in)
Axle Load: 29,545kg (65,000lb)

Fuel: 21,364kg (47,000lb)
Grate Area: 7.5m² (81sq ft)
Water: 54,480lit (12,000gal) (14,400 US gal)
Heating Surface: 352m² (3,791sq ft)
Superheater: 143m² (1,542sq ft)
Steam Pressure: 19.3kg/cm² (275psi)
Adhesive Weight: 88,162kg (194,000lb)
Tractive Effort: 20,548kg (45,300lb)

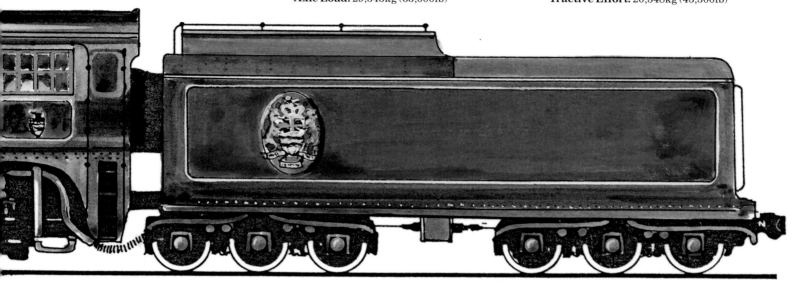

CLASS GS-2 4-8-4
Railway: Southern Pacific Railroad (SP)
Date: 1937
Length Overall: 30.91m (101ft 5in)
Total Weight: 401,364kg (883,000lb)
Cylinders: 2 648 × 813mm (25.5 × 32in)
Driving Wheels: 1.87m (6ft 1.5in)
Axle Load: 31,330kg (68,925lb)

Fuel: 22,263lit (4,900 gal) (5,900 US gal) oil
Grate Area: 8.4m² (90.4sq ft)
Water: 88,984lit (19,600gal) (23,500 US gal)
Heating Surface: 454m² (4,887sq ft)
Superheater: 194m² (2,086sq ft)
Steam Pressure: 21.1kg/cm² (300psi)
Adhesive Weight: 125,455kg (276,000lb)
Tractive Effort: 32,285kg (71,173lb)

CLASS J 4-8-4
Railway: Norfolk & Western Railway (N&W)
Date: 1941
Length Overall: 30.759m (100ft 11in)
Total Weight: 396,818kg (873,000lb)
Cylinders: 2 686 × 813mm (27 × 32in)
Driving Wheels: 1.778m (5ft 10in)
Axle Load: 32,727kg (72,000lb)

Fuel: 31,818kg (70,000lb)
Grate Area: 10m^2 (107.5sq ft)
Water: 75,818lit (16,700gal) (20,000 US gal)
Heating Surface: 490m^2 (5,271sq ft)
Superheater: 202m^2 (2,177sq ft)
Steam Pressure: 21kg/cm^2 (300psi)
Adhesive Weight: 130,909kg (288,000lb)
Tractive Effort: 36,287kg (80,000lb)

BIG BOY 4-8-8-4
Railway: Union Pacific Railroad (UP)
Date: 1941
Length Overall: 40.487m (132ft 10in)
Total Weight: 540,682kg (1,189,500lb)
Cylinders: 4 603 × 812mm (23.75 × 32in)
Driving Wheels: 1.727m (5ft 8in)
Axle Load: 30,795kg (67,750lb)

Fuel: 25,455kg (56,000lb)
Grate Area: 13.9m^2 (150sq ft)
Water: 94,500lit (20,800gal) (25,000 US gal)
Heating Surface: 547m^2 (5,889sq ft)
Superheater: 229m^2 (2,466sq ft)
Steam Pressure: 21.1kg/cm^2 (300psi)
Adhesive Weight: 245,455kg (540,000lb)
Tractive Effort: 61,422kg (135,375lb)

H-8 ALLEGHENY 2-6-6-6
Railway: Chesapeake & Ohio Railway (Chessie)
Date: 1941
Length Overall: 39.653 (130ft 1in)
Total Weight: 489,091kg (1,076,000lb)
Cylinders: 4 571 × 838mm (22.5 × 33in)
Driving Wheels: 1.701m (5ft 7in)
Axle Load: 39,250kg (86,350lb)

Fuel: 22,727kg (50,000lb)
Grate Area: 12.5m^2 (135sq ft)
Water: 94,500lit (20,800 gal) (25,000 US gal)
Heating Surface: 673m^2 (7,240sq ft)
Superheater: 296m^2 (3,186sq ft)
Steam Pressure: 18.3kg/cm^2 (260psi)
Adhesive Weight: 214,091kg (471,000lb)
Tractive Effort: 50,000kg (110,200lb)

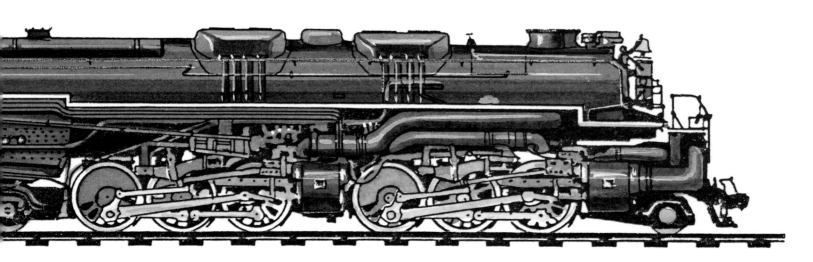

P-1 4-6-4
Railway: Wabash Railroad (WAB)
Date: 1943
Length Overall: 26.64m (87ft 5in)
Total Weight: 264,850kg (582,680lb)
Cylinders: 2 660 × 711mm (2ft 2in × 2ft 4in)
Driving Wheels: 2.03m (6ft 8in)
Axle Load: 32,727kg (72,000lb)
Fuel: 17,272kg (38,000lb)
Grate Area: 5.5m² (59sq ft)
Water: 37,868lit (8.333 gal) (10,000 US gal)
Heating Surface: 393m² (4,225sq ft)
Superheater: 98m² (1,051sq ft)
Steam Pressure: 15.5kg/cm² (220psi)
Adhesive Weight: 543,800kg (1,196,360lb)
Tractive Effort: 20,074kg (44,244lb)

CHALLENGER CLASS 4-6-6-4
Railway: Union Pacific Railroad (UP)
Date: 1942
Length Overall: 37.16m (121ft 11in)
Total Weight: 486,818kg (1,071,000lb)
Cylinders: 4 533 × 813mm (21 × 32in)
Driving Wheels: 1.753m (5ft 7in)
Axle Load: 30,909kg (68,000lb)
Fuel: 25,455kg (56,000lb)
Grate Area: 12.3m^2 (132sq ft)
Water: 94,500lit (20,800 gal) (25,000 US gal)
Heating Surface: 431m^2 (4,642sq ft)
Superheater: 162m^2 (1,741sq ft)
Steam Pressure: 19.7kg/cm^2 (280psi)
Adhesive Weight: 184,545kg (406,000lb)
Tractive Effort: 44,100kg (97,400lb)

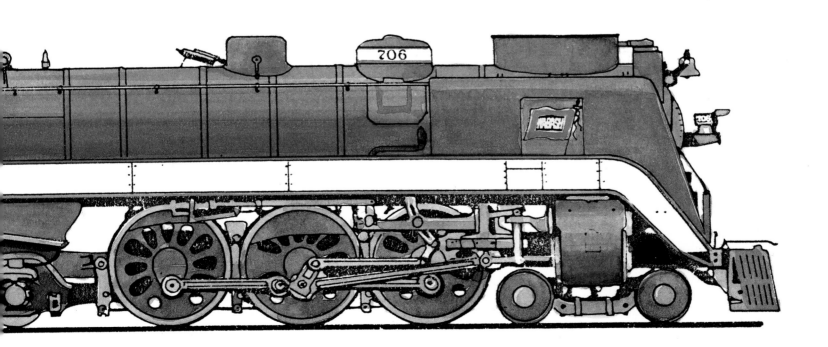

CLASS A-5 4-8-4
Railway: Northern Pacific Railroad (NP)
Date: 1943
Length Overall: 34.391m (112ft 10in)
Total Weight: 432,727kg (952,000lb)
Cylinders: 2 711 × 762mm (28 × 30in)
Driving Wheels: 1.956m (6ft 5in)
Axle Load: 33,636kg (74,000lb)
Fuel: 24,545kg (54,000lb)
Grate Area: 10.7m^2 (115sq ft)
Water: 95,340lit (21,000gal) (12,000 US gal)
Heating Surface: 433m^2 (4,660sq ft)
Superheater: 185m^2 (1,992sq ft)
Steam Pressure: 18.3kg/cm^2 (260psi)
Adhesive Weight: 13,409kg (295,000lb)
Tractive Effort: 31,660kg (69,800lb)

CLASS UL-F 4-8-2
Railway: Canadian National Railways (CNR)
Date: 1944
Length Overall: 28.426m (93ft 3in)
Total Weight: 290,000kg (638,000lb)
Cylinders: 2 610 × 762mm (24 × 30in)
Driving Wheels: 1.854m (6ft 1in)
Axle Load: 27,045kg (59,500lb)
Fuel: 18,182kg (40,000lb)
Grate Area: 6.6m^2 (70.2sq ft)
Water: 52,210lit (11,500gal) (13,800 US gal)
Heating Surface: 333m^2 (3,584sq ft)
Superheater: 146m^2 (1,570sq ft)
Steam Pressure: 18.3kg/cm^2 (260psi)
Adhesive Weight: 107,727kg (237,000lb)
Tractive Effort: 23,814kg (52,500lb)

2900 CLASS 4-8-4
Railway: Atchison, Topeka & Santa Fe Railway (AT&SF)
Date: 1944
Length Overall: 36.830m (120ft 10in)
Total Weight: 436,818kg (961,000lb)
Cylinders: 2 711 × 813mm (28 × 32in)
Driving Wheels: 2.032m (6ft 8in)
Axle Load: 33,636kg (74,000lb)

Fuel: 26,488lit (5,830 gal) (7,000 US gal) oil
Grate Area: 10m² (108sq ft)
Water: 92,616lit (20,400gal) (24,500 US gal)
Heating Surface: 494m² (5,313sq ft)
Superheater: 220m² (2.366sq ft)
Steam Pressure: 21kg/cm² (300psi)
Adhesive Weight: 133,636kg (294,000lb)
Tractive Effort: 36,270kg (79,960lb)

NIAGARA CLASS 4-8-4
Railway: New York Central Railroad (NYC)
Date: 1945
Length Overall: 35.192m (115ft 5.5in)
Total Weight: 405,000kg (891,000lb)
Cylinders: 2 648 × 813mm (25.5 × 32in)
Driving Wheels: 2.007m (6ft 7in)
Axle Load: 31,818kg (70,000lb)

Fuel: 41,818kg (92,000lb)
Grate Area: 9.3m² (100sq ft)
Water: 68,100lit (15,000gal) (18,000 US gal)
Heating Surface: 4.48m² (4,827sq ft)
Superheater: 191m² (2,060sq ft)
Steam Pressure: 19.3kg/cm² (275psi)
Adhesive Weight: 124,545kg (274,000lb)
Tractive Effort: 27,936kg (61,570lb)

FEF-3 CLASS 4-8-4
Railway: Union Pacific Railroad (UP)
Date: 1944
Length Overall: 34.696m (113ft 10in)
Total Weight: 412,727kg (908,000lb)
Cylinders: 2 635 × 813mm (25 × 32in)
Driving Wheels: 2.032m (6ft 8in)
Axle Load: 30,455kg (67,000lb)

Fuel: 22,727kg (50,000lb)
Grate Area: 9.3m² (100sq ft)
Water: 89,052lit (19,600gal) (23,500 US gal)
Heating Surface: 393m² (4,225sq ft)
Superheater: 130m² (1,400sq ft)
Steam Pressure: 21kg/cm² (300psi)
Adhesive Weight: 121,136kg (266,500lb)
Tractive Effort: 28,950kg (63,800lb)

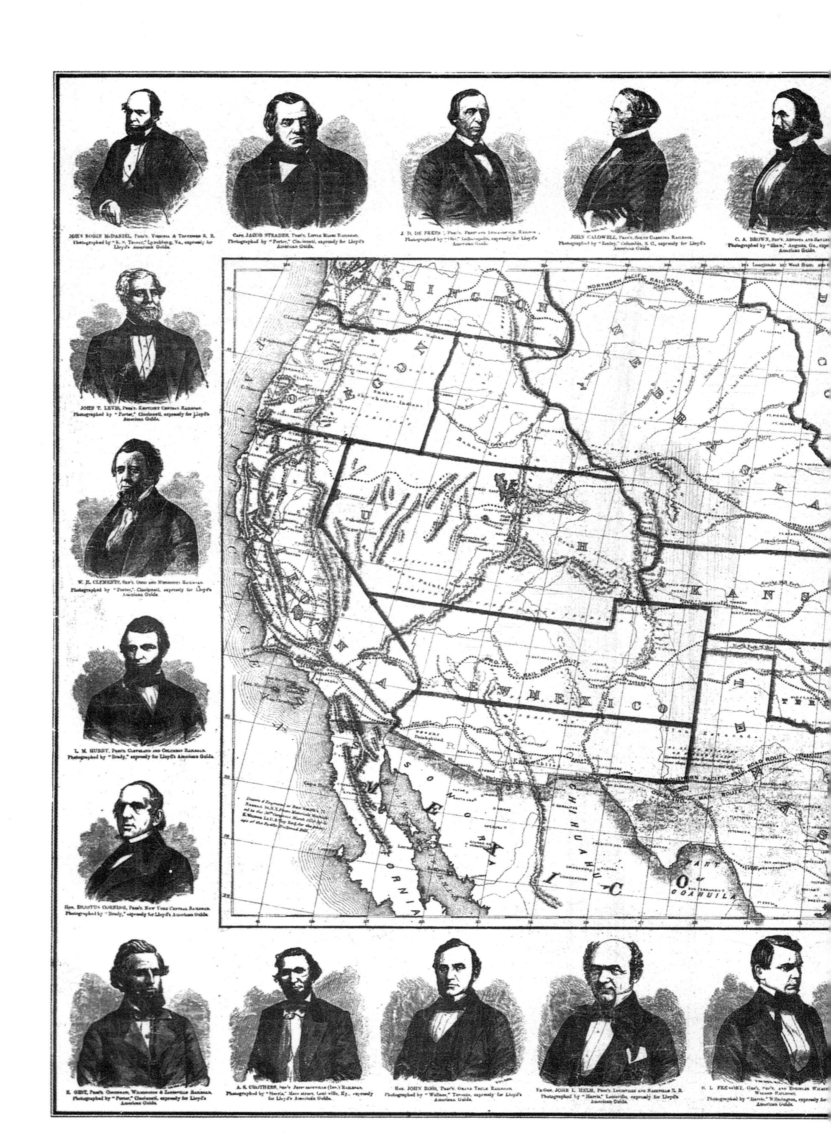

JOHN ROBIN McDANIEL, Pres't, Virginia & Tennessee R. R.
Photographed by "S. N. Tirene," Lynchburg, Va., expressly for
Lloyd's American Guide.

Capt. JACOB STRADER, Pres't, Little Miami Railroad.
Photographed by "Porter," Cincinnati, expressly for Lloyd's
American Guide.

J. D. DE FREES, Pres't, Pres't and Indianapolis Railroad,
Photographed by "Otto," Indianapolis, expressly for Lloyd's
American Guide.

JOHN CALDWELL, Pres't, South Carolina Railroad.
Photographed by "Kenley," Columbia, S. C., expressly for Lloyd's
American Guide.

C. A. BROWN, Sup't, Atlanta and Savannah
Photographed by "Shaw," Augusta, Ga., expressly

JOHN T. LEVIS, Pres't, Kentucky Central Railroad.
Photographed by "Porter," Cincinnati, expressly for Lloyd's
American Guide.

W. H. CLEMENTS, Sup't, Ohio and Mississippi Railroad.
Photographed by "Porter," Cincinnati, expressly for Lloyd's
American Guide.

L. M. HUBBY, Pres't, Cleveland and Columbus Railroad.
Photographed by "Brady," expressly for Lloyd's American Guide.

Hon. ERASTUS CORNING, Pres't, New York Central Railroad.
Photographed by "Brady," expressly for Lloyd's American Guide.

E. GEST, Pres't, Cincinnati, Wilmington & Zanesville Railroad.
Photographed by "Porter," Cincinnati, expressly for Lloyd's
American Guide.

A. S. CROTHERS, Sup't, Jeffersonville (Ind.) Railroad.
Photographed by "Harris," Main street, Louisville, Ky., expressly
for Lloyd's American Guide.

Hon. JOHN ROSS, Pres't, Grand Trunk Railroad.
Photographed by "Wallace," Toronto, expressly for Lloyd's
American Guide.

Ex-Gov. JOHN L. HELM, Pres't, Louisville and Nashville R. R.
Photographed by "Harris," Louisville, expressly for Lloyd's
American Guide.

S. L. FREMONT, Civ'l, Pres't, and Engineer Wil
Weldon Railroad.
Photographed by "Harris," Wilmington, expressly for
American Guide.

THE MAJOR RAILROADS

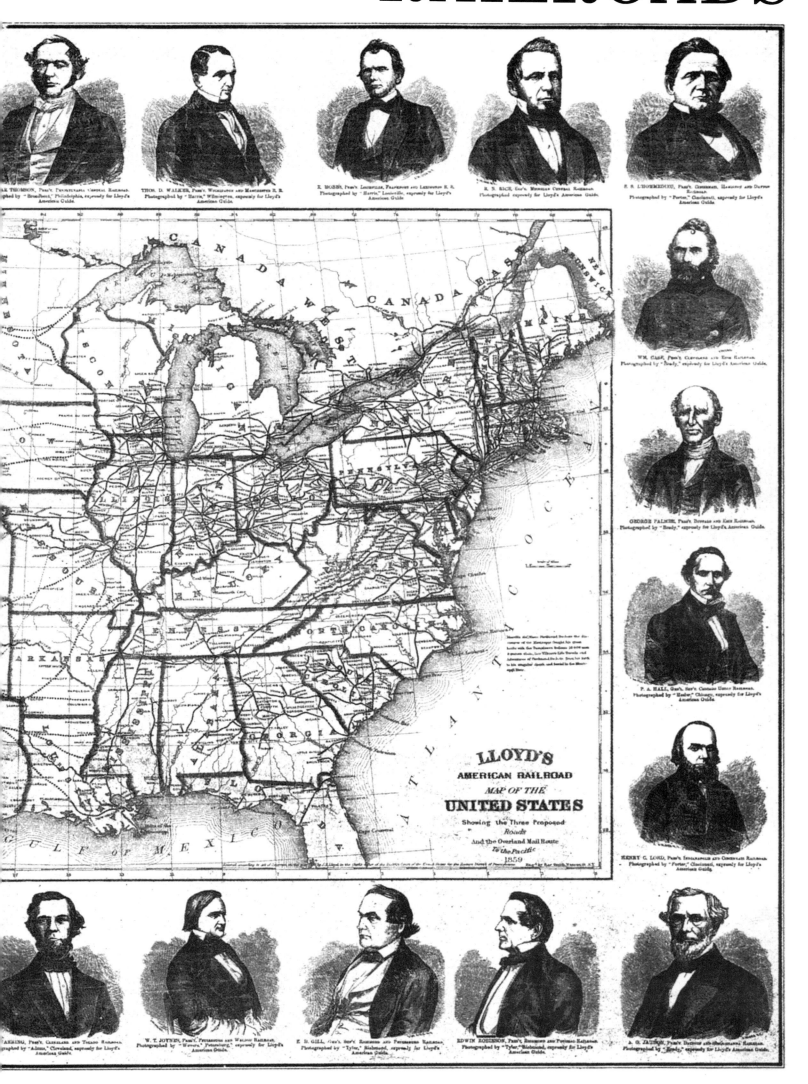

ABERDEEN AND ROCKFISH RAILROAD

Incorporated: 1892

Completed: 1913

Previously: N/A

Operations: Between Aberdeen and Fayetteville, North Carolina

Miles operated: 47 (75.6km)

Locomotives: 3

Freight cars: 224

Passenger cars: Nil

Services: Freight, concentrating on building materials, chemicals, food grains and animal by-products.

Address: PO Box 917, Aberdeen, North Carolina 28315.

ALASKA RAILROAD

Incorporated: Authorised by Congress in 1912

Completed: 1923

Previously: Alaska Northern and Tanana Valley

Operations: Between Seward and Fairbanks, serving Whittier, Anchorage and Denali Park. Branch lines serve Eielson Air Force Base, Fairbanks International Airport and Sutrana Coalfield

Miles operated: 526 (846km)

Locomotives: 65

Freight cars: 1,251

Passenger cars: 42

Services: Coal, petroleum, sand and gravel. Iron and steel products. Special tourist trains.

Notes: Expanded during construction of Alaska Pipeline in mid-1970s. Financial problems in early 1980s but now fully recovered.

Address: PO Box No 7-2111, Anchorage, Alaska 99510.

ALGOMA CENTRAL RAILWAY

Incorporated: Chartered in 1899

Previously: Algoma Central and Hudson Bay Railway until 1965

Operations: Sault Ste Marie to Hearst (via Ontario Wilderness)

Miles operated: 322 (518km)

Locomotives: 34

Freight cars: 1,223

Passenger cars: 42

Services: Iron ore and forest products.

Notes: A tourist service runs to the Agawa River Canyon Wilderness Park. During the 1960s the company diversified into water, rail and road transport.

Address: PO Box 7000, Sault Ste Marie, Ontario P6A 5P5.

Three GMD SD40-2 3,000-hp locomotives of the DRF-30 Class head a unit train of empty hopper cars along a river valley on a sunny winter's day.

ALTON AND SOUTHERN RAILROAD

Incorporated: 1913

Previously: Owned by the Missouri Pacific and St. Louis Southwestern Railroads

Operations: Transfers railroad cars in the east St. Louis, Illinois, area

Miles operated: 32 (51km)

Locomotives: 20

Services: A belt line serving other major railroads.

AMERICAN CIVIL WAR RAILROAD

Completed: (1861-65)

Operations: Throughout the war zone

Notes: Both the Union and Confederacy relied heavily upon railroads for the speedy movement of troops and material. Prior to 1861, the North possessed 22,000 miles of track compared with the South's 9,000. Although initially border lines suffered, others prospered, though some in outlying areas were commandeered and moved in their entirety. As the Union drove deep into the South so it relied more heavily on railroads, destroying those of the enemy wherever it went.

APALACHICOLA NORTHERN RAILROAD

Incorporated: 1903

Operations: Throughout Western Florida panhandle, southeastern Alabama and southwestern Georgia

Miles operated: 96 (154km)

Locomotives: 11

Freight cars: 261

Services: Lumber, pulpwood, paper products and coal.

Notes: Main route from Port St. Joe, Florida, to Chattahoochee, Florida, to link with the Seaboard System.

Address: PO Box 50, Port St. Joe, Florida 32456.

ARKANSAS AND LOUISIANA MISSOURI RAILROAD

Incorporated: 1920

Previously: Arkansas and Louisiana Midland Railways

Operations: Monroe, Louisiana, to Crossett, Arkansas

Miles operated: 54 (87km)

Locomotives: 4

Freight cars: 374

Services: Fertilizer, pulpwood and paper products.

Notes: Owned by Olin Corporation through Olinkraft Inc. subsidiary.

ASHLEY, DREW AND NORTHERN RAILROAD

Incorporated: 1905

Completed: An amalgamation of Crossett Lumber Company (1905), Crossett, Monticello and Northern Railway (1912)

Previously: Purchased by Georgia Pacific Corporation in 1963

Operations: Between Crossett, Fordyce and Monticello, Arkansas

Miles operated: 41 (66km)

Locomotives: 6

Freight cars: 2,076

Services: Paper products, pulpwood and other pine tree-derived products.

Address: PO Box 757, Crossett, Arkansas 71635.

ATCHISON, TOPEKA AND SANTA FE RAILWAY COMPANY (SANTA FE)

Incorporated: 1872

Operations: Western United States from Chicago to Gulf of Mexico and Pacific Coast

Miles operated: 12,079 (19,439km)

Locomotives: 2,000

Freight cars: 62,610

Services: General. Note use of aerodynamically shaped "fuel-foiler" containers in figure "A" configuration (legs of "A" allow freight cars to be stacked in pairs).

Notes: First diesel service in 1935 (hauling the "Super Chief"). Surrendered all passenger services to Amtrak in 1973. Merged with Southern Pacific to form Santa Fe Southern Pacific Corporation in 1983. History of innovation among rolling stock. Leading intermodal railroad with 38 major terminals.

Address: 80, East Jackson Boulevard, Chicago, Illinois 60604.

An emotional farewell for a passenger about to board the Santa Fe Railroad's 'California Limited' in May 1905.

ATLANTA AND ST. ANDREWS BAY RAILWAY (THE BAY LINE)

Incorporated: Organized in 1906

Operations: Panama City, Florida, to Dothan, Alabama

Miles operated: 89 (143km)

Locomotives: 13

Freight cars: 828

Services: Grain, paper products, pulpwood and chemicals.

Notes: Owned by Southwest Forest Industries.

Address: PO Box 729, 514 East Main Street, Dothan, Alabama 36302.

ATLANTIC AND WESTERN RAILROAD

Incorporated: 1927

Operations: Originally from Lillington to Sanford, North Carolina, but now from Lillington to Jonesboro.

Miles operated: Originally 26 (42km) but now 3 (5km)

Locomotives: 2

Freight cars: 1,600

Services: Sand and gravel, scrap iron and furniture.

Notes: Note the huge ratio of freight cars per mile of track.

The railway bridge spanning the Ohio River at Bellaire, Ohio, photographed in 1872.

BALTIMORE AND OHIO RAILROAD

Incorporated: 1827

Completed: Reached Ohio River in 1853 before continuing west

Operations: From Baltimore west across the Ohio River

Miles operated: 9,806 (15,791km)

Locomotives: 1,014 (including 115 switchers)

Freight cars: 44,896

Services: Basically coal, but all general freight carried.

Notes: Controlled by Chesapeake and Ohio Railroad. Affiliated within the Chessie System.

Address: Chessie System Railroads (holding company): Terminal Tower, Cleveland, Ohio 44101.

BANGOR AND AROOSTOOK RAILROAD

Incorporated: 1891

Operations: Searsport (Maine coast) to Fort Kent, Van Buren and Caribou, Maine

Miles operated: 494 (795km)

Locomotives: 45

Freight cars: 3,590

Passenger cars: Discontinued in 1961

Services: Pulpwood and other forest products.

Notes: Also runs a bus service north from Bangor.

Address: Northern Maine Junction Park, RR2, Bangor, Maine 04401.

Diesel electric No. 717 of the British Columbia Railway runs through spectacular scenery on its journey between Vancouver and Fort Nelson.

BAY COLONY RAILROAD

Incorporated: 1982

Previously: Track purchased from Conrail and New York, New Haven and Hartford

Operations: Various routes in Massachusetts including Cape Cod peninsula between Hyannis, Falmouth, Buzzards Bay and Middleboro: Plymouth and Braintree: Westport and Watuppa: Medfield Junction and Needham Junction.

Miles operated: 124 (200km)

Locomotives: 5

Freight cars: 47

Services: Route incorporates a vertical lift bridle spanning Cod Canal at Buzzards Bay.

BELT RAILWAY OF CHICAGO

Incorporated: Built between 1880 and 1882

Previously: Belt division of Chicago and Western Indiana Railroad

Operations: Provides connections between line-haul railroads in Chicago area

Miles operated: 48 (77km)

Locomotives: 41

Services: Acts as locating and switching service for over 325 industries.

Notes: Clearing yard has a working capacity of 12,600 cars and the ability to hump four trains simultaneously during classification.

Address: 6900 South Central Avenue, Chicago, Illinois 60638.

BESSEMER AND LAKE ERIE RAILROAD

Incorporated: 1865

Previously: Bear Creek Railroad

Operations: North Bessemer, Pennsylvania to Erie, Pennsylvania and Conneaut, Ohio

Miles operated: 205 (328km)

Locomotives: 64

Freight cars: 9,555

Services: Primarily coal, coke, iron ore and limestone.

Notes: Route contains two of the longest bridges in North America (Osgood – 1724 feet – and foot bridge over Allegheny river – 2327 feet).
Western Allegheny Railroad (purchased from Pennsylvania Railroad) is operated as a separate division.

Address: PO Box 68, Monroeville, Pennsylvania 15146.

BIRMINGHAM SOUTHERN RAILROAD

Incorporated: 1899

Previously: Owned by Southern Railway and Louisville and Nashville Railroad

Operations: Port Birmingham, Alabama, to Fairfield and Bessemer

Miles operated: 91 (146km)

Locomotives: 22

Freight cars: 796

Services: Steel, iron ore and associated raw materials.

Notes: Operates ancillary general terminal service in Birmingham, Alabama.

Address: PO Box 579, Fairfield, Alabama 35064.

BRITISH COLUMBIA RAILWAY

Incorporated: Chartered in 1912

Previously: Pacific Great Eastern

Operations: Vancouver to Fort Nelson and Dease Lake

Miles operated: 1,261 (2,029km)

Locomotives: 125

Freight cars: 9,790

Passenger cars: 6 (plus 5 diesel railcars)

Services: Forest products and coal. A limited rail diesel car passenger service operates between Vancouver and Prince George ("Cariboo Dayliner").

Notes: Summer steam service with former Canadian Pacific "Royal Hudson" operates between Vancouver and Squamish.

Address: West Pender Street, Vancouver, British Columbia VGE 2N6.

BURLINGTON NORTHERN RAILROAD

Incorporated: 1970

Previously: Amalgamation of Chicago, Burlington and Quincy Railroad, Great Northern Railway, Northern Pacific Railway and Spokane, Portland and Seattle Railway

Operations: Southern and western states. Operates in 25 US States and 2 Canadian provinces. From Gulf coast at Houston and Pensacola through midwest to northern states and westward to Pacific coast of Washington and Oregon

Miles operated: 29,200 (46,992km)

Locomotives: 3,205

Freight cars: 108,600

Passenger cars: 141

Services: Coal, grain and forest products. Commuter service between Chicago and Aurora, Illinois. Amtrak routes including Chicago–Denver ("California Zephyr"); St. Paul–Seattle; Seattle–Portland ("Coast Starlight"); Spokane–Portland ("Empire Builder").

Notes: Linked with St. Louis–San Francisco ("The Frisco") in 1980. Absorbed the Colorado and Southern Railway Company and Denver Railway Company in 1981. Largest railroad route-mileage in United States. Two longest tunnels in United States. Wholly-owned by Burlington Northern Inc.

Address: 176 East Fifth Street, St. Paul, Minnesota 55101.

BUTTE, ANACONDA AND PACIFIC RAILWAY

Incorporated: 1893

Operations: Butte to Brown, Montana

Miles operated: 43 (69km)

Locomotives: 8

Freight cars: 427

Services: Copper ore.

Address: Box 1421, 300 West Commercial Avenue, Anaconda, Montana 59711.

CALIFORNIA WESTERN RAILROAD

Incorporated: 1885

Previously: Fort Bragg Railroad

Operations: Fort Bragg to Willits, California

Miles operated: 40 (64km)

Locomotives: 4 diesel, 2 steam

Freight cars: Nil

Passenger cars: 10

Services: Steam trains carry tourists through scenic routes in summer, diesels in winter.

Address: PO Box 907, Foot of Laurel Street, Fort Bragg, California 95437.

CAMBRIA AND INDIANA RAILROAD

Incorporated: 1904

Previously: Blacklick and Yellow Creek Railroad

Operations: Between Colver, Nanty Glo and Manver in western Pennsylvania

Miles operated: 62 (100km)

Locomotives: 18

Freight cars: 956

Services: Originally logging, but now basically coal and steel.

Address: 1275 Daly Avenue, Bethlehem, Pennsylvania 18015

CAMDEN AND AMBOY RAILROAD

Incorporated: Charter granted in 1830

Operations: No longer operational

Notes: Formed by John Stevens and his son Robert, the railroad was one of the first to operate in the United States. Originally, engines and track were imported from Britain, but later a large 30-ton locomotive ("The Monster") was produced domestically.

The 'Empire Builder' of the Great Northern Railroad approaches the summit of the Continental Divide in the Rocky Mountains in 1947. The railroad later became part of the Burlington Northern.

CANADIAN NATIONAL RAILWAYS

Incorporated: 1922

Previously: An amalgamation of several existing railroads including the Canadian Northern, Grand Trunk Railway and Grand Trunk Pacific. Later joined by Northern Alberta Railroad and Newfoundland Railway

Operations: Coast-to-coast and north to Hudson Bay

Miles operated: Approx. 22,520 (36,241km)

Locomotives: 1,830

Freight cars: 80,690

Services: Passenger services taken over by "Via Rail" in 1978. General freight, with recent emphasis on container transport.

Notes: A commuter service is operated under contract for the Montreal Urban Community Transportation Commission.

Address: PO Box 8100, Montreal, Quebec H3C 3NA, Canada.

C P RAIL (CANADIAN PACIFIC LIMITED)

Incorporated: 1881

Previously: Originally Canadian Pacific, now C P Rail

Operations: Coast-to-coast from New Brunswick to Vancouver (not Newfoundland or Prince Edward Island)

Miles operated: 21,500 (34,600km)

Locomotives: 1,178

Freight cars: 55,300

Services: Grain, coal, potash, sulfur, copper, iron, nickel ores, forest products, liquid petroleum gas, oil, gasoline and chemicals.

Notes: Bulk of passenger travel passed to VIA Rail in 1978. However, community services operated under contract for Montreal Urban Community Transportation Commission and Government of Ontario Transit.

Address: Windsor Station, Montreal, Quebec H3C 3E4.

This map, produced in 1892, was intended for tourists using Canadian Pacific's railroads and steamships.

RAND AVERY SUPPLY CO., BOSTON. 1896

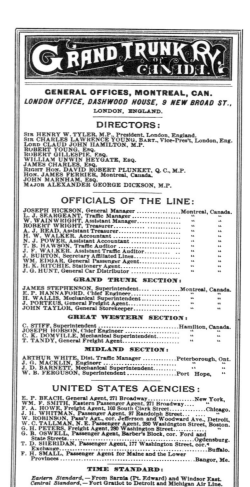
REID-NEWFOUNDLAND COMPANY

	Miles
Rail	625
North Sydney to Port-au-Basques, Steamer	102
Port-au-Basques, Placentia Steamer	371
Placentia Bay Steamer	296
Trinity Bay Steamer	182
Bonavista Bay Steamer	146
Notre Dame Bay Steamer	262
St. John's and Labrador (Summer Service)	1021
Bay of Islands and Battle Harbor Service	579
Total Miles Operated	**3464**

USEFUL INFORMATION.

Ticket Offices—Passengers are requested to procure tickets at ticket offices and in ample time to enable the proper checking of baggage. When tickets are procured on train the Conductor will collect ten (10) cents additional to regular fare.

Tickets, Direction Honored—Tickets of all classes are good for passage only in the direction printed.

Round Trip Tickets—Round trip through tickets can be obtained at reduced fares; they are good only for time specified and are not transferable nor good for stop-over at any intermediate station, unless specially stamped "Good to stop off."

Children—Children not exceeding five years of age, accompanied by their parents or friends will be carried free. Children over five and under twelve will be carried at half fare.

Stop-Over will be allowed in exchange on such tickets as entitle holders to stop-over and when so stamped.

Lost Tickets—Proper care should be taken so as to guard against the loss of a ticket, as Railways are not responsible for lost tickets; also, care should be taken of baggage checks, making a memorandum of check numbers for use in case of loss.

Personal Baggage—Consisting of wearing apparel only, and not exceeding 150 lbs. weight, will be checked free on each whole fare ticket, and 75 lbs. free on each half fare ticket. Baggage in excess of free allowance will be charged for, and passengers paying excess charges will receive an excess baggage ticket which must be delivered to Agent with baggage check when baggage is claimed. Storage will be charged on each piece of baggage, either checked or not checked, remaining at stations over twenty-four hours.

Baggage for Flag Stations—Must be claimed at baggage car door immediately on arrival, otherwise it will be carried to next station where agent is on duty and held for further orders.

Caution—It is unlawful to carry dangerous articles, such as gunpowder, matches, etc., in baggage.

Customs—When baggage is examined at Canadian and Newfoundland points, passengers are required to attend to this personally, otherwise baggage will be held by the Customs.

Time of Trains—It is not guaranteed that the starting time or the arriving time of trains shall be as published herein, neither will this Railway be liable for loss or damage arising from delays or detentions, nor will this railway assume any responsibility beyond its own line.

Reference Marks—
*—Flag Station—Trains stop only when signalled or when there are passengers to set down, and under the conditions named herein.
†—Indicates that trains do not stop.

Disputes—Conductors and Agents are governed by rules which they are not authorized to change, therefore, in the event of any disagreement about tickets required, privileges allowed, etc., passengers should pay Conductor's or Agent's claim, obtain receipt and refer the matter to the General Passenger Agent for his decision.

Seat Space—A passenger is entitled only to seat space in car sufficient for one person, baggage and parcels that cannot be placed under car seat or in the passenger's portion of the parcel rack must not be taken into the car. Baggage which cannot be stowed away as above mentioned should be delivered at the baggage room. If found in the car it will be removed.

Obstruction of the Car Aisles Will Not Be Permitted.

SEASON OF 1908

REID NEWFOUNDLAND COMPANY

RAILWAY AND STEAMSHIP SYSTEM

Both the Grand Trunk Railway, whose 1896 brochure is shown above, and the Reid-Newfoundland Company later became part of Canadian National Railways.

CENTRAL VERMONT RAILWAY

Incorporated: 1849

Operations: New London, Connecticut north to Vermont and New York state

Miles operated: 377 (607km)

Locomotives: 29 (all leased)

Freight cars: 549

Services: General freight.

Address: 2 Federal Street, St. Albans, Vermont 05478.

CHESAPEAKE AND OHIO (C & O) RAILWAY

Incorporated: 1836 (name assumed in 1867)

Previously: Louisa Railroad

Miles operated: 9,571 (15,412km)

Locomotives: 957 (including 76 switchers)

Freight cars: 58,722

Services: General freight.

Notes: Grew progressively between 1880 and 1910. Took over Chicago, Cincinnati and Louisville line in 1910. Took control of Baltimore and Ohio Railroad and Chicago, South Shore and South Bend in 1960s. In 1940s operated H-8 Allegheny 2-6-6-6 engines, then the most powerful in the world; later withdrawn as unreliable, despite ability of two engines to pull 140 cars weighing 11,500 U.S. tons.

Address: Chessie System Railroads: Terminal Tower, Cleveland, Ohio 44101

The Chicago and North Western's *Pioneer* (below) was the first locomotive to operate in Chicago.

CHESSIE SYSTEM RAILROADS

Incorporated: Wholly-owned subsidiary of CSX Corporation

Previously: Amalgamation of: Chesapeake and Ohio Railway, Baltimore and Ohio Railroad and Western Maryland Railway (operating as associates within the Chessie System)

Operations: Mid-Atlantic states to Kentucky, Ohio, western Pennsylvania, Michigan, Indiana, Illinois and Missouri

Miles operated: 16,300 (26,232km)

Locomotives: 1964

Freight cars: 108,230

Passenger cars: 6

Services: Coal and merchandise freight.

Notes: A component of CSX Corporation. Lines extended to Rochester, Buffalo and southern Ontario. Largest coal-hauling system in the United States. Serves over 400 mines.

Address: Terminal Tower, Cleveland, Ohio 44101.

CHICAGO AND ILLINOIS MIDLAND RAILWAY

Incorporated: 1888 (present name assumed in 1905)

Previously: Pawnee Railroad

Operations: Between Peoria, Cimic and Taylorville, southern Illinois

Miles operated: 121 (195km)

Locomotives: 20

Freight cars: 1,076

Services: Coal to power stations.

Address: PO Box 139, Springfield, Illinois 62705.

CHICAGO, MILWAUKEE, ST. PAUL AND PACIFIC RAILROAD (THE MILWAUKEE ROAD)

Incorporated: Reorganized in 1977

Previously: Milwaukee and Mississippi Railroad (incorporated 1847)

Operations: Chicago northward to Milwaukee, via Wisconsin to Minneapolis and Duluth, west to Sheldon, Iowa, southwest to Kansas City and south to Terre Haute and Louisville

Miles operated: 3,200 (5,150km)

Locomotives: 327

Freight cars: 12,489

Services: Food products, wood, lumber and coal. Pulp, paper and chemicals.

Notes: Until 1980, operated approx. 9,800 route-miles (13,780km) in 16 states. In March 1980 embargoed 6,000 route-miles (9,650km) including all track west of Miles City, Montana and most in South Dakota. Hoped to incorporate grain routes between Iowa and southern Minnesota. Chicago area passenger commuter services transferred to Regional Transportation Authority in October 1982. Amtrak intercity passenger trains operate over Milwaukee Road between Chicago, Milwaukee and St. Paul.

Address: 516, West Jackson Boulevard, Chicago, Illinois 60606.

CHICAGO AND NORTH WESTERN TRANSPORTATION COMPANY

Incorporated: 1836 (adopted present name in 1972)

Previously: Galena and Chicago Union Railroad

Operations: Chicago south to St. Louis, southwest to Kansas City, north to Duluth and west to Nebraska and South Dakota

Miles operated: 6,899 (11,103km)

Locomotives: 1,103

Freight cars: 33,269

Passenger cars: 18

Services: Grain, coal and food products.

Address: One North Western Center, Chicago, Illinois 60606.

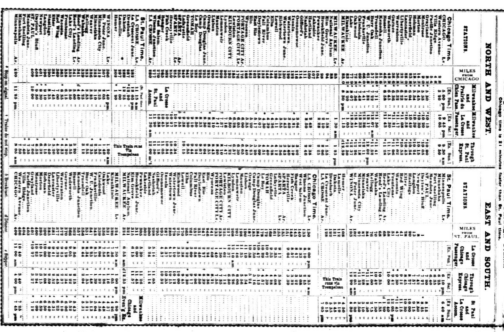

CHICAGO, SOUTH SHORE AND SOUTH BEND RAILROAD

Incorporated: 1901

Previously: Chicago and Indiana Air Line Railway

Operations: Commuter service between Chicago and South Bend, Indiana

Miles operated: 76 (122km)

Locomotives: 10

Freight cars: 27

Passenger cars: 50 (electric)

Services: Passengers and mixed freight.

Address: Carroll Avenue, Michigan City, Indiana 46360.

Shown above is the 1874 timetable of the Chicago, Milwaukee and St. Paul.

COLORADO AND WYOMING RAILWAY

Incorporated: 1900

Operations: Between Pueblo and Allen Mine, Colorado, via Trinidad and Jansen

Miles operated: 110 (177km)

Locomotives: 18

Freight cars: 168

Services: Coal.

Address: PO Box 316, Pueblo, Colorado 81002.

COLUMBUS AND GREENVILLE RAILWAY

Incorporated: 1878

Operations: Greenville to Columbus, Mississippi

Miles operated: 168 (270km)

Locomotives: 19

Freight cars: 1,160

Services: Agricultural products, steel, furniture, pulpwood and coal.

Notes: Purchased by local interests in 1975.

Address: PO Box 6000, 201 19th Street North, Columbus, Mississippi 39701.

CONRAIL (CONSOLIDATED RAIL CORPORATION)

Incorporated: By statute in 1975

Previously: Penn Central (collapsed in 1970). Also took track from Central of New Jersey, Erie Lackawanna, Lehigh and Hudson River, Lehigh Valley and Hudson River

Services: Coal, coke, iron ore, iron and steel, food products, chemicals and automobiles.

Miles operated: 14,967 (23,652km)

Locomotives: 3,572

Freight cars: 104,640

Operations: 15 states in north-east United States and in 2 Canadian provinces.

Notes: A government-sponsored amalgamation of several bankrupt railroads. Operates through five regions with 17 divisions. Became profitable in 1983 when made available for private sector purchase. Transported approx. 177 million tons of freight in 1982. 34 daily services between Atlantic seaboard and mid-west, including 4 mail runs.

Address: Six Penn Center Plaza, Philadelphia, Pennsylvania 19104.

DELAWARE AND HUDSON RAILWAY

Incorporated: 1823

Previously: Delaware and Hudson Canal Company

Operations: New York, Pennsylvania, New Jersey, Maryland, District of Columbia, Vermont and Quebec

Miles operated: 1,709 (2,750km)

Locomotives: 136

Freight cars: 4,764

Services: Iron, pulp, paper, agricultural products.

Notes: Purchased by Guildford Transportation Industries in 1983.

Address: D & H Railway Building, 40 Beaver Street, Albany, New York 12207.

DENVER AND RIO GRANDE WESTERN RAILROAD

Incorporated: 1873

Operations: Denver and Pueblo, Colorado, to Salt Lake City and Ogden, Utah

Miles operated: 1,840 (2,961km)

Locomotives: 284

Freight cars: 740

Services: Coal, food products, iron and steel.

Notes: A few narrow-gauge passenger routes retained for tourists. Last railroad to operate passenger services independently of Amtrak (agreed to take over in 1983 when 6 "Zephyr" cars sold to Amtrak). Railroad wholly-owned by Rio Grande Industries Inc. (Denver). Recent increase in intermodal/trailer-on-flat-car (TOFC) traffic, particularly in West Coast wines and canned goods.

Address: PO Box 5482, 1 Park Central, 1515, Arapahoe Street, Denver, Colorado 80217.

Facing page: A Conrail freight hauls one of its numerous loads of coal.

Below: This 1883 brochure extols the benefits to be gained from farming in Colorado.

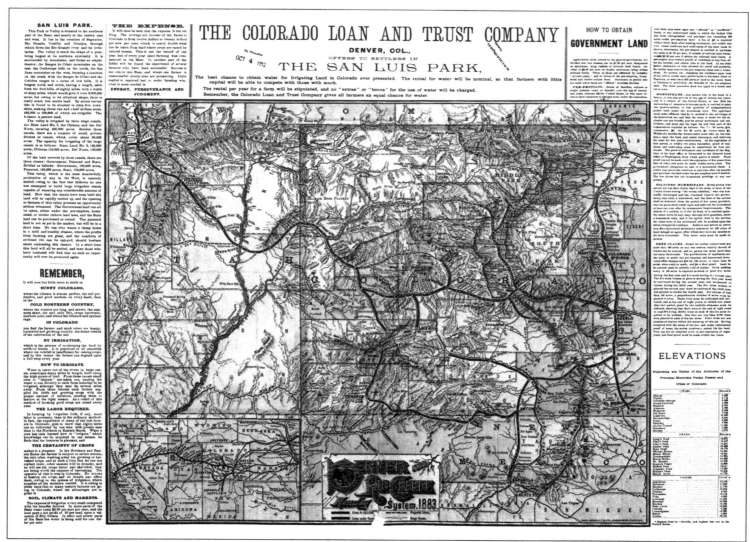

DETROIT AND MACKINAC RAILWAY

Incorporated: 1878 (converted to standard gauge in 1888)

Previously: Lake Huron and South-western

Operations: Northern two-thirds of Michigan's lower peninsula

Miles operated: 405 (652km)

Locomotives: 12

Freight cars: 1,320

Services: Gravel, shale, wood products and gypsum.

Address: Tawas City, Michigan 48763.

DULUTH, MISSABE AND IRON RANGE RAILWAY

Incorporated: 1874 (adopted present name in 1937)

Previously: Duluth and Iron Range Rail Road

Operations: North-eastern Minnesota to Lake Superior

Miles operated: 357 (575km)

Locomotives: 66

Freight cars: 7,405

Services: Iron ore.

Address: Missabe Building, Duluth, Minnesota 55802.

DULUTH, WINNIPEG AND PACIFIC RAILWAY (THE "PEG")

Incorporated: 1901 (name adopted in 1909)

Previously: Duluth, Virginia and Rainy Lake

Operations: Virginia, Minnesota, to Duluth

Miles operated: 167 (269km)

Locomotives: 13

Freight cars: 2,430

Services: Lumber, paper and potash.

Notes: Today operated by Grand Trunk Corporation.

ELGIN, JOLIET AND EASTERN RAILWAY (CHICAGO OUTER BELT)

Incorporated: 1898

Operations: Waukegan, Illinois to Porter, Indiana, with branch line between Griffith, Indiana, and South Chicago

Miles operated: 231 (372km)

Locomotives: 100

Freight cars: 10,190

Services: Iron, coal and steel.

Notes: Runs a semi-circular route 30-40 miles from Chicago city center.

Address: PO Box 880, Maple Road, Joliet, Illinois 60434.

ESCAMBIA AND LAKE SUPERIOR RAILROAD

Incorporated: 1898

Operations: Northern Wisconsin and Upper Peninsula, Michigan

Miles operated: 325 (523km)

Locomotives: 8

Freight cars: 130

Services: Iron ore, paper and pulpwood.

Notes: The line forms an asymmetrical X with Channing, Michigan, at the center and Green Bay, Escanaba, Onantagon and Republic, Michigan, at its extremes.

Address: PO Box 158, Wells, Michigan 49894.

FLORIDA EAST COAST RAILWAY

Incorporated: 1883

Previously: Jacksonville, St. Augustine and Halifax

Operations: Jacksonville to Miami, with branch line from Fort Pierce to Lake Harbor on Lake Okechobee

Miles operated: 534 (859km)

Locomotives: 66 (including four switchers)

Freight cars: 2,546

Services: Agricultural products.

Address: 1, Malaga Street, St. Augustine, Florida 32084.

GRAND TRUNK WESTERN RAILROAD

Incorporated: 1852 (present name assumed in 1928)

Previously: Grand Trunk Railway

Operations: Port Huron, Michigan, to Chicago, south to Toledo and Cincinnati and west to central Michigan

Miles operated: 1,515 (2,438km)

Locomotives: 262

Freight cars: 11,870

Services: Automobiles and automobile parts. Owned by Canadian National Railways through its subsidiary, Grand Trunk Corporation.

Address: 131, West Lafayette Boulevard, Detroit, Michigan 48226.

GREAT WESTERN RAILWAY

Incorporated: 1901

Operations: Central Colorado

Miles operated: 58 (93km)

Locomotives: 4

Freight cars: 150

Services: Sugar beet, sugar, molasses and coal.

Notes: Steam engine Decapod No. 900 was once operated on this line but now operates on Strasburg (Pennsylvania) Railroad as a tourist attraction

Address: Loveland Depot, PO Box 537, Loveland, Colorado 80537.

GREEN BAY AND WESTERN RAILROAD (GREEN BAY ROUTE)

Incorporated: 1866

Previously: Green Bay and Lake Pepin

Operations: Winona, Minnesota (on Mississippi River), to Kiwaunee, Wisconsin, via Green Bay

Miles operated: 255 (410km)

Locomotives: 19

Freight cars: 2,060

Services: Paper (originally wheat and lumber).

Address: PO Box 2507, Green Bay, Wisconsin 54306.

GREEN MOUNTAIN RAILROAD

Previously: Rutland Railway

Operations: Bellous Falls to Rutland, Vermont

Miles operated: 50 (80.5km)

Locomotives: 6

Freight cars: 500

Services: Talc.

Address: PO Box 468, Bellows Falls, Vermont 05101.

HILLSIDE COUNTY RAILWAY

Incorporated: 1976

Previously: Purchased from New York Central assets

Operations: Steubenville, Indiana to Litchfield, Michigan

Miles operated: 62 (100km)

Locomotives: 3

Freight cars: 60

Services: Grain, agricultural products, manufactured goods.

ILLINOIS CENTRAL GULF RAILROAD

Incorporated: 1851

Completed: 1856

Previously: Illinois Central

Operations: Gold Coast to Great Lakes via states bordering the Mississippi. Cities served include: Chicago, St. Louis, Omaha, Kansas City, Indianapolis, Louisville, Memphis, Birmingham, Mobile and New Orleans

Miles operated: 7,100 (11,426km)

Locomotives: 1,100

Freight cars: 39,200

Passenger cars: 175

Services: Grain, coal and chemicals in south; steel, automobiles and component parts in north. Commuters between Chicago and southern suburbs.

Address: Two Illinois Center, 233N Michigan Avenue, Chicago, Illinois 60601.

An early Illinois Central sleeping car (left) contrasts with an E6 passenger locomotive.

INDIANA HARBOR BELT RAILROAD

Incorporated: 1896 (present name assumed in 1907)

Previously: East Chicago Belt

Operations: Southern end of Lake Michigan to Franklin Park, Illinois, forming a belt around Chicago

Miles operated: 114 (183km)

Locomotives: 106

Freight cars: 33

Services: General freight.

Address: Union Station, Chicago, Illinois 60606.

LAKE ERIE, FRANKLIN AND CLARION RAILROAD

Incorporated: 1913

Previously: Member of Pennsylvania Northern, Pennsylvania Southern and Pittsburgh, Clarion and Franklin

Operations: Franklin to Clarion

Miles operated: 15 (24km)

Locomotives: 6

Freight cars: 1,120

Services: Coal, raw materials, glass.

Address: PO Box 430, East Wood Street, Clarion, Pennsylvania 16214.

LITTLE ROCK AND WESTERN RAILWAY

Previously: Purchased from bankrupt stock of Chicago, Rock Island and Pacific Railroad

Operations: Perry to Pulaski, Arkansas

Miles operated: 54 (87km)

Locomotives: 2

Freight cars: 350

Services: Paper.

IOWA RAILROAD

Incorporated: 1981

Operations: Iowa state between Omaha and Bureau, Illinois

Miles operated: 456 (739km)

Locomotives: 12

Freight cars: 296

Services: Grain.

Notes: Shares track with Chicago, Milwaukee, St. Paul and Pacific Railway.

LAKE SUPERIOR AND ISHPEMING RAILROAD

Incorporated: 1896

Operations: Mines in Michigan's Upper Peninsula to ports on Lake Superior

Miles operated: 60 (97km)

Locomotives: 23

Freight cars: 2,175

Services: Iron ore.

Address: 105 East Washington Street, Marquette, Michigan 49855.

MAINE CENTRAL RAILROAD

Incorporated: 1862

Previously: Merger of Androscoggin and Kennebec Railroad and Penobscot and Kennebec Railroads

Operations: Southern Maine, northern New Hampshire and Vermont. Main lines from Portland via Lewiston and Waterville to Bangor, with branch lines north to Mattawamkeag and Vanceboro and south to Calais

Miles operated: 819 (1,318km)

Locomotives: 65

Freight cars: 4,377

Services: Paper products.

Address: 242 St. John Street, Portland, Maine 04102.

KANSAS CITY SOUTHERN RAILWAY

Incorporated: 1890

Completed: First stretch in 1897

Previously: Kansas City, Pittsburgh and Gulf Railroad

Operations: Kansas City and Gulf Coast ports of Lake Charles, Louisiana, and Port Arthur, Texas; also Shreveport, Louisiana to Dallas, Texas

Miles operated: 1,663 (2,676km)

Locomotives: 300

Freight cars: 7,130

Services: Chemicals, coal, petroleum.

Address: 114 West 11th Street, Kansas City, Missouri 64105.

LAMOILLE VALLEY RAILROAD

Incorporated: 1869

Completed: 1888

Previously: St. Johnsbury and Lake Champlain Railroad

Operations: St Johnsbury to Swanton, Northern Vermont

Miles operated: 50 (80km)

Locomotives: 4

Freight cars: 50

Services: Talc, paper, grain.

Address: RFD 21, Stafford Avenue, Morrisville, Vermont 05661.

MARINETTE, TOMAHAWK AND WESTERN RAILWAY

Incorporated: 1894

Operations: Bradley to Wausau, Wisconsin

Miles operated: 13 (21km)

Locomotives: 3

Freight cars: 595

Services: Paper and coal.

Notes: Wholly-owned by Owens-Illinois Inc.

MARYLAND AND DELAWARE RAILROAD

Incorporated: 1977

Previously: Operates on track once owned by defunct New York, Philadelphia and Norfolk Railroad (originally incorporated in 1884)

Operations: Delmarva Peninsula with branch line south to Pockomoke

Miles operated: 148 (238km)

Locomotives: 4

Freight cars: 135

Services: Paper products, fertilizers and foodstuffs.

Address: 106, Railroad Avenue, Federalsburg, Maryland 21632.

MARYLAND AND PENNSYLVANIA RAILROAD ("MA AND PA")

Incorporated: 1867

Previously: Maryland Central Railroad (narrow gauge)

Operations: Hanover to York, Pennsylvania

Miles operated: 66 (106km)

Locomotives: 6

Freight cars: 2,190

Services: Paper products, furniture and foodstuffs.

Notes: Purchased by Emons Industries in 1971. Produces excess railcars for leasing.

Address: 490, East Market Street, York, Pennsylvania 17403.

McCLOUD RIVER RAILROAD

Incorporated: 1897

Operations: Northern California between Mt Shasta and Lookout, California, and on to Burney via branch line

Miles operated: 96 (154km)

Locomotives: 4

Freight cars: 247.

Services: Lumber.

Notes: Connects with Southern Pacific at Mt Shasta and with Burlington Northern at Lookout.

Address: PO Box A, McCloud, California 96057.

MERIDIAN AND BIGBEE RAILROAD

Incorporated: 1917

Completed: Began operations in 1928

Previously: Meridian and Bigbee River Railway

Operations: Meridian, Mississippi, to Myrtlewood, Alabama

Miles operated: 51 (82km)

Locomotives: 5

Freight cars: 475

Services: Chemicals, pulp and paper products.

Notes: Owned by James River Corporation.

MICHIGAN INTERSTATE RAILWAY

Incorporated: 1869

Previously: Ann Arbor Railroad

Operations: Ann Arbor, Michigan, to Toledo, Ohio

Miles operated: 49 (79km)

Locomotives: 3

Freight cars: 520

Services: Automobiles, automobile parts and cement.

Notes: The victim of several mergers and financial disputes. Bought by the state of Michigan in 1973, the line is now independent.

MICHIGAN NORTHERN RAILWAY

Incorporated: 1975

Previously: Operates on track originally owned by Pennsylvania Railroad and not subsequently purchased by Conrail

Operations: Grand Rapids to Mackinaw City, Michigan. Services to Alma, Frankfort and Charlevoix also provided

Miles operated: 430 (700km)

Locomotives: 7

Freight cars: 42

Passenger cars: 2

Services: Lumber, sand, foodstuffs and LP gas.

Notes: Seasonal passenger service to resort areas also provided.

Address: PO Box 359, 110 W North Street, Cadillac, Michigan 49601.

MISSOURI–KANSAS– TEXAS RAILROAD ("KATY")

Incorporated: 1865

Completed: Present name assumed in 1923

Previously: Union Pacific Railway, Southern Branch

Operations: Kansas City and St. Louis in the north to Oklahoma City, Tulsa and Altus, Western Oklahoma, south via Dallas and Fort Worth to San Antonio and Galveston in Texas

Miles operated: 2,175 (3,500km)

Locomotives: 203

Freight cars: 5,464

Services: Wheat, lumber, steel products, coal, crushed stone, automobiles and trucks.

Notes: Texas City terminal owned jointly by Missouri Pacific and Atchison, Topeka and Santa Fe.

Address: 701, Commerce Street, Dallas, Texas 75202.

MOHAWK AND HUDSON RAILROAD

Incorporated: 1826

Previously: Incorporated into New York Central Railroad in 1853

Operations: Originally from Albany to Schenectady between the Hudson and Mohawk Rivers

Miles operated: Originally 15 (24km)

Notes: Designed originally as a horse-drawn line, it obtained its first steam locomotive in 1831.

MONONGAHELA RAILWAY

Incorporated: 1915

Previously: Merger of Monongahela Railroad and the Buckhannon and Northern Railroad

Operations: Brownsville to Blacksville, Pennsylvania, on one branch and Brownsville to Keyport, West Virginia on another

Miles operated: 136 (219km)

Locomotives: 11

Freight cars: 10

Services: Coal.

Notes: Jointly owned by Baltimore and Ohio component of Chessie System, Conrail and Pittsburgh and Lake Erie Railroads.

Address: P&LE Terminal Building, Pittsburgh, Pennsylvania 15219.

NATIONAL RAILROAD PASSENGER CORPORATION (AMTRAK)

Incorporated: Created by Rail Passenger Service Act in 1970 (first operational trains in 1971)

Completed: First nationwide passenger operations in 1971

Operations: Owns Boston–New York–Washington Northeast Corridor track and small line between Porter, Indiana, and Kalamazoo, Michigan. Elsewhere, track owned and run by freight-hauling railroads (who are responsible for its maintenance)

The Amtrak 'Coast Starlight', running between Los Angeles and San Francisco, has replaced the Southern Pacific's 'Daylight'.

Miles operated: 23,400 (37,658km)

Locomotives: 220 diesel, 62 electric, 14 gas-turbine cars and 109 emu cars

Passenger cars: 1,390

Services: Major nationwide passenger service (took over last independent passenger line – southern railway – in 1980)

Notes: Wholly-owned commuter services in Northeast Corridor operated by several state and regional agencies. Locomotives and cars originally inherited from participating railroads, and known as "Heritage Fleet", now being replaced by custom-built stock. Bi-level "super-liner" cars used on long distance hauls west of Chicago. Amtrak owns and operates Washington Terminal Company with facilities adjacent to Washington's (federal) Union Station. Commuter cars from other railroads serviced under contract at Amtrak's Beech Grove facilities near Indianapolis.

Address: 400, N Capitol Street NW, Washington DC 20001.

NEW ORLEANS PUBLIC BELT RAILROAD

Incorporated: 1900

Operations: Switch service in New Orleans port area

Miles operated: 47 (76km)

Locomotives: 10

Freight cars: 1,250

Services: General freight.

Notes: Track crosses Huey P. Long Bridge, the longest railway bridge in North America. 4.5 miles long, it has a central span of 3,524 feet.

NEW YORK, NEW HAVEN AND HARTFORD RAILROAD

Incorporated: 1872

Previously: Merger of New York and New Haven Railroad and Hartford and New Haven Railroad

Operations: Originally New York to Boston, covering Connecticut, Massachusetts, Rhode Island and eastern New York

Notes: Went into bankruptcy in 1961 due to competition from Connecticut Turnpike running parallel. Absorbed into Penn Central.

NORFOLK AND WESTERN RAILWAY

Incorporated: 1850

Completed: 1858 (original Norfolk to Petersburg track)

Previously: Norfolk and Petersburg Railroad

Operations: Norfolk, Virginia, to Buffalo, New York, in east; Kansas City, St. Louis and Omaha in west, via 14 states and one Canadian province

Miles operated: 8,000 (12,874km)

Locomotives: 1,320

Freight cars: 85,900

Passenger cars: 23

Services: Coal and agricultural products. Also serves coal fields of West Virginia, southern Ohio and eastern Kentucky.

Notes: Operates commuter service between Chicago and Highland Park, Illinois, for Regional Transportation Authority. Resisted dieselization until 1960s; in 1959 merged with Virginian Railway. Bought Atlantic and Danville in 1962, Wabash and New York, Chicago and St. Louis in 1964. Operates mining, docks and hotels subsidiaries.

Address: 8, North Jefferson Street, Roanoke, Virginia 24042.

OCTORARO RAILWAY

Incorporated: First track purchased in 1971

Previously: Majority of track purchased from Penn Central, Octoraro branch

Operations: Southeastern Pennsylvania and northern tip of Delaware

Miles operated: 68 (109km)

Locomotives: 4

Freight cars: 142

Services: General freight.

Notes: Track is X-shaped with Chadds Ford Junction at the center, one track from Wawa to Colora, Pennsylvania, the other between Modena, Pennsylvania, and Wilmington, Delaware. Excursions run by Historic Red Valley Inc as Wilmington and Western Railroad on former Baltimore and Ohio track between Wilmington and Hockessin, Delaware.

Address: PO Box 146, Kennett Square, Pennsylvania 19348.

This Ontario Northland locomotive has a particularly narrow nose, designed to allow the engineer increased visibility when it is in operation.

NORFOLK AND PORTSMOUTH BELT LINE RAILROAD

Incorporated: 1896

Completed: Received present name in 1898

Previously: Southeastern and Atlantic Railroad

Operations: Switching service in Norfolk, Virginia, area

Miles operated: 30 (48km)

Locomotives: 15

Services: General freight.

Notes: Owned by Chessie System, Norfolk and Western, Seaboard System and Southern Railway.

NORTH LOUISIANA AND GULF RAILWAY

Incorporated: 1906

Operations: Gibsland to Hodge, Louisiana

Miles operated: 40 (64km)

Locomotives: 5

Freight cars: 990

Services: Pulpwood, finished paper products and wood chips.

Notes: Owned by Continental Group and run in conjunction with its sister line, Central Louisiana and Gulf.

Address: PO Drawer 550, Hodge, Louisiana 71247.

ONTARIO NORTHLAND RAILWAY

Incorporated: 1902

Completed: Reached Cochrane in 1909 and Moosonee in 1931

Previously: Temiskaming and Northern Ontario Railway

Operations: North Bay to Moosonee, Ontario, on James Bay. Branches to Elk Lake, Timmins, Iroquois Falls and from Swastika to Noranda, Quebec

Miles operated: 574 (924km)

Locomotives: 39

Freight cars: 930

Passenger cars: 45

Services: Minerals and forest products.

Notes: Passenger services include Northlander service between Toronto and Timmins. Operated by the Ontario Northland Transportation Commission.

Address: 195, Regina Street, North Bay, Ontario P1B 8L3

OREGON, CALIFORNIA AND EASTERN RAILWAY

Incorporated: 1917

Completed: 1928

Operations: Klamath Falls to Bly, Oregon

Miles operated: 66 (106km)

Locomotives: 11

Freight cars: 150

Services: Logging.

Notes: Owned by Weyerhauser Company.

Address: PO Box 1088, Klamath Falls, Oregon 97601.

OREGON NORTH-WESTERN RAILROAD

Incorporated: 1904

Operations: Seneca to Hines, Oregon

Miles operated: 51 (82km)

Locomotives: 4

Freight cars: 440

Services: Lumber.

Notes: Connects with a line of the Union Pacific at Burns. Owned by Edward Hines Lumber Co.

Address: PO Box 557, Hines, Oregon 97738.

PITTSBURGH AND LAKE ERIE RAILROAD

Incorporated: 1875

Completed: 1879

Operations: Ashtabula, Ohio, on Lake Erie to Brownsville Junction and Connellsville, south of Pittsburgh

Miles operated: 273 (439km)

Locomotives: 95

Freight cars: 17,380

Passenger cars: 5

Services: Iron ore, coal, coke and limestone, finished steel products.

Notes: Tracks used by Baltimore and Ohio for commuter service to Pittsburgh. Operates subsidised commuter service between College, Pennsylvania, and Pittsburgh.

Address: Commerce Court, 4, Station Square, Pittsburgh, Pennsylvania 15219.

PITTSBURGH AND SHAWMUT RAILROAD

Incorporated: Present name adopted in 1910

Previously: Brookville and Mahoning Railroad

Operations: Western Pennsylvania between Brockway and Freeport Junction, northeast of Pittsburgh

Miles operated: 96 (154km)

Locomotives: 12

Freight cars: 1,290

Services: Coal.

Address: 1 Glade Park, RD3, Kittaning, Pennsylvania 16201.

PRAIRIE CENTRAL RAILWAY

Previously: Part of Wabash Railroad

Operations: L-shaped route between Decatur and Mt Carmel, Illinois

Miles operated: 165 (266km)

Locomotives: 7

Freight cars: 160

Services: Grain and fertilizer.

Notes: Line owned by Trans-Action Lines Ltd.

PROVIDENCE AND WORCESTER RAILROAD

Incorporated: 1844

Previously: Reincorporated in 1968 (previously part of New York, Providence and Boston Railroad)

Operations: Southeastern New England, serving Gardner, Worcester, Fall River and Newport, Massachusetts; Providence, Rhode Island; Willimantic, New London and Old Saybrook, Connecticut

One of the 76 locomotives employed by the Quebec North Shore and Labrador Railway in hauling freight cars loaded with iron ore.

Miles operated: 370 (595km)

Locomotives: 12

Freight cars: 1,070

Services: Chemicals, newsprint, general freight. Weekend excursion trains run between Worcester and Uxbridge, Massachusetts.

Address: PO Box 1490, 1, Depot Square, Woonsocket, Rhode Island 02940-9205.

QUEBEC NORTH SHORE AND LABRADOR RAILWAY

Incorporated: 1949 (construction commenced in 1951)

Completed: 1954

Operations: Ungava along Newfoundland–Quebec border to ports along St Lawrence River. Termini at Schefferville, Quebec and Sept-Iles. Branch line from Ross Bay Junction to Wabush Lake completed in 1960

Miles operated: 397 (639km)

Locomotives: 76

Freight cars: 4,235

Services: Iron ore.

Notes: Bi-weekly passenger trains operated. Line does not link with main US network. Operates some of the longest (average 1.5 miles) and heaviest (average 28,000 tons) trains in North America.

Address: PO Box 1000, Sept-Iles, Quebec G4R 4LS.

RICHMOND, FREDERICKSBURG AND POTOMAC RAILROAD

Incorporated: 1834

Completed: Final link from Potomac River to Washington completed in 1872

Operations: Washington, DC and Richmond, Virginia

Miles operated: 1,620 (2,607km)

Locomotives: 41

Freight cars: 1,620

Services: Paper products, foodstuffs, chemicals, general freight.

Notes: Owned by CSX Corporation.

Address: PO Box 11281, 2134 West Laburnum Avenue, Richmond, Virginia 23227.

ROBERVAL AND SAGUENAY RAILROAD

Incorporated: 1911

Previously: Ha!Ha! Bay Railway

Operations: Port Alfred to Arvida, Quebec

Miles operated: 55 (89km)

Locomotives: 14

Freight cars: 290

Services: Bauxite from company mine.

Notes: Owned by Aluminium Company of America.

ST MARIES RIVER RAILROAD

Incorporated: 1980

Previously: Original line purchased from Milwaukee Road

Operations: Plummer Junction to Bovill, Idaho

Miles operated: 71 (114km)

Locomotives: 5

Freight cars: 515

Services: Logs, plywood and wood chips.

Notes: Operated by Kyle Railways through its subsidiary, Idaho Western Inc.

SEABOARD SYSTEM RAILROAD

Incorporated: 1967

Previously: A series of mergers including Seaboard Air Line Railroad, Atlantic Coast Line and Louisville and Nashville

Operations: Southeastern United States, through Kentucky to Cincinnati, Indianapolis, St Louis and Chicago

Miles operated: 15,400 (24,783km)

Locomotives: 2,365

Freight cars: 116,500

Services: Coal, fresh fruits, vegetables (via "Orange Blossom Special"), chemicals, phosphate rock, wood and paper.

Notes: Owned by CSX Corporation. Serves more ocean ports than any other US railroad.

Address: PO Box C-32222, Richmond, Virginia 23261

SEATTLE AND NORTH COAST RAILROAD

Incorporated: 1980

Previously: Track originally operated by Milwaukee Road

Operations: Port Angeles and Port Townsend, Washington, along coast of the Strait of Juan de Fuca

Miles operated: 50 (80km)

Locomotives: 7

Freight cars: 300

Passenger cars: Experimenting with passengers on Port Angeles to Port Townsend line ("Olympic Peninsula Route")

Services: Paper and general supplies to various paper mills.

Notes: Company began experimenting with loading intermodal containers direct, to take advantage of Far East and domestic markets.

Address: 2150, North 107th Street, Washington 98133

Facing page: Southern Pacific's locomotive No. 4449, in 'Daylight' livery, is the only one of its type to survive. It was completely refurbished in 1958 and presented to the citizens of Portland, Oregon.

SIERRA RAILROAD

Incorporated: 1890

Previously: Sierra Railway

Operations: Standard to Oakdale, California

Miles operated: 50 (80km)

Locomotives: 3

Freight cars: 250

Services: Lumber and wood. Operates seasonal passenger excursions.

Notes: Used for film productions such as *High Noon* and *Petticoat Junction*.

Address: 13645, Tuolumu Road, Sonora, California 95370

SOUTH CENTRAL TENNESSEE RAILROAD

Incorporated: 1978

Previously: Track originally owned by Louisville and Nashville Railroad

Operations: Colesburg to Hohenwald, Tennessee

Miles operated: 50 (80km)

Locomotives: 3

Freight cars: 95

Services: Wood chips and carbon black.

Notes: A subsidiary of Kyle Railways.

SOUTHERN PACIFIC COMPANY

Incorporated: 1850s

Previously: Can trace history, via numerous mergers, from Sacramento Valley Rail Road. Merger of Northwestern Pacific Railroad and St Louis South-western Railway (the Cotton Belt)

Operations: Midwestern and southwestern United States, north from San Francisco to Portland, Oregon, west to Ogden, Utah and south to Los Angeles. Also "Sunset Route" from Houston, west to New Orleans and northwest to Memphis and St Louis

Miles operated: 10,110 (16,270km)

Locomotives: 2,621

Freight cars: 67,933

Passenger cars: 92

Notes: One of the first railroads to adopt diesel power (mid-1930s). Operates a commuter service between San Francisco and San Jose under auspices of State of California.

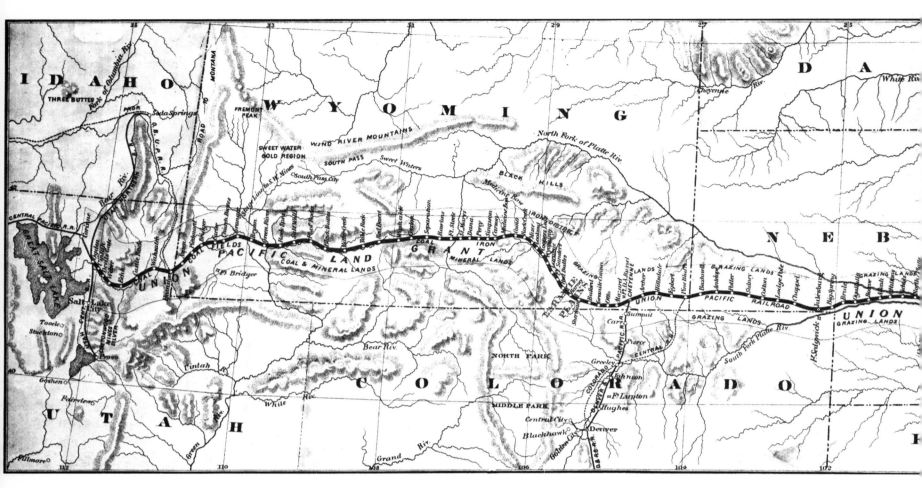

A map of the land grant and connections of the Union Pacific Railroad, published in Philadelphia in 1872.

ST LOUIS SOUTH-WESTERN RAILWAY (COTTON BELT)

Locomotives: 319

Freight cars: 18,961

Miles operated: 2,180 (3,508km)

Address: Southern Pacific Building, One Market Plaza, San Francisco, California 94105

TEXAS MEXICAN RAILWAY ("TEX-MEX")

Incorporated: 1875

Previously: San Diego and Rio Grande Narrow Gauge Railroad

Operations: Flour Bluff on Gulf of Mexico to Laredo, Texas

Miles operated: 157 (253km)

Locomotives: 16

Freight cars: 1,121

Services: Chemicals, grain, gravel and scrap iron.

Notes: The majority of freight interchanges with National Railways of Mexico.

Address: PO Box 419, Laredo, Texas 78042-0419

TOLEDO, PEORIA AND WESTERN RAILROAD

Incorporated: 1863

Completed: 1868

Previously: Toledo, Peoria Warsaw Railroad

Operations: Logansport, Indiana Keokuk, Iowa

Miles operated: 472 (760km)

Locomotives: 29

Freight cars: 382

Notes: A full merger with Santa Fe is anticipated.

Address: 2000, East Washington Street, East Peoria, Illinois 61611

TORONTO, HAMILTON AND BUFFALO RAILWAY

Incorporated: 1884

Completed: 1895

Operations: Southern Ontario peninsula between Port Colborne and Waterford, via Hamilton

Miles operated: 111 (179km)

Locomotives: 17

Freight cars: 1,120

Services: Fertilizer, chemicals, iron and steel.

Notes: Wholly-owned by Canadian Pacific.

TUSCOLA AND SAGINAW BAY RAILWAY

Incorporated: 1977

Previously: Track originally used by New York Central railroad

Operations: Eastern Michigan between Ann Arbor, Alma and points in the Saginaw Bay area, including Saginaw, Munger and Colling

Miles operated: 208 (335km)

Locomotives: 6

Freight cars: 159

Services: Molasses, coal, grain and auto parts.

Address: 538, E. Huron Street, Vassar, Mississippi 48768

UNION PACIFIC RAILROAD COMPANY

Incorporated: Charter granted in 1862, via Pacific Railroad Act

Previously: Union Pacific, Missouri, Pacific and Western Pacific merged in December 1981. (Western Pacific became subsidiary, Missouri Pacific continued to operate independently)

Operations: 13 states from Kansas City and Council Bluffs, Iowa, westward to Ogden/Salt Lake City. Lines extend southwest to Los Angeles and northwest to Portland and Seattle, via Wyoming, Montana and Idaho

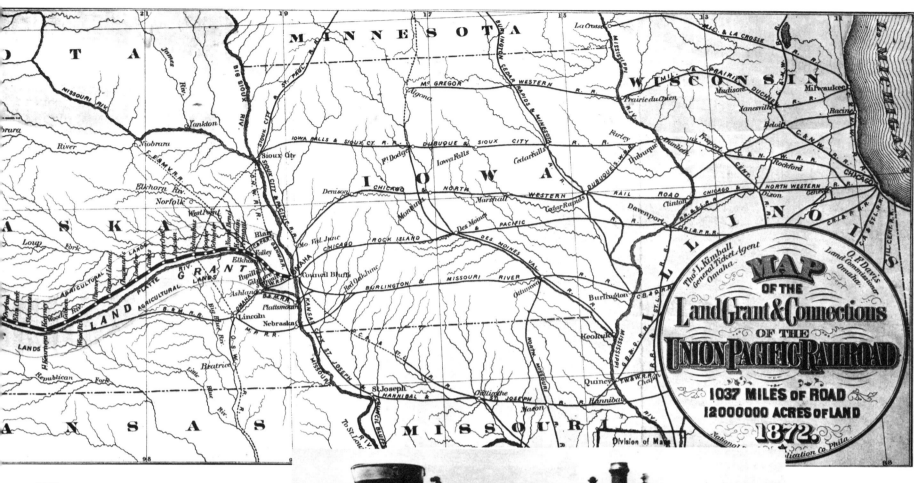

Miles operated: 1,432 (2,305km)

Locomotives: 1,742

Freight cars: 67,778

Services: General freight, with emphasis on coal (25 trains per day).

Notes: Important coal exportation line of 784 miles (1,262km) between Salt Lake City and Pacific Coast at Long Beach and Los Angeles. Big Boy locomotives (introduced in 1941) were the largest in the world. 4-runner intermodal sets now running successfully between Chicago and Los Angeles. At the end of their laden westbound journey, freight cars are rented to Transway International Corporation, which carries the majority of its freight from west to east.

Address: 1416, Dodge Street, Omaha, Nebraska 68179

UTAH RAILWAY

Incorporated: 1914

Operations: Provo to Mohrland, central Utah

Miles operated: 95 (153km)

Locomotives: 8

Services: Coal.

Notes: Owned by Sharon Steel Corporation and operates on tracks bought from Denver and Rio Grande Railroad.

The final section of the Central Pacific and Union Pacific was completed at Promontory, Utah, on 10 May, 1869. A golden spike used in the ceremony is now owned by Stanford University and can be seen there.

VERMONT RAILWAY

Incorporated: Originally in 1843; bankrupted; reformed in 1961

Previously: Rutland Railroad

Operations: Throughout Vermont; lines also from Rutland to Bellows Falls, and St Johnsbury to Stanton

Miles operated: 130 (209km)

Locomotives: 7

Freight cars: 1,260

Services: General freight.

Address: 267, Battery Street, Burlington, Vermont 05401

WISCONSIN AND SOUTHERN RAILROAD

Incorporated: 1980

Previously: Track purchased from Milwaukee Road

Operations: Milwaukee, northwest to Oshkash, Cambria, including Ripon, Brandon and Iron Ridge

Miles operated: 147 (237km)

Locomotives: 19

Freight cars: 420

Services: General freight.

THE NEW AGE OF US RAILROADING

A GE 3,000 hp C30-7A in Conrail colours.

If it had hit ten years earlier, an economic recession of the severity experienced in the early 1980s would have had Wall Street analysts forecasting a fresh wave of bankruptcies which ravaged US railroads in the late 1960s. In 1980-82 the industrial downturn knocked away more than 13 percent of the gross ton-mileage registered by the 30 freight-hauling Class I US railroads, which in the Association of American Railroads (AAR) classification ruling since the start of 1978 are those pulling in over $50 million operating revenue a year (the purely passenger-operating Amtrak also meets this qualification). However though one or two Class I systems slid into the red, it was no more than a temporary inconvenience. Still more of a contrast to valuation of railroad prospects a decade earlier was the view of a good many market seers, not only that the railroads would revive in step with the national economy, but that in many cases their stocks were a sound growth buy.

One reason for this confidence was the much healthier financial state of the railroad industry as it faced the 1980s slump. Adjusted to constant dollar values, the combined net revenue of the Class I railroads in 1981 was more than three times their income at the start of the 1970s. Even in the two dire years that followed, 1982-83, they posted a total net well up on their results in the early 1970s.

Plenty more statistics testified to the railroads' steadily advancing technical and commercial efficiency, but just one comparison must suffice here. In 1971 the Class I railroads together logged 740 billion freight ton-miles, but were then employing over 544,300 men. In 1980 the figures were 919 billion ton-miles, with staff down to just under 459,000. By 1983 the recession had cut ton-mileage to 825,000, but the total of Class I system employees had dropped much more steeply, to a little below 335,300. That represented an 80 percent improvement in the productive use of labor in a dozen years. (In 1949, incidentally, Class I railroad employees numbered over 1.19 million!)

Federal action takes some of the credit for the upturn in US railroad fortunes. It became inescapable when, in the fading 1960s, the US passenger train was heading for extinction (how that was forestalled is discussed elsewhere); and, far graver, railroading generally throughout the Northeast faced total collapse as economic trends peculiar to that region aggravated problems that were common to the whole railroad industry.

By the 1960s the railroads' financial performance had deteriorated to the extent that the average return on the

Right: A celebrated Union Pacific location, the Keddie Wye junction in California, with four of UP's heavily predominant road-haul power type, the GM-EMD SD40-2.

Below: In 1979, more than 15 miles of new track was installed on CP Rail's Calgary-Vancouver main line. The new lines handle westbound trains while the existing main line, in the background, is used for lighter eastbound trains.

Class I systems' capital was less than 3 percent. Neither Washington nor railroad managements had responded positively to the impact of post-war trucking's upsurge on traditional rail transportation patterns and method. Spurred by the spread of new highways, by cheap fuel, and by vehicle development, it had robbed the railroads of a huge tonnage of lucrative general merchandise traffic and left them increasingly dependent on lower-rated bulk mineral and commodity freight.

Reaction to the rapid expansion of domestic air services, to keener intercity bus competition from Greyhound and others, and to wider-ranging use of the private automobile was more lively. But it was not swift enough to stem industry-wide losses averaging almost $650 million a year in the second half of the 1950s, despite the thousands of passenger-route miles that were already being abandoned and which by 1967 had more than halved the percentage of the national rail network carrying passenger trains. Some railroads were already out of the passenger business altogether.

To be fair, the pace of withdrawal from financially debilitating passenger service was to an extent dictated by the need to seek Interstate Commerce Commission (ICC) approval for each and every abandonment. This was just one of the shackles inherited from the late 19th-century legislation enacted to prevent railroads abusing their monopoly on economic bulk transportation, whether of passengers or freight. Much

more crippling, though, were the archaic statutes which still strictly limited railroads' freedom of commercial maneuver – and which consequently stifled managerial initiative in face of drastically changed freight market conditions. Sparkling new railroad managerial talent became progressively harder to recruit as the 1960s progressed, in fact.

The railroad labor unions, one ought to add, saw nothing in the railroads' deepening financial crisis to justify a relaxation of their historic work-rules. Moreover, the courageous Florida East Coast refused in the early 1960s to be enslaved by the rigidity of 100-mile train-crew working days or a five-man train-crew requirement, and withdrew from the national railroad labor negotiations and deals that accepted such conditions. It had to withstand not only a year of strikes and sabotage, but also heavy pressure from the Kennedy Administration to settle on the labor unions' terms, before it established its right to attack its long-running deficit on its own terms.

Contraction of investment resources was the obvious consequence of the railroads' dwindling income. Track maintenance was the principal casualty. On the more financially unsound systems the gap between track repair or renewal need and achievement was widening by the year. This meant that speed restrictions over bad-order sections were proliferating, extending transits, and injecting new unreliabilities into the quality of service, to make

even more forlorn the battle with truckers for the well-paying categories of freight.

Several major railroads had sought greater financial strength through merger since World War II, either to rationalize parallel, competing systems or to stitch systems together end-to-end for longer through-haul opportunities. At the start of 1959, for instance, the Virginian had been absorbed by Norfolk & Western, merging two of the chief coal hauliers from the eastern mines to the east coast shipment ports. Four years later Chesapeake & Ohio had taken control of neighboring Baltimore & Ohio and the Central of Georgia had passed into Southern Railway hands. The most amazing marriage was that first announced in 1957, to the astonishment of the rest of the industry: the alliance of the giant arch-rivals of the East, the Pennsylvania and New York Central. Both were desperately in need of economies, chiefly because of horrendous losses on passenger operation – $54.7 million in Pennsy's case, $48.5 million in NYC's in 1956; in 1957 NYC's net revenue was slashed by two-thirds, Pennsy's by almost half, and neither on its own looked capable of plugging the drain.

However the merger of the two systems as Penn-Central was not effected until 1968. Every claim of disadvantage from the merger had to be heard and dissected by the ICC; and at that time there was no statutory obligation on the ICC to pronounce on the case within a reasonable time-scale. The ICC's

leisurely deliberation was not the end of the rigmarole either, as appellants dissatisfied with their findings could always seek to get ICC judgments overruled in the courts: the last hurdle cleared by the Penn-Central merger was, in fact, the US Supreme Court. Even so, Penn-Central was not a record in protracted consideration of a merger case. In the 1960s and early 1970s the ICC took 12 years, no less, to summon up an endorsement of Rock Island's application to merge with Union Pacific. By then Union Pacific had lost interest and the Rock was left to slip back into bankruptcy, which eventually destroyed it as an independent system in the early 1980s.

By the time the Penn-Central merger was finally approved, an archangelic management team would have had its work cut out to stave off financial catastrophe. Its railroad operations were losing around $150 million a year, chiefly because PC was running almost three-quarters of the US surviving inter-city passenger trains; they were responsible for almost half the deficit purely on their avoidable costs – that is, the obvious direct expenses of running the trains, with no account taken of their share of track, signaling, and other fixed railroad costs. Neither constituent

Left: Four SD40-2s head a trailer-train of 59 bogies out of Cheyenne yard under the C & S overbridge. They immediately hit the gradient up Sherman Hill, heading west.

Above: A Pennsylvania Railroad electric GGI locomotive hauls the 18-car Congressional.

company had managed better than 0.6 percent return on capital employed since 1961. The ICC then compounded their financial troubles by insisting that the merged system embrace the hopelessly sick New Haven system, north of New York. Worse yet, the Pennsy had been borrowing heavily to follow Union Pacific and others into diversification, especially into property development countrywide. With the country's economy regressing at the close of the 1960s, that was yielding a return well below expectations. Add to all this the onset of cost inflation, and the outlook was in any event grim.

It was hopeless when, from board to ground level, age-old Pennsy-NYC jealousies and dogmatic differences were immediately allowed not merely to surface but to permeate every reorganization and rationalization project.

None of the financial economies forecast from the merger were realized; managers from the two former systems who were now thrown together often refused to collaborate; and dogfights aggravated an operational confusion arising from the incompatibility of the two railroads' data transmission systems, which had freight customers decamping to the highways in droves.

In the background, sagging US industrial output and labor strikes were accelerating the drain on PC resources – so much so that in the first quarter of 1970 PC losses were already soaring beyond the system's full 1969 deficit. In May that year, Wall Street sensed irreversible descent to disaster and refused any more loans. A desperate PC sought help from Washington, which had just bailed out another industrial giant, aircraft manufacturer Lockheed, but was rebuffed by Congress. The only course left was to file a bankruptcy petition. It was the largest-scale collapse of an industry in US history.

The fall of PC had a domino effect on its smaller northeastern neighbors, all of which had been teetering on the brink of insolvency. One of the external factors contributing to PC's downfall was the downward trend of the Northeast's heavy industrial traffic, the result partly of a move out of coal and into oil or gas as a fuel, partly of the depression in the steel and auto industries, and partly of the drift of smokestack industry out of the region. So the 1970 bankruptcy of the 1,100-mile Lehigh Valley was unsurprising; that railroad had been built essentially to transport anthracite coal. The 3,189-mile Erie-Lackawanna went the same way in 1972. Others to tumble in the late 1960s and early 1970s were the Central of New Jersey, the Reading, the Lehigh & Hudson River, and the Ann Arbor (though the Reading Company, like PC, is among former railroad concerns still involved in the activities into which it diversified).

In the wake of PC's bankruptcy, the trustees appointed to attempt a reorganization of the corporation's railroad business (under a section of US law specifically allowing US railroads a tax-free and debt-free moratorium to essay a financial turnround) struggled to rationalize the system's gross excess of duplicate routes and terminals; to trim its labor costs; to counter the loss of heavy industrial freight by developing a competitive intermodal system for high-rated merchandise; and to offload

Mechanized track relaying. This machine secures the clips which hold the foot of the rail to the concrete sleepers.

heavily loss-making commuter passenger operations in Boston, New York, and Philadelphia on to the relevant state administrations. Success was scant. All the time the railroad assets were sinking further into disrepair and decrepitude.

Washington had to intervene. The first step was the Regional Rail Reorganization Act of 1973 – since known as the "3-R" – which set up the United States Railway Administration (USRA) to contrive a viable scheme for a rationalized rail system in the Northeast. That was followed in 1976 by the Rail Revitalization & Reform Act – the "4-R" –which, under USRA's supervision, set up the Consolidated Rail Corporation, or Conrail, to run a conglomeration of PC and the six other railroads which it had helped to suck into bankruptcy.

The 4-R Act also tackled the inability of railroads to generate adequate funds for essential plant upkeep by creating a $1.6 billion fund with which the Federal Railroad Administration (FRA) – a component of the Department of Transportation (DOT) – could underwrite and get moving the overdue infrastructure rehabilitation of many busy routes interlining major markets. This money, incidentally, was additional to the considerable funds established to launch Conrail and the new national intercity passenger train operator, Amtrak.

The 4-R Act further clamped a 2½-year time limit on the ICC's consideration of merger applications. That reflected not only a chastened Washington's embarrassment at its failure to foresee and forestall disaster in the Northeast, but also its arousal to the irrelevance of so many historic antipathies to mega-railroad proposals. This was apparent with the patent benefits quickly realized from the March 1970 forging of the country's longest system, the 26,500-mile Burlington Northern (BN) after years of hearings which, as in the Penn-Central case, reached their climax in the US Supreme Court.

Amalgamation of railroads participating in or competing for traffic between the Great Lakes and the West Coast had been attempted more than once, starting with the effort of railroad empire-builder James J Hill in 1893. All had been blocked by variations on the theme of antitrust paranoia. Ultimate achievement in BN was no shotgun marriage in the face of financial difficulty, but a voluntary alliance of four companies which recognized the overwhelming advantages of concen-

Above: Conrail's track geometry car gives maintenance engineers a panoramic view of the railroad.
Left: ICG is an important coal carrier, utilizing unit trains for almost all of its coal traffic.

trating their transcontinental freight on the easiest of two parallel routes through the Cascade Mountains, for example; and of through diesel locomotives and trains running from West Coast ports to Chicago, instead of the much less productive operation involved in traction changes and train reclassification at each others' frontiers.

The four original constituents of BN were the Great Northern, Northern Pacific, the Chicago, Burlington & Quincy, and the Spokane, Portland & Seattle. In 1980 BN also gathered in the St Louis-San Francisco, best-known as the 'Frisco,' followed in 1981 by the Colorado & Southern, a former CB & Q subsidiary, and at the start of 1983 by the Fort Worth & Denver.

Today BN is a network of over 29,200 route-miles, operating in 25 US states and two Canadian provinces, and stretching from Washington and Oregon in the west to Minneapolis-St Paul, Chicago, and St Louis and as far south as Houston, Texas, and Pensacola, Florida. Almost two-thirds of its gross revenue derives from movement of three commodities: coal, grain, and forest products. In two of these departments, coal and grain, it is a national leader in tonnage hauled annually: indeed, as a grain mover it has no equal.

Like a number of other major railroads, BN is part of a conglomerate. As the earlier postwar years stripped the financial gloss from railroading, several companies looked to offset the worsening performance of their prime business by diversifying – the hapless Pennsylvania's move into property development has already been mentioned. Elsewhere, the Atchison, Topeka & Santa Fe (ATSF) or Santa Fe, became in 1968 the subsidiary of Santa Fe Industries, whose interests today embrace other transportation modes, natural resources, real estate, construction, and forest products. Southern Pacific (SP) is a member of the Southern Pacific Transportation Co, with very extensive land ownings, timberland, and mineral rights in its portfolio as well as pipeline operations. To cite just one more example, Union Pacific Corporation, the parent of the Union Pacific Railroad (UP), own major petroleum/petro-chemical and mining companies as well as an industrial development enterprise. As for BN, the activities of Burlington Northern Inc, of which it is a subsidiary, run the gamut from forestry products to oil and gas exploration and ore mining.

The striking feature of this diversification is that to date only two major companies have found other industrial activities profitable enough that they would be better out of their founding business, railroading. In the 1950s the dynamic Ben Heinemann fought to weld together some of the financially

Above: Santa Fe operates this vast automobile unloading yard at Horton, Texas.

sick railroads in the Midwest into an integral, viable system. By 1966 he had achieved a Chicago & North Western (C&NW) that turned in a resounding operational surplus of some $26 million. However further Heinemann schemes to enlarge the C&NW railroad empire, notably the acquisition of the Rock Island and Milwaukee Roads to establish virtually a single network for the region, were frustrated.

Its momentum checked, C&NW slid back into the red. Back in 1965 Heinemann had formed Northwest Industries to diversify into non-rail business; this proved tremendously profitable and by the end of the decade Northwest Industries was eager to be rid of C&NW. A disenchanted Heinemann, so recently the eagerest beaver on the US rail scene industry, now owned that he had become "totally discontented with the railroad industry . . . its rate of return is disgustingly inadequate." In 1972 the sale of C&NW and certain of its subsidiaries to the railroad's employees was completed and in that guise the railroad functions today under the title of Chicago & North Western Transportation Co.

Disposal of another Class I system, the Illinois Central Gulf (ICG), created through the 1972 merger of Illinois Central and Gulf, Mobile & Ohio encompassing a 9,660 route-mile system stretching from Chicago, Omaha, and Sioux City southward to Montgomery, Mobile, and New Orleans, was still only an intention in early 1984. Illinois Central had a diversification frontrunner, forming IC Industries as early as 1962, and this conglomerate became ICG's parent. Since the 1972 merger that established ICG the parent has already presided over a 28 percent truncation of route-mileage, but it has been aiming for an ultimate core system of little more than 5,000 route-miles, to fine down to the highest-volume routes on its books. A further 700 route-miles, along with 30 locomotives and 1,500 freight cars, were being sold in eastern Mississippi and neighboring states in the course of 1984, for operation by Kyle Railways of San Diego under L B Foster & Co (Pittsburgh) ownership. Nevertheless, IC Industries, now big in the food and drink business and with other interests in automotive and machinery component manufacture, and in defense items, pronounced sale of ICG to be a priority objective as soon as an acceptable buyer materialized.

Although the economic disruption engaged the railroads in the mid-1970s, driving the average return on Class I system investment to an abysmal 1.24 percent in 1977, none of the other big railroads were denied investment by their parent corporations. BN, for instance, has been allowed since 1976 to plow over $1,500 million into infrastructure improvements and more than $600 million into new traction and cars to enlarge its coal-carrying capacity in face of the rising demand for export coal, also of increased domestic consumption as industry shied away from high-priced oil fuel, and clean-air legislation put a premium on low sulphur coal mined in BN's Wyoming and Montana territory. On the other hand the depressed financial state of railroading in the mid-1970s, together with the clear testimony that the technical means to recoup some of the lost intercity merchandise freight had been perfected, swelled railroad executive clamor for release from the chains of ICC regulatory law. In its essentials this was encompassed in the hallowed provision of the Interstate Commerce Act of 1887.

The Kennedy Administration had professed its intention to attack the

Right, top: Maintenance and repair of the railroad track is nowadays fully mechanized.

Right: Two SD40-2s of the Burlington Northern are needed in order to haul the large number of cars in this unit train.

problem, but deregulation of transport did not get underway until Carter's presidency. First to be thrown to the free play of market forces, in October 1979, was air transport. Deregulation unleashed an internecine fare-cutting war on plum routes and spawned a rash of small airlines to take over the less remunerative routes abandoned by the majors. Next followed the deregulation of the trucking industry: but no more than 40 percent of motor-carrier tonnage had been subject to ICC regulation anyway.

Meanwhile the railroads stayed almost completely regulated. Apart from recent exemption in respect of fresh fruit and vegetable traffic, they were still hog-tied by the same restrictions on their rate-making and freedom to contract for long-term business – or contract out of loss-making routes and services – as applied before more than 40,000 miles of Interstate Highway were laid across the country, and at the price of over 100 billion taxpayers' dollars which trucker users were in no way fully contributing toward. The railroads were not only financially responsible for the full maintenance of their right-of-way, but obliged to pay local taxes on it.

The airline and trucking industries had fought fiercely to abort their deregulation, principally for fear of its opening up the business to new entrants who would dilute the profits of established concerns. That was obviously not a risk in the railroad industry. Nevertheless, rail chiefs were not unanimous in pressing for deregulation. For example, Norfolk & Western's (NW) then President, John P Fishwick, argued in 1979 that it should wait until the potential inter-railroad competition had been diminished by further mergers. He knew his industry. When deregulation was enacted, the retrograde response of some railroads was to go for their neighbors' traffic with riskily low-priced offers, and not develop a marketing expertise to broach markets that had

Below: A Southern Pacific unit coal train just west of Reno, Nevada, on its way to a northern Californian port.

been previously inaccessible. But then, not one railroad executive of 1979 had ever been born when a US railroad last had any need to learn how to turn a marketplace deal on price.

After a tortured Congressional passage, during which it barely escaped derailment by determined coal-mining and coal-burning public utility interests convinced that deregulation would make them captive to rail transportation rate exploitation, President Carter signed the necessary legislation in October 1980. It is known as the Staggers Act, in honor of sponsoring Representative Harley O Staggers, a Democrat of West Virginia.

In brief, the Staggers Act allowed market forces much more play in setting railroad freight rates. The rigid enforcement of ICC maximum and minimum rates was over. Too often in the past the ICC had set a ceiling on rates with far more solicitude for powerful shippers or the clout of a geographical area than for the railroads' desperate need of a fair return to finance the upkeep of their tracks and rolling stock, and never mind their stockholders. The poor state of a good deal of track and vehicles was an inevitable result. The Staggers Act enshrined the importance of allowing railroads a fair margin above the direct costs of moving traffic, and set a floor for that margin: if a railroad's return fell below it, then the railroad could hike its rate back on the right side without reference to the ICC.

Staggers further authorized the ICC to exempt entirely any traffic and services it deemed needless of regulation; only when railroads exercised "market dominance" was much control still thought reasonable. The most important traffics completely deregulated up to the end of 1984 were perishables, intermodel traffic (this release was accompanied by license for railroads to run their own complementary trucking – nationwide if they wished to apply for such authority – so as to offer total door-to-door transportation), and export coal.

Another widely welcomed provision of Staggers was freedom for railroads to negotiate individual price and service contracts with their customers, regardless of terms offered by other systems or carriers, or of any rates already offered for comparable traffic. Less universally applauded was abolition of the "joint rate" principle, whereby the same tariff had previously to be charged over all competing rail routes between two points, no matter what their disparity in distance (any alteration of that rate was debarred unless each railroad concerned consented to the change, moreover).

An end to joint rate-setting naturally benefited many shippers, who could play the field to get a better rate. It squeezed railroads untouched by the mega-mergers of the 1980s, as the new

giant systems moved to keep traffic on their own tracks for the maximum mileage of each transit. Missouri-Kansas-Texas (the "Katy"), for instance, has had to battle with pinched rates to keep from the clutches of Burlington Northern and the Union Pacific-Missouri Pacific alliance its shipment freight between its Kansas City and St Louis gateways and the Gulf ports.

Some Jeremiahs forecast that the compression of railroads into a few giant networks which deregulation would encourage, would simply create mammoths content to turn an easy profit by persistent price-raising on convenient traffics like coal. In time that would build up such customer resistance that the only option left would be the unthinkable, railroad nationalization.

Certainly the railroads' exploitation of deregulation has begun to worry the competition. By 1984 efforts to restore at least a measure of regulation were being mounted, one sponsored by the barge operators. The export coal industry's persistent litigation over its new rates had achieved the success of a Washington Appeal Court judgment that the ICC's deregulation of its traffic was an "improper" interpretation of the Staggers Act's intent.

But most of the complaints were unwarranted. Statistics issued by the Association of American Railroads in

early 1982 showed that since the Staggers Act's passage far more rates had been cut than raised. More significantly, there were already signs of the railroads grabbing a bigger share of some markets, and of lifting their net earnings. That was reinforcing the faith of the holding companies in their railroad subsidiaries, to the extent that these conglomerates were plowing between 64 and 78 percent of their total investment resources into their rail subsidiaries. A high proportion of those dollars was being wisely invested in track upgrading of routes carrying traffic particularly sensitive to quality of service.

Belief that deregulation would be followed by new grouping moves in the railroad industry was not unjustified, however. Before 1980 was out, three massive new mergers were before the ICC. In November 1980 the ICC pronounced its blessing on the molding of a new mega-railroad boasting even more route-miles than Burlington Northern at the latter's birth. What had once been 16 separate railroads, with an aggregate of 28,212 miles, were assembled under the wing of a new CSX Corporation, though by the fall of 1980 these 16 systems had already sorted themselves

Below: A BN unit train snakes around Horseshoe Curve in northwestern Nebraska.

A Chessie GP40-2 is the lead diesel heading this unit grain train near Fustoria, Ohio.

into two large groups.

One was the Chessie System, incorporated in 1973. This had fused the Chesapeake & Ohio, Baltimore & Ohio, Western Maryland (which by 1963 was 43 percent B&O-owned), and the Chicago South Shore & South Bend, an electrified interurban system with an important commuter passenger role which the C&O had acquired in 1967. B&O and C&O retain separate operating organizations within the Chessie System – as, naturally, does the Chicago South Shore & South Bend – but Western Maryland lost its identity and became part of B&O in 1983.

The Chessie System as a whole is the major US railroad coal haulier. C&O's chief routes link the coalfields of southern West Virginia, eastern Kentucky, and southern Ohio with the eastern seaboard, above all the shipment port of Newport News, Virginia; to the north with Detroit; and in the west with Chicago, Cincinnati, and Louisville. Another key route connects Chicago with Detroit and Buffalo. B&O's princi-

pal main lines run from Philadelphia through Baltimore and Washington, DC to Cumberland, Maryland, and from there by separate routes to Chicago and St Louis. Another trunk reached from Cincinnati to Toledo, and B&O also penetrates the West Virginia coalfield.

The other constituent of the CSX Corporation was in 1980 the Seaboard Coast Line (SCL), though since the mid-1970s it had been promoting itself under the unofficial tag of the "Family Lines." This title coalesced a number of railroads, which had been assembled by a process of mergers spanning many years and too complex to recount here, and which blanketed the whole southeast of the country, from Chicago, Cincinnati, and Norfolk, Virginia, down to New Orleans, Tampa, and Miami, Florida. Chief components were the Atlantic Coast Line, Seaboard Air Line,

Louisville & Nashville, Clinchfield, Georgia, and Atlanta & West Point Railroads, and the Western Railway of Alabama. The Louisville & Nashville was not formally merged with SCL until December 1982, whereupon the charter of SCL was rewritten under a new title, the Seaboard System Railroad.

Seaboard has both a crucial north-south transportation role and also important east-west routings throughout its territory. It reaches all the Atlantic coast ports from Richmond, Virginia, down to New Orleans on the Gulf, and also caters for several significant ports on the Mississippi and Ohio Rivers. Seaboard is, too, another of the coal-hauling majors, tapping reserves put at over 12,000 million tons in the Appalachian Mountains areas of Kentucky, Tennessee, southwest Virginia, and Alabama, and in the Midwestern states

of Indiana and Illinois. Coal generates almost a quarter of Seaboard revenues, much of it fed to electric power utilities in the Southeast, Midwest, and along the Gulf coastline.

SCL had sought alliance with the neighboring Chessie System in 1978 to escape the clutches of Southern Pacific, owner of nearly 10 percent of SCL stock, which was bent on achieving the dream of a true transcontinental railroad. Marriage with another coal-hauling giant in the eastern half of the US made more immediate sense. At the time

Left: Four GM-EMD GP40-2 diesels working hard with Conrail freight.

Above: More GP40-2s, this time in Chessie System service, powering a unit train of crushed rock near Daswell, VA.

Chessie was flush with traction and coal hoppers, and with its own hopper-car manufacturing capacity, whereas the L&N member of the Seaboard family in particular was being harried by the ICC as well as its shippers for service short-comings traceable to inadequate equipment.

Within the CSX fold, the Chessie and Seaboard Systems retain not only their separate identities, but also their own management and control of operations. CSX also has a controlling interest in the Richmond, Fredericksburg & Potomac (RF&P), a system of much greater significance than its mere 113.8 miles of route might suggest. Fringing Conrail

and the B&O at Washington, DC, and Seaboard at Richmond, Virginia, it is a vital bridge, particularly for intermodal traffic, and logs a volume of traffic worth $55 million in 1983. In that year RF&P's operating ratio – direct operating costs in relation to income – was a very robust 65.7 percent.

The reaction of the two other Class I systems confronting CSX with a giant, unified railroad overlapping their territory was predictable. In April 1979 Norfolk & Western and Southern likewise opened merger talks. The courtship was chequered. For a period in 1979-80 talks foundered on a clash both of forward strategies and of powerful

personalities, but once differences were resolved the ICC cleared the application to merge in only 15 months. In March 1982 it approved formation of Norfolk Southern Corporation (NS) as a holding company to coordinate the merger, which became fully effective at the start of the following June.

Norfolk & Western (NW), which in the 1950s and 1960s had accumulated

Left: A pair of Seaboard System's GM-EMD SD50 diesels ride a steel trestle with Appalachian coal.

Above: 'Orange Blossom Special' units TOFC train en route from Florida to Delaware.

several other roads by merger or lease, notably the Virginian, Nickel Plate, Pittsburgh & West Virginia, and Wabash, was the archetypal coal-hauling US railroad – and consequently the last to surrender steam traction to diesel. It still counts almost two-thirds of its total tonnage in coal. With a network stretching from the port (and NS base) of Norfolk, Virginia, westward to Kansas City and north to industrial Chicago, Detroit, and Cleveland, N&W digs deep into the rich coalfields of West Virginia, southern Ohio, and eastern Kentucky.

Southern also draws a considerable income from coal, though not so much as N&W; today coal accounts for about 40 percent of the combined NS railroads' revenue. Southern ranges over 13 states east of the Mississippi River, from St Louis, Cincinnati, Washington, DC, and Norfolk, Virginia, down to New Orleans and Jacksonville, Florida, taking in a chain of Atlantic coast ports from Norfolk southward. Consequently NS was essentially an end-to-end merger of the two railroads, which connect principally at East St Louis and Cincinnati, and at points in Virginia and North Carolina. In route-length, 17,860 miles at the time of merger, NS forged a network that trailed some way behind the extent of BN and CSX, but one that was and still is the most profitable in the whole Class I railroad industry: in 1983 its net income after taxes was $356.5 million on gross revenues of $3,148.1 million.

From the outset freight cars of the two NS systems were pooled, likewise workshop capacity, terminal, and yard installations, and rationalization of traction employment was followed by application of not particularly prepossessing corporate locomotive livery.

Above: Chessie System coal piers at Newport News, Va.

Left: A Richmond, Fredericksburg and Potomac diesel tests Road-Railers.

Right: Three GP-5s (one in front), one GP-30 and one GP18 in pre-NS merger livery.

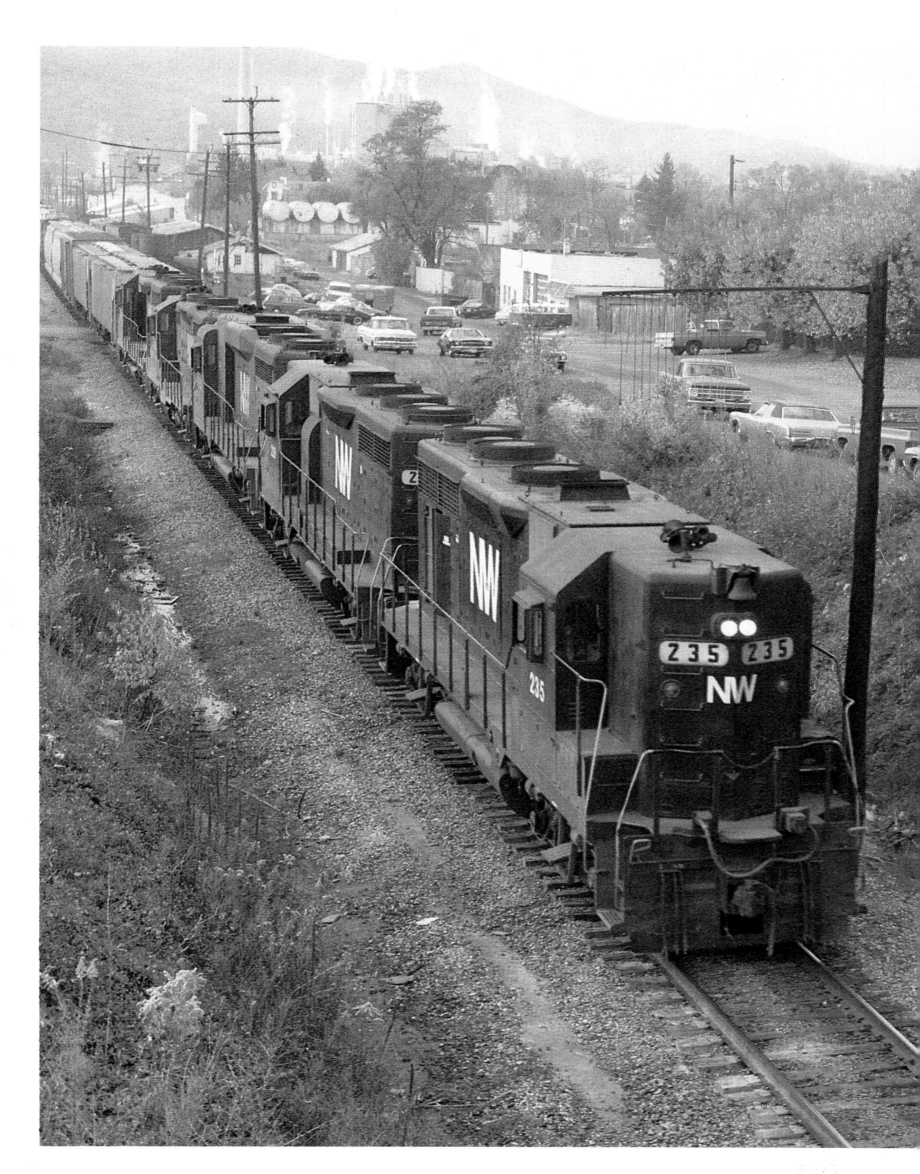

But in general the two systems operate autonomously. An obvious benefit was the opening up of several efficient new single-system routes to and from the south-eastern US, in one case backed by the immediate construction of a new intermodal yard at Landers, Chicago.

The CSX and NS mergers, welding together as they did new single-system links between the south and not only the Midwest but also parts of the Northeast, naturally threatened erosion of Conrail traffic and raised fresh question marks against the prospects of that system. By the end of 1980, coming up to its fifth anniversary, Conrail had already gobbled up almost $3.3 billion of Federal money, and it was still losing heavily. This was much less Conrail management's fault than failures on the part of its founders. USRA, created by Congress to plot a potentially viable Northeastern rail network, then to sit at its progeny's elbow as banker and consultant, had hopelessly overestimated the likely growth of Conrail's coal tonnage by about 25 percent. That it did not foresee depression in the steel and auto industries, or the migration of heavy industry from the territory, was perhaps less culpable. Be that as it may, the combined effect was a 20 percent shortfall on USRA's projections of Conrail freight as a whole.

USRA also grossly misjudged the state of the fixed plant, traction, and freight cars which Conrail had inherited from its bankrupt forebears. In its first four years Conrail had to lay 3,873 miles of new rail, replace 18.4 million ties, resurface over 35,500 miles of track, buy 675 new locomotives, put 3,110 more through a heavy overhaul,

Left: Southern before the merger: two SD45s and an SD40-2 with 147 freight cars in tow.

Above: Norfolk Southern keeps N & W black as basic livery but enlivens it with a prancing horse.

Conrail's employees were coaxed into wage increase concessions which gave impetus to the Congressional enactment of NERSA, and which promised to yield the railroad some $350 million savings up to mid-1984. Then NERSA's revision of employee terms of service, substituting the once-for-all-time Federally-funded severance payments for the original long-term wage or job guarantees, freed Conrail to start the overdue rationalization of its route system. By 1982, in a first-phase scheme branded "Window I," abandonment

purchase 8,136 new freight cars and treat over 73,000 more to heavy repairs before it could fully satisfy its shippers.

Conrail itself was slow to tackle the oversized network it had been handed; and because its hauls were short by comparison with those of other big Class I systems, the cost of its excess of terminals loomed large in its balance sheet. But it was not easy to prune the overlapping facilities of the pre-Conrail system, or to develop new strategies based on a slimmed down network, when Conrail had been forced to cede extravagant job concessions to the staff it had taken over. Those concessions had saddled Conrail with ratio of labor costs to total operating expenses way above the Class I norm. Finally, Conrail's founders had required it to continue the city commuter operations of its predecessors, on terms that were far from meeting the losses these passenger services incurred.

To the incoming Reagan Administration at the start of 1981, the Conrail concept was clearly anathema. Its immediate aim of a fire sale was frustrated by Congress, but the legislature had obviously to take some remedial action. The outcome was the Northeast Rail Services Act (NERSA) of 1981.

Regional transportation authorities were ordered to take over the commuter services by the start of 1983, or else contract with a newborn Amtrak subsidiary for their assumption. In the event the Amtrak subsidiary was still-

born. Each commuter operation was taken over locally – though not without traumas, as some of the authorities had to withstand protracted labor walkouts before they could impose more realistic pay-scales and terms than those in which the men had luxuriated under Conrail.

But on Conrail itself NERSA rescinded the very indulgent job protection clauses written into the system's initial constitution. Conrail was further required to sell off all its lines in Connecticut and Rhode Island, and in part of Massachusetts. Finally, Conrail was given until mid-1983 to prove to USRA that it had the capability to be viable. If it passed that test, NERSA bound the Administration to seek a buyer for Conrail as an intact railroad, not take the easy course of selling Conrail's most profitable segments piecemeal.

At the beginning of 1981 Conrail took on a new Chairman, former Southern Railway executive L Stanley Crane. Under him Conrail staged an extraordinary turnround. First, in May 1981,

Above: Conrail Chairman and Chief Executive, L. Stanley Crane, sees for himself in the control tower of the railroad's big Elkhart, Ind., classification yard.

Right: These new 3500hp SD50 diesels from GM-EMD typify the rejuvenation of Conrail's fleet in the 1980s.

applications had been filed for no fewer than 360 superfluous and profitless branch-line segments aggregating 2,607 miles; by the 1983-84 winter 1,777 miles had been discarded or approved for abandonment by the ICC, and 765 miles had been sold off to short lines (of which more later) or others for continued operation. In the spring of 1984 Central had a further 431 segments of line totaling 1,641 miles tabled for disposal as generating insufficient revenue, under the "Window II" continuation of the rationalization drive.

Meanwhile the massive plant and rolling stock rehabilitation program launched at Conrail's inception, which seasoned observers acknowledged was creating some of the most handsomely manicured main-line track in the country, had been complemented by innovative marketing and such discrimination in favor of the best-paying traffic as a US railroad's common carrier obligations decently allowed. Conrail had begun life with some 8,000 miles of its network subject to slow orders because of inferior track. By the end of 1983 the

total had been trimmed to a mere 200 miles or so on the core trunk network, and 2,600 route-miles elsewhere. Most of the main lines had been relaid with continuous welded rail which was continuous on the ex-New York Central's so-called Water Level Route from New York to Chicago via Albany, Buffalo, Cleveland, and Toledo. Concentration on high-volume flows had made Conrail's dedicated Trailvan intermodal trains, up to 36 of them daily, conveying piggy-back trailers and maritime containers between its 34 eastern and

midwestern terminals, one of the territory's showpieces.

The pay-off started to show in 1981, when Conrail posted the first, if very modest, full-year net income in its short history. Thereafter the surplus climbed steadily, scaling $313 million on revenues of $3,076 million in 1983, and on the outcome of 1984's first three-quarters promising close to $500 million for that year. Since June 1981, moreover, Conrail had not had to seek any Federal money. It has been able to secure its capital investment needs in the private sector (though by the end of 1983, admittedly, its drawings there had topped $1 billion).

So it was as an integral concern that the DOT put Conrail on the market in 1984. The 14 bids submitted by the mid-June deadline included offers from CSX, NS, the Allegheny Corporation (onetime controllers of New York Central) and a New England railroad conglomerate this chapter has yet to discuss, Guildford Transportation Industries (GTI). By the fall, the Department of Transportation had given a thumbs-down to 11 of the contestants and short-listed NS (despite initial coolness to Conrail's acquisition by another railroad), the Allegheny Corporation and another financial group fronted by international hotelier J Willard Marriott. The bidders frozen out included Conrail's own staff, but at the end of October Conrail responded with a proposal which, with a cash offer of $1.4 billion, topped those already on the table; Conrail aimed to fund its offer partly with its own dollars, partly by a bank loan, and partly by a common stock flotation. The Department's reaction was very dismissive, but then a political ground-swell of antipathy to a quick sale of Conrail to another party was detectable. Conrail's fresh attempt to keep the system under its existing management had the support of both Pennsylvania's republican senators.

The Reagan Administration was also divesting itself of the Alaska Railroad, the core of which was constructed in 1913-23 with Federal money to link up two existing short lines in the Seward and Fairbanks areas. In the 1970s the railroad's carrying slumped and it slipped into losses when completion of the Alaska pipeline ended a bonanza of construction materials traffic. But by

An EMD SD-50 in smart new Conrail colours. It has an updated 16-cylinder version of the 645 series engine.

1983 both passenger and freight business had rebounded to record levels, benefitting moreover from a railroad that was in good shape because of the shrewd investment of pipeline era profits in track and rolling stock upgrading. The outlook was brighter yet, thanks to a contract with South Korean interests for unit train movement of coal 360 miles from a mine at Healey to a new transshipment terminal at the port of Seward (the first deep-draft installation of this kind on the US west coast, incidentally), and also to developing intermodal traffic in roll-on/roll-off barges with Seattle via the two Alaskan ports of Seward and Whittier. Transfer of the railroad to the state of Alaska for $22.3 million was to be completed by January 1985.

Above: The caboose of a 1983 Alaska Railroad diesel locomotive.

The least expected early-1980 move on the merger scene was the successful bid of multimillionaire Timothy Mellon to mold into a single, 4,050-mile system three smaller railroads twined among the giants of the Northeast from Maryland to the Canadian border.

The investment hardly looked gilt-edged, since two of the systems, the Boston & Maine and Delaware & Hud-

Top: Alaska Railroad passenger stock includes ten dome cars acquired secondhand from the Milwaukee, Denver and Rio Grande Western and Canadian railroads.

Centre: Alaska Railroad operates a thriving passenger service that includes connections with cruise ships calling at Whittier.

son, were financially embarrassed (there had been some Congressional effort to propel both into Conrail in the run-up to NERSA's 1981 passage). Furthermore, all three were operating in territory where hauls were comparatively short and trucking competition consequently vicious. But Mellon was convinced such deterrents were outweighed by the traffic prospects of a rationalized single system in the region. "The times are such that railroads are more and more important in terms of the economic viability of this country," he wrote in 1981. "They seem like a good investment."

In June 1981 Mellon opened his account with purchase by his Guildford Transportation Industries (GTI) of the 817-mile Maine Central. Then, after negotiation of Boston & Maine's debts with the bankruptcy court, that railroad was absorbed by GTI in June 1983 and the Delaware & Hudson at the start of 1984. The three railroads have retained their individual identities, but they are under the command of the same chief executive and are operated as a unified network, with interchangeability of locomotives.

GTI's future prospects could be clouded by a sale of Conrail. Its east-west trade is reliant on trackage rights to Newark (NJ), Buffalo, Philadelphia, and Washington over Conrail metals which were captured by GTI's Delaware & Hudson constituent at Conrail's birth. Without them, D&H, left to the limited potential of its own thin stem from the Canadian border through Albany to eastern Pennsylvania, would surely have foundered. A new Conrail owner would probably hike the rental for those rights. But if the buyer were NS, it would freeze out GTI and keep its New England traffic on its own trains right to Albany. If that eventuated, depriving GTI of some 600 freight carloads a day, GTI's Chief Executive has conceded that he "would have to fold up the tent at D&H."

While GTI was taking shape, a massive regrouping of railroads in the western US had reached its conclusion. Union Pacific had betrayed no ambitions to expand since its second thoughts in the early 1970s about strengthening its Midwestern presence through acquisition of the hapless Chicago, Rock Island & Pacific – the "Rock." With the non-rail activity of its parent corporation generating more than half the latter's revenue and attracting about 60 percent of its investment, it seemed unlikely that UP would want to extend its commitment to railroading. Besides, the existing 9,420-mile UP network, joining limbs from Los Angeles and Seattle/Portland into a double-track main from Ogden to Omaha that was arguably, in relation to its length, the busiest rail freight highway in the whole country, already

Above: Missouri Pacific SD40-2s head a run-through Pacific Coast-southeastern US freight, fruit of a merger with Union Pacific.

boasted the longest average freight hauls in the US. Married to UP's traditionally efficient operating method, that made the railroad look nicely contoured for profit as it was.

Early in 1980, however, UP stunned its railroad neighbors by announcing that, after negotiations which – no less surprisingly – had been kept a hermetically-sealed secret from the rest of the industry, it had concluded an agreement in principle to take over the 11,277-mile Missouri Pacific, along with that company's subsidiary gas exploration, production, and pipeline interests. The price was around $1 billion. Then, just two weeks later, it bid a further $25 million for the 1,482-mile Western Pacific. With Missouri Pacific, or the "Mo-Pac," UP's empire would reach further east to Chicago and St Louis, and drive a broad wedge southward through Kansas, Missouri, Oklahoma, and Arkansas to El Paso, Laredo, and Houston in Texas, and to New Orleans. Western Pacific would give it direct access from Salt Lake City to Oakland and San Francisco, in parallel with Southern Pacific.

The shock waves from these proposals naturally whipped up strong reaction from anxious neighbors, mostly expressed in the usual demands for extravagant trackage rights over parts of the mega-system to offset the latter's breakout from the historic UP midwest gateway of Council Bluffs, Indiana, Kansas City, and Ogden, Utah. But Santa Fe strove to block the alliance completely as fundamentally inimical to the public interest, however indulgently it was circumscribed by grants of trackage rights to adjacent railroads. However, in approving BN's takeover of the Frisco the ICC had shown it was far

less susceptible than it had been in mid-century to exorbitant trackage rights claims, and to threats that their refusal would condemn the appellants to creeping penury. Late in 1982 it endorsed the consolidation of the three railroads with a rider agreeing only a proportion of the trackage right demands, principally those of Southern Pacific (Kansas-St Louis), Denver & Rio Grande Western (Pueblo-Kansas City) and Missouri-Kansas-Texas, the "Katy" (Kansas City-Omaha/Council Bluffs, Lincoln and Topeka). Shortly afterwards Santa Fe, Kansas City Southern, Denver & Rio Grande Western, and Southern Pacific had their appeals against the ICC rulings rejected by the US Supreme Court and the merger became effective on 22 December 1981.

Western Pacific was subsequently absorbed as a fourth UP operating district, but UP and Mo-Pac have preserved their separate identities, though they are now promoted as one enterprise under the Union Pacific System brand and their locomotives are all taking on the traditional UP Armor yellow color scheme. The three traffic departments have been merged for development and marketing of the combined network as a unitary system, with common operating, service, and pricing policies.

With the BN-Frisco and UP System alliances sealing off respectively the northern and central regions of the western US, defensive action by one or more of the remaining railroads in the area was a certainty. It came in May

340

1980, but in a form none had anticipated: an announcement by traditional antagonists Santa Fe and Southern Pacific that their two boards had agreed in principle to SP's absorption by Santa Fe.

Santa Fe's assumption of lead role was surprising. It had evinced no enthusiasm for aggrandizement since the start of the century and seemed content with its southwestern span of the US from San Francisco, Los Angeles and San Diego to Chicago, Kansas City, Dallas, and Houston. Though its anxiety at the UP-MoPac-WP alliance had been expressed in court action, Santa Fe had seemed initially prepared to ride the consequences of that merger if its litigation failed.

SP, on the other hand, was in 1980 seeking a firmer bridgehead in the Midwest. Its network fringing the Pacific coast and the Mexican border from Portland through San Francisco, Los Angeles, Tucson, and El Paso round to Dallas, Houston, and New Orleans was projected on to Memphis and St Louis over the metals of what was legally its principal subsidiary, the Cotton Belt Railroad (officially the St Louis Southwestern, but rarely dignified with that title). However, the "Cotton Belt" lettering of the subsidiary's vehicles is nowadays the only evidence that it is treated as anything but an SP operating division. To add Midwestern access to the SP system, the Cotton Belt in 1980 bought the bankrupt Rock Island's 973-mile line from Santa Rosa, New Mexico, through Kansas City to St Louis; and SP promptly put in hand a $97 million

rehabilitation of its Tucumcari-Topeka stretch to restore fitness for 60mph freight operations, then bargained trackage rights over MoPac from Kansas City to St Louis. All this would have SP equipped with a transcontinental route to St Louis some 400 miles shorter than its previous, circuitous approach.

It was not a scheme calculated to delight competitor Santa Fe, already well-placed to handle transcontinental freight between the Pacific coast and the Midwest. Nor did SP dump its plan to redevelop the Rock Island share of what was known as the Golden State Route when the merger move was agreed. That was undoubtedly one factor in the May 1980 collapse of the

Above: The engineer mounts the lead SD40-2 of a UP System Oakland, California-Midwest run-through freight at North Platte, Nebraska.

discussions with Santa Fe. In any event, there was skepticism abroad that the ICC would approve a merger which concentrated in one conglomerate 5,388 of the 7,244 rail route-miles in California.

Below: A Union Pacific snowplow carves a path through formidable drifts between Ashton and Tetonia, Idaho, in April 1982.

Mature consideration of the effects of the UP-MoPac-WP merger prompted second thoughts. In September 1983 Santa Fe and SP announced that they had settled their differences and agreed to combine under the aegis of a holding company ponderously titled the Santa Fe Southern Pacific Corporation. In the resultant 25,200-mile system Santa Fe would have the majority, 54 percent share. The marriage was effected at the end of 1983, but pending ICC approval,

sought the following March, the stock of SP was placed in trust.

The future of the Class I railroads so far untouched by the mega-system mergers was the topic absorbing analysts of the US railroad scene. Illinois Central Gulf's openness to offers has already been mentioned. Expectedly, another railroad to announce early in 1984 that it was seeking a buyer was Denver & Rio Grande, dwarfed by surrounding BN and UP System – and, furthermore,

Above: A Maine Central GP38 prepares to leave Bangor, Maine, yard with a morning freight for the Canadian border.

Below: SP was first with lightweight new-generation 'Impack' TOFC cars in full trains. These are loading 'Golden Pig' trailers at Oakland, California.

since 1969 only a component of an expanding conglomerate, Rio Grande Industries.

The focus of interest in 1984 was the Midwest. One bankrupt, the Rock Island, had already been dismantled and its worthwhile segments sold off to neighbors or to new short line companies. The remaining question was who would get the Chicago, Milwaukee, St Paul & Pacific, more compactly known as the Milwaukee Road, which had survived two bankruptcies, in 1921 and 1935, more or less unscathed, but not yet one more insolvency in 1977. The reorganization by a trusteeship ensuing from this final debacle had shorn the Milwaukee of all its western territory, which once reached Tacoma in Washington state, and pared it down from 9,800 to only some 3,800 route-miles interconnecting Chicago, Kansas City, Minneapolis/St Paul, and (via trackage rights over other roads) Duluth and Louisville. For purchase of that rump Chicago & North Western, Soo Line, and Grand Trunk Western were in contention.

Grand Trunk Western (GTW) is a Canadian property, the chief constituent of the Grand Trunk Corporation set up in 1970 to gather in the US subsidiaries of the state-owned Canadian National (CN); its other constituents are the Duluth, Winnipeg & Pacific (DWP) and Central Vermont (CV), neither qualifying for Class I status. CV has been badly pinched both by the consolidation of neighboring New England systems in Mellon's GTI and by the sharper competition arising from deregulation, so much so that in 1982 CN was trying to sell CV off, but then withdrew it from the market the following year.

GTW runs a main line from Port Huron (Mich) on the Great Lake of that name to Chicago and another south through Detroit to Jackson (Mich), enjoying access from the latter to Cincinnati and exchanges there with Seaboard and Southern through trackage rights from Conrail. It has been on an expansionist tack in the 1980s. From less than 1,000, GTW's route-mileage has jumped to 1,699, largely through

Above: Five Denver and Rio Grande Western SD40s haul 73 carloads of coal over the Craig branch in northwestern Colorado.

1980 acquisition of the 478-mile Detroit, Toledo & Ironton (DTI) – its present Detroit-Jackson line – and of Conrail's discarded Michigan trackage. As a result it has lately adopted the more opulent title of Grand Trunk Rail System. If the Milwaukee were tacked on to this network, Grand Trunk would have commanded a seamless system right around the south of Lake Michigan, would improve its net income through longer average freight hauls, and not least would tap business to reduce the extent of its present dependence for freight on the erratically-performing automotive industry.

For a while Grand Trunk's bid for the Milwaukee looked unchallenged and the two systems had already launched collaborative exercises when rivals stepped in. The interest of Soo Line – or, to be pedantic, the Minneapolis, Sault St Marie & Atlantic, though few people

nowadays are aware of the full title – was foreseeable. For one thing, Soo parallels the Milwaukee in the Chicago-Minneapolis/St Paul-Duluth region. For another, it is a subsidiary of CN's great rival on the Canadian system's home ground, Canadian Pacific (CP). The 4,433-mile Soo derives a major part of its income from maritime container traffic shipped through Canadian ports on the St Lawrence Seaway.

The 8,200-mile Chicago & North Western, the third bidder, is also a near carbon copy of the Chicago-Milwaukee-Twin Cities-Duluth area, beyond which it reaches south to Kansas City and St Louis, and west through Omaha and across Nebraska and South Dakota into Wyoming. Thus it is affected not only by the future of the residual Milwaukee system but also by some of the mega-railroad groupings already described. Since 1980 CNW has already developed its presence in the Midwest by taking over some 800 miles of the defunct Rock Island's trackage, including RI's Kansas City-Twin Cities main line, and about 150 miles of Milwaukee grain-gathering branches in Iowa. In 1983-84 CNW was embarked on a $57 million scheme to hoist the capacity of the ex-RI Kansas City-Twin Cities single track to 20 million gross tons annually, but its major enterprise in 1984 was completion of a scheme for greater participation in coal movement out of Wyoming.

The state of Milwaukee Road play in the fall of 1984 was that the ICC had stated a preference for Soo ownership, but CNW had tabled the highest bid. If CNW won, it was certain to adopt the Milwaukee as its prime Chicago-Twin Cities route, since that threaded more commercially fruitful areas than its own. However, neither CNW or Soo would get as appealing a Milwaukee as they first thought. Defeated GTW

reacted to this snub by switching to Burlington Northern the heavy traffic which since 1982, anticipating a smooth Milwaukee takeover of its own, it had been channeling on to the Milwaukee in Chicago. The 49,000 carloads a year that represented was widely credited as the force behind the sharply contracted Milwaukee's return to the black.

Another Class I railroad with a keen interest in the Powder River basin is the 1,663-mile Kansas City Southern (KCS), which mates with BN to ferry coal from Wyoming to utilities in Arkansas, Louisiana, and Texas. KCS, which includes the Louisiana & Arkansas, is a slender chord south from Kansas City to Port Arthur, Texas, and New Orleans, with an offshoot to Dallas by grace of Santa Fe trackaging rights. Thus it has been in the thick of the mega-system mergers of the 1980s. But so far the diversified conglomerate of which it is a subsidiary, Kansas City Southern Industries, has seemed relatively unmoved.

Equally menaced by the BN/Frisco and UP-MoPac mergers was the Missouri-Kansas-Texas (MKT), generally known as the "Katy," which operates from Kansas City and St Louis in the north down through Oklahoma to Dallas, Forth Worth, San Antonio, and Galveston in Texas. It is another beneficiary of the Rock Island break-up, and operates some 600 former "Rock" route-miles focussed on the bankrupt's Salina (Kansas)-Dallas line under its Oklahoma & Texas Railroad subsidiary.

"Katy's" traffic is naturally dominated by shipment freight to and from the southern ports, with coal and grain outstanding. Although, as remarked earlier, it has conceded trackage rights over MoPac to Lincoln, Omaha and Council Bluffs, and west to Topeka, to preserve its vital northern connections

Above: Cotton Belt is the commonly-used title of the St. Louis Southwestern, a subsidiary of Southern Pacific.

in face of the UP-Mopac merger, "Katy" has been penalized by shut-out from other routes and gateways as a result of mergers; and also, as already mentioned, by the pinching of its rates as the new giants set their single-system tariffs for traffic to and from "Katy" territory which they were obviously reluctant to match in joint rates for freight channeled through the "Katy" routes.

Of the remaining small Class I railroads, four are locked into the steel industry and consequently debilitated by the latter's depression. The 273-mile Pittsburgh & Lake Erie, which shares with Chessie and Conrail ownership of the 136-mile Monongahela Railway (or Monon) on the borders of Pennsylvania and West Virginia, counts three-quarters of its traffic in raw material and finished product transport for the steel industry. Substantial 1970s investment in anticipation of traffic that did not materialize has saddled P&LE with serious debt and in the early 1980s it was working in the red, at an operating ratio worse than 125 percent.

The other three steel-based systems are in fact owned by the United States Steel Corporation, which following its costly 1982 purchase of Marathon Oil announced that it was open to offers for any or all of them. So far there have

Right, top: The final livery of the Milwaukee Road, acquired in 1985 by Soo Line.

Right: A GM-EMD SD50 in the stark white styling of Kansas City Southern.

A pair of Missouri-Kansas-Texas ('Katy') SD40-2s flank a leased Conrail unit as they trundle a Fort Worth freight past the Regency Hotel, Dallas, Texas.

been no takers. The three railroads are: the 205-mile Bessemer & Lake Erie, from the Pittsburgh area to Conneaut on Lake Erie; the 357-mile Duluth, Missabe & Iron Range, the major ore carrier among US railroads, ferrying the mineral from the Missabe range in northeastern Minnesota to ports at the western end of Lake Superior; and the 231-mile Elgin, Joliet & Eastern, which traces a semicircle around Chicago, from Waukegan (Ill) on Lake Michigan to Porter (Ind), with a key branch to the US steel plant at Gary (Ind), and which in the course of that arc intersects every railroad serving Chicago.

The one jaunty system among the smaller Class Is is the iconoclastic Florida East Coast (FCE), the 554-mile railroad fringing the Atlantic coast from Jacksonville down to Miami. Its boldness in opting out of the industry-wide pay negotiation system in 1963 and determination to break the mold of anachronistic work rules, which committed it to eight years increasingly bitter confrontation with the labor unions, has already been outlined. The reward of its obduracy is striking.

Able to run trains the whole length of its main line with a two-man crew, instead of halting them twice en route for changes of the once mandatory five-man crews – and, incidentally, running the trains without cabooses, an eco-nomy to which other railroads did not win labor consent until 1982 – FCE can schedule its freights at an average speed of almost 40mph. It can also afford to run trains of no more than 15-20 cars to keep both loads and re-turning empties flowing continuously day and night. The pay-off is that though FCE competes in all its prime traffic centers with the far bigger Sea-board System arm of mighty CSX, it turned in the best operating ratio (80.2 percent) of all Class I railroads in 1984. FCE is also as high as eighth in the intermodal league in terms of annual carloadings, even though its main line is only some 350 miles long.

To deal adequately with the many US railroads not aspiring to Class I status would need a book twice the size of this one. Some of them are very size-able enterprises. The Providence & Worcester, for example, is a 371-mile system in New England, while the Ban-gor & Aroostook extends for 494 miles from north to south of Maine.

At the bottom end of US railroading scale is the most rapidly expanding type of system in recent years – the short-line. In 1984 the shortline total was over 400, with an average length of less than 30 miles.

The great majority of shortlines have been created to serve shippers and industries not directly connected to a major railroad, and which a local company with modest overheads can achieve more economically than its big neighbors. (But it follows, of course, that shortline is very dependent on the service and rates it gets from the major railroad – or railroads – into which it feeds for its prosperity.) Besides scope to adopt more flexible work-rule, a short-line scores over a bigger carrier by striking up closer relationships with its clients, and by stimulating a degree of local support that can open up local in-dustrial development funds for its use.

In the 3R and 4R Acts, Congress acted to safeguard existing shortlines and encourage new ones with the offer of start-up subsidies. The Reagan Admi-nistration, however, shut off Federal funding and now shortline aid is de-rived chiefly from state or local agen-cies and shippers groups. Many recent additions to the shortline total are takeovers of branches discarded as uneconomic by the major railroads. The NERSA legislation of 1981, by per-mitting Conrail to put its redundant branches on the market at rock-bottom prices, alone promoted creation of 21 new shortlines, which in concert with 57 already in existence, kept alive 591 miles of the trackage Conrail had to abandon as unremunerative. Conrail now regards these shortlines as invalu-able retailers of its trunk service.

INDEX

Illustrations are indicated by figures in *italic* numerals.

Aberdeen, 288
Aberdeen and Rockfish Railroad, 288
Abilene, 252
Adrian, 17
Agawa River Canyon, 288
Alabama, 27
Alaska Northern and Tanana Valley Railroad, 288
Alaska Pipeline, 288
Alaska Railroad, 288, 338, *339*
Albany, 14, 15, 20, 64, *183*, 305, 337, 340
Albany and Hudson Railroad, *17*
Albany and Susquehanna Railroad, 64
Alberta, 114, 126, *247*
Albion, 183
Albuquerque, 49
Algoma Central and Hudson Bay Railway, 288
Algoma Central Railway, 288
Allegheny Corporation, 76, 338
Allegheny River, 293
Allegheny Summit, *81*, 185
Allen, Horatio, 13, 14, 15
Allen Mine, 298
Alma, 305, 312
Alton and Southern Railroad, 288
Altus, 305
Aluminium Company of America, 310
Alyth Yard, 248, *249*, *251*
Amarillo, *256*
American Civil War Railroad, 288
American Locomotive Company (ALCO), 182, 184, 186, *189*, 199
Ames, Oakes, *49*
Amtrak (*see* National Railroad Passenger Corporation)
Amtrak Superliner, *229*
Anchorage, 288
Androscoggin and Kennebec Railroad, 304
Ann Arbor Railroad, 92, 305, 312
Apalachicola Northern Railroad, 288
Appleyard, *164*
Arizona, 48, 49
Arkansas, 26
Arkansas and Louisiana Midland Railways, 290
Arkansas and Lousiana Missouri Railroad, 290
Arkansas River, 48
Arvida, 310
Ashley, Drew and Northern, 290
Ashtabula, 309
Ashton, *341*
Association of American Railroads, 81, 84, 251, 316, 325
Atchison, Topeka and Santa Fe Railway Company, 38, *39*, 48, 49, 72, 93, *169*, *173*, 184, 185, *185*, 198, *203*, 205, 220, *220*, *226*, *245*, 249, *249*, 251, *252*, *254*, *256*, *284*, 290, 305, 322, *322*, 340, 341, 342, 344
Athens, 17, *84*
Atlanta, 17, 27
Atlanta and West Point Railroad, 329
Atlanta and St Andrews Bay Railway (The Bay Line), 291
Atlantic and Danville Railroad, 308
Atlantic and Pacific Railroad, 49
Atlantic and Western Railroad, 291
Atlantic City, 177
Atlantic Coast Line, 90, 310, 329
Aurora, 294
Auto-Train, 229
Auto-Train Corporation, 223, *231*
Avery, 57

Baldwin Locomotive Works, 177, 195
Baldwin, Matthias, 16, *17*, 23, 182, 183, 185, 186, 199
Baltimore, 12, 13, 14, 193, 291, 329
Baltimore and Ohio Railroad, *12*, *13*, 13, 14, 17, *20*, 20, 22, 26, 65, 72, 76, 81, *84*, 90, *167*, *171*, 177, *179*, 184, *185*, 193, *193*, 198, *203*, *213*, *226*, *243*, *260*, *261*, 291, 297, 305, 308, 309, 317, 328
Banff Springs Hotel, *124*
Bangor, 292, 304, *342*
Bangor and Aroostook Railroad, 292, 347
Bank of Montreal, 109
Barstow, *249*, 249
Barstow Yard, *252*
Bay Chaleur, 100
Bay Colony Railroad, 292
Bay Line (*see* Atlanta and St Andrews Bay Railway)
Bear Creek Railroad, 293
Bear River City, *37*, *41*
Beech Grove, 307
Bellows Falls, 303, 313
Belpaire firebox, 181
Belt Railway of Chicago, 292
Benton, 39
Bessemer and Lake Erie Railroad, 183, 293, 347

Billings, Frederick, *49*, 52
Binghamton, 64
Birmingham, 293, 303
Birmingham Southern Railroad, 293
Bismarck, 49
Bitter Creek, 39
Bitter Root Mountains, 57
Black Butte, 39
Black Hills, 39
Blacklick and Yellow Creek Railroad, 295
Black Mesa, 196, 207
Blacksville, 305
Bluefield, 194
Bly, 309
Bond, 165
Boston, 12, 14, 93, 96, 196, 207, *208*, 307, 308, 321
Boston and Maine Railroad, 76, 92, 194, 340
Bow River, 157
Bradley, 304
Bragg, Braxton, 27
Brainerd, 49, 52
Braintree, 292
Brandon, 313
Brighton and Saco River Railroad, *269*
British Columbia, 106, 115, *143*, 157
British Columbia Railway, 148, *148*, 152, *292*, 293
British North America Act (1867) 100
Broadway Limited, 219
Brockway, 309
Brookville and Mahoning Railroad, 309
Brown, John, 26
Brownsville Junction, 305, 309
Buckhannon and Northern Railroad, 305
Budd Company, 207, 220
Budd Metroliner, 205, 223, 232
Buffalo, 20, 96, 97, 216, 308, 328, 337, 340
Buffalo and Albany Railroad, *20*
Buffalo and Lake Huron Railway, *217*
Bull Run, 27
Bureau, 304
Burlington Northern Inc., 322
Burlington Northern Railroad, 93, 173, *203*, *243*, *245*, 250, *250*, 294, *295*, 305, 321, 322, 323, *323*, 325, *325*, 329, 331, 342, 344
Burlington Route, *83*, 196, *199*, *223*, 223, *224*
Burns, 309
Butte, 294
Butte, Anaconda and Pacific Railway, 294
Buzzards Bay, 292

Caboctin Mountains, 13
Calgary, 109, *118*, 248
Cairo, 17, 22, 173
Cajon Pass, *162*, 165
Calais, 304
Calgary, *316*
California, 23, 35, 36, 48, 49, 185, *203*, 254
California Zephyr, 223, *226*, 294
California Western Railroad, 295
Cambria and Indiana Railroad, 295
Camden, 177
Camden and Amboy Railroad, 16, *259*, *262*, 295
Campbell, Henry, 16
Canadian *143*, *153*, *224*, *229*
Canadian National Railway Company, 120, *126*, 126, 132, *133*, *135*, 136, *140*, 152, 153, 173, 207, 223, 229, *247*, *282*, 296, 302, *339*, 343
Canadian National Station, 194
Canadian Northern Railway, 114, 115, 120, 126, *138*, 148, 296
Canadian Pacific Railway Company, 52, 109, *109*, *113*, *114*, 114, *115*, 115, *118*, *119*, 120, *120*, *123*, *124*, *125*, *126*, *127*, *129*, 132, *135*, 136, *136*, *143*, *146*, 152, 153, *153*, 157, *158*, *164*, 165, 167, 171, 172, *181*, 196, 223, *224*, *229*, 245, 248, *249*, *251*, *277*, 293, 299, 312, *316*, 344
Cannonball, 218
Canton, 76
Cariboo Dayliner, 293
Caribou, 292
Carillon and Grenville Railway, 96
Carlin, 40
Carol Lake, 141, 196
Carson River, 23
Carter, President, 92, 251, 324, 325
Cartier Railroad, 141, *152*
Cascade Mountains, 322
Cascade Tunnel, *164*, 165, 194
Casement, Daniel, 38
Casement, General John S., 38
Centennial, *220*
Central Louisiana and Gulf Railroad, 308
Central Pacific Railroad, 23, 30, *35*, 35, 36, 39, 40, 41, *42*, 46, 48, *161*, 162, *169*, 172, 183, *313*
Central Railroad of Georgia, 17, 23, 317
Central Railroad of New Jersey, 92, 299, 320
Central Vermont Railway, 114, 297, 243
Centralized train control, 250
Chadds Ford Junction, 308
Chambersburg, 214

Champlain and St. Lawrence Railroad, 96
Channing, 302
Charleston, 14, 17
Charleston and Hamburg Railroad, 15, 16, 22
Charlevoix, 305
Chattahoochee, 288
Chattanooga, 17, 27
Chesapeake and Ohio Canal, 12
Chesapeake and Ohio Railroad, *81*, 90, 93, 186, *278*, 291, 297, 317, 328
Chesapeake Bay, 245
Chessie System Railroads, 93, 249, 250, 252, 291, 297, 305, 308, *327*, 328, 329, *329*, 331, *332*, 344
Cheyenne, 39, 48, 156, 184, *186*, *319*
Cheyenne Pass, 156
Chicago 22, 26, 37, 41, 57, 65, 66, *78*, 90, *93*, 109, 181, 182, 183, 194, 196, *199*, 207, 216, 219, 220, *223*, 223, 246, 250, 251, 252, *252*, 254, 290, 292, 294, 297, 298, 302, 303, 304, 307, 308, 310, 313, 322, 323, 328, 332, 337, 340, 341, 343, 344, 347
Chicago and Alton Railroad, 216, *219*
Chicago and Eastern Illinois Railroad, *23*
Chicago and Galena Union Railroad, 22, 298
Chicago and Illinois Midland Railway, 297
Chicago and Indiana Air Line Railroad, 298
Chicago and Northwestern Transportation Company, 22, 39, *83*, 93, *205*, 298, 322, 343, 344
Chicago, Burlington and Quincy Railroad, 22, 57, 65, 66, 93, 220, *226*, *240*, 254, 294, 322
Chicago, Milwaukee, St. Paul and Pacific Railroad (The Milwaukee Road), *57*, *83*, 93, 109, 165, 182, *182*, 194, *195*, 220, *224*, 274, 298, 304, 310, 313, 322, *339*, 343, 344, *344*
Chicago Railway Exposition, 1884, 14
Chicago, South Shore and South Bend Railroad, 297, 298, 328
Chickamauga, 27
Chisholm Trail, 252
Churchill, 148
Cimic, 297
Cincinnati, 17, 20, 173, 297, 302, 310, 328, 329, 332, 343
Cincinnati Union Terminal, *81*
Cincinnatian, *84*
City of Denver, *236*
City of Los Angeles, 223, *236*
City of Portland, 223
City of Salina, *201*, 220
City of San Francisco, 223
City Point, *26*, 177
Civil War, American, 38, 46, 49, 60, 65, 100, *157*
Clarion, 304
Cleburne, *203*
Cleveland, 20, 22, 76, 297, 332, 337
Clinchfield Railroad, 329
Clinton, 22
Clipper Gap, 36
Coast Daylight, 223, 307
Coast Starlight, 223, 294, 307
Cochrane, 308
Colesburg, 310
Colling, 312
Collingwood, 96
Colora, 308
Colorado, 216
Colorado and Southern Railroad Company 294, 322
Colorado and Wyoming Railway, 298
Colorado Midland Railway, 172
Colorado River, 48, 49
Colton, *162*, 165
Columbia River, 49, 52
Columbian, *226*
Columbian Express, *203*
Columbus, 20, *224*, 300
Columbus and Greenville Railway, 299
Colver, 295
Congress, 26, 27, 35, 37, 38, 46, 67, 76, 92, 254
Congressional, *197*, *319*
Connaught Tunnel, *123*, 132, *164*, *167*, 167
Conneaut, 293
Connecticut, 23, 114
Connellsville, 309
Conrail (*see* Consolidated Rail Corporation)
Consolidated Rail Corporation (Conrail), 92, 93, 292, 299, 305, *314*, 321, *321*, *328*, 331, 334, 336, *336*, *337*, 337, 338, 340, 343, 344, *346*, 347
Continental group, 308
Continental Limited, *135*
Contract and Finance Corporation, 36, 48
Cooke, Jay, 49
Cooper, Peter, 14
Council Bluffs, 22, 39, 312, 340, 344
Crane, L. Stanley, 336, *336*
Credit Mobilier of America, 38, 46, 48, *49*, 49
Crocker, Charles, 23, 35, 36, 40, 41
Crossett, 290
Crossett Lumber Company, 290
Crossett, Monticello and Northern Railway, 290
Crows Nest Pass, 126, 127, 245
C.S.X. Corporation, 250, 297, 310, 325, 329, 331, 332, 334, 338, 347

Cumberland, 20, 329
Cumberland Valley Railroad, 214
Custer, 49

Dakota, 49, 170
Dallas, 48, 304, 305, 341, 344
Daswell, *329*
Davenport, 22
Davis, Phineas, 14
Dawson Creek, 148
Daylight, *311*
Dease Lake, 152, 293
Decatur, 309
Decker, *245*
Delaware and Hudson Canal Company, 13, 14, 64, 90, *259*, 299, 340
Delaware and Hudson Railway, 299
Delmarva, 305
Dempsey, William H., 251
Denali Park, 288
Denver, 48, 57, 165, 196, *199*, 223, 294, 300
Denver and Rio Grande Western Railroad, 48, 57, *57*, 92, 165, 185, *265*, *272*, 300, 313, *339*, 340, 342, *343*
Denver Railroad Company, 294
Denver Zephyr, *199*
Department of Transportation, 321, 338
Detroit, 96, 97, 194, 216, 328, 332, 343
Detroit and Mackinac Railway, 302
Detroit, Toledo and Ironton Railroad, 343
Dey, Peter, 38
Dix, John A., 37
Dodge City, 48, 252
Dodge, General Grenville, 38, 39, 48, 156, 157
Dome cars, *226*
Donner Lake, 37
Donner Pass, 23, 37
Dothan, 291
Dotsero, 165
Douglas, Stephen A., 23, 26
Drew, Daniel, 46
Dubuque and Sioux City Railroad, 65
Duluth, Jay, 49, 298, 302, 343, 344
Duluth and Iron Range Rail Road, 302
Duluth, Missabe and Iron Range Railway, 302, 347
Duluth, South Shore and Atlantic Railroad, 114, 136
Duluth, Virginia and Rainy Lake Railroad, 302
Duluth, Winnipeg and Pacific Railway (the PEG), 302, 343
Dunkirk, 20
Duplex car, *223*
Durango, 57
Durant, Thomas, 37, 38, 41, 48

Eagle Pass, 157
East Chicago Belt Railroad, 304
Eastern Airlines, 232
Edmonton, 106, 114
Edward Hines Lumber Co., 309
Eielson Air Force Base, 288
El Gobernador, 183
El Paso, 48, 340, 341
Electromotive Engine Company, 196, 198, 199, *203*, 204, *205*, 205, 220
Elgin, Joliet and Eastern Railroad, 347
Elgin, Joliet and Eastern Railway (Chicago Outer Belt), 302
Elk Lake, 308
Elkhart, *336*
Elkhorn Tunnel, 194
Elkins Act (1903), 68
Ellicott's Mills, 14
Emergency Transportation Act (1933), 81
Emerson, 109
Emons Industries, 305
Empire Builder, *93*, 294, *295*
Erie, 293
Erie and Kalamazoo Railroad, 17
Erie Canal, 12, 15, 17, 20, 181
Erie-Lackawanna Railroad, 92, 299, 320
Erie Railroad, 60, 64, 65, 76, 90, *181*, 185, 219
Escambia, 302
Escambia and Lake Superior Railroad, 302

Fairbanks, 288
Fairbanks International Airport, 288
Fairbanks-Morse, 199
Fairfield, 293
Fall River, 309
Falmouth, 292
Family Lines System, 90, 250
Farnam, Henry, 22
Fayetteville, 288
Federal Railroad Administration, 321
Field Hill, 167
First World War, 69, 120, 148, 184, 219, 246
Fishwick, John P., 324
Fisk, Jim, 46, 64, *64*
Fleming, Sandford, 100, 106, *113*, 114, 136, 157, 160

Florida East Coast Railway, 302, 317, 347
Flour Bluff, 312
Ford Motor Company, 229
Fordyce, 290
Fort Bragg Railroad, 295
Fort Kent, 292
Fort Madison, *173*
Fort Nelson, 152, *292*, 293
Fort St. James, 152
Fort Worth, 48, 305, 344, *346*
Fort Worth and Denver Railroad, 322
Foster, L.B. & Co., 323
Foster, Rastrick, 13
Franklin, 304
Franklin Park, 304
Franco-Prussian War, 49
Frankfort, 305
Fraser River, 106, *135*, 157
Fraser Valley, 148, 157
Freeport Junction, 309
Fremont, Elkhorn and Missouri Valley Railroad, *240*
Frisco Line, The, 294, 322, 344
Frisco System, 250
Fustoria, *327*

Galena, 17, 216
Galveston, 305, 344
Galveston, Harrisburg and San Antonio Railroad, 48
Gardner, 309
Gary, 347
General Bonding Law (1869), 64
General Electric, 196, 199, 204, 207, 228
General Motors, 196, 198, *203*
Genoa, *66*
Georgia, 38
Georgia Central Railway, 183
Georgia Pacific Corporation, 290
Georgia Railroad, 17, 329
Gibsland, 308
Gillette, 245
Gould, George, 57
Gould, Jay, 46, 47, 48, 49, 64, 65, 72
Grafton, *106*
Grand Central Station, *79*, 183, 193, 219
Grand Rapids, 305
Grand Trunk Corporation, 343
Grand Trunk Pacific Railroad, 115, 120, 296
Grand Trunk Railway, 96, 100, *103*, *106*, 114, 120, 126, 148, 194, 296, 302, 343
Grand Trunk Western Railroad, 302, 343
Grant, 40, 216
'Grasshopper' engines, 14
Great Lakes, 17, 23, 47, 181, 245
Great Northern Railway, 57, *63*, 65, 93, 109, *164*, 165, 194, *195*, *197*, 220, *269*, 294, *295*, 322
Great Salt Lake, 162, 172
Great Slave Lake Railway, 152
Great Trestle, 172
Great Western Railway, 96, *101*, *104*, 216, 302
Green Bay, 302
Green Bay and Lake Pepin Railway, 302
Green Bay and Western Railway, 302
Green Mountain Railroad, 303
Green River, 39, 184
Greenville, 299
Griffith, 302
Guilford Transportation Industries, 338, 340
Gulf, Mobile and Ohio, 323
Gulf of Mexico, 12, 23, 312

Halifax, 96, 97, 100, 136
Hamburg, 17
Hamilton, *118*, 312
Hannibal and St. Joseph Railroad, 22, 23, 30, 254
Hanover, 305
Harlem Railroad, 46
Harlem Valley Bridge, 171
Harlowtown, 57, *57*
Harmon, *78*, 193
Harper's Ferry, 26, 171
Harriman, Edward, 65, *66*, 66, 67, 72, 322
Harrisburg, 195, 214
Harrison, Joseph, 16
Hartford and New Haven Railroad, 308
Haupt, Brigadier-General Herman, *30*
Hay River, 152
Hayes, Charles, 114, 115
Healey, *339*
Hearst, 288
Heath's Ravine, *161*
Hepburn Act (1906), 68
Hiawatha, *82*, 182, 220, 223, *224*
Highland Park, 308
High Speed Ground Transportation Program, 207
Hill, James J., 52, *52*, 57, 65, *66*, 66, 67, 72, 93, 109, 114, 157, 321
Hillside County Railway, 303
Hines, 309
Historic Red Valley Inc., 308

Hockessin, 308
Hodge, 308
Hohenwald, 310
Holliday, Cyrus K., 38
Honesdale, 13
Hopkins, Mark, 23
Hoosac Tunnel, 194
Horseshoe Curve, *325*
Horton, *322*
Houston, 294, 310, 322, 340, 341
Howe Sound, *146*
Howse Pass, 157
Hudson Bay, 148, 296
Hudson Bay Company, 101
Hudson Bay Railway, 148
Hudson River, 12, 65, 219, 305
Hudson River Railroad, 20
Huey P. Long Bridge, 173, 308
Huntingdon, Collis P., 23, 30, 35, 36, 48, 65, *66*
Hyannis, 292

IC Industries, 323
Idaho, 170
Idaho Western Inc., 310
Illinois, 12, 17, 22, 23, 26
Illinois Central Gulf Railroad, 250, 251, *252*, *266*, 303, *321*, 322, 323, 342
Illinois Central Railroad, 17, 22, 23, 65, 109, 173, 194, 245, 303, *303*
Indiana, 12, 17
Indiana Harbor Belt Railroad, 304
Indianapolis, 303, 307, 310
Industrie (Joliette), 96, 170
Intercolonial Railway, 97, 100, 101, *113*
International Bridge, *101*
Interoceanic Company, 109
Interstate Commerce Act (1888), 67, 68
Interstate Commerce Commission, 67, 72, 76, 81, 84, 90, 92, 93, 251, 317, 319, 324, 325, 331, 340, 341, 342, 344
Iowa, 26, 65
Iowa Railroad, 304
Iron Ridge, 313
Iroquois Falls, 308
Ivanhoe Pass, 172

Jackson, 17, 343
Jackson, Stonewall, 26
Jacksonville, 302, 332, 347
Jacksonville, St. Augustine and Halifax Railway, 302
James Bay, 148, 308
James, Henry, 60
James River Corporation, 305
Janney automatic coupler, 214
Jansen, 298
Jasper, *133*
Jersey City, 14, 46
Jervis, John B., 13, 15, *17*
Jonesboro, 291
Judah, Theodore, 23, 30, 156
Kalamazoo, 307
Kamloops Lake, 157
Kansas City, 22, 23, 26, 35, 38, 48, 57, 182, 220, *245*, 249, 251, 252, 298, 303, 304, 305, 308, 312, 325, 332, 340, 341, 343, 344
Kansas City Chief, *220*
Kansas City, Pittsburgh and Gulf Railroad, 304
Kansas City Southern Railway, 304, 340, 344, *344*
Kansas Pacific, 48, 49
Keddie Wye Junction, *316*
Kennebec Railroad, 304
Kennedy, President, 317, 323
Kentucky, 17, 185, 245, 297, 310
Kentucky River, 173
Keokuk, 312
Kettle Valley, 132
Keyport, 305
Kicking Horse Pass, 114, *114*, 120, 127, *129*, 157, 165
King George VI, *124*
Kiwaunee, 302
Klamath Falls, 309
Klondyke, 152
Knob Lake, 136, 141
Kootenay Pass, 157
Kyle Railways, 310, 323

La Junta, 48
Labrador, 136
LAC Jeannine, 141
Lachine Bridge, 173
Lackawanna and Western Railroad, 64, 76, 90
Lake Charles, 304
Lake Erie, 12, 309, 347
Lake Erie, Franklin and Clarion Railroad, 304
Lake Erie Railroad, 17, 167
Lake Harbor, 302
Lake Huron, 96
Lake Huron and South Western Railway, 302

Lake Louise, *118*
Lake Manitoba Railway, 114
Lake Michigan, 304, 347
Lake Nipissing, 114
Lake Okechobee, 302
Lake Ontario, 96
Lake Powell, 207
Lake Powell Railroad, 196
Lake Superior, 23, 49, 106, *109*, 114, 115, 120, 220, 302, 304, 347
Lake Superior and Ishpeming Railroad, 304
Lamberts Point, 245, 249
Lamoille Valley Railroad, 304
Landers, 335
Laprairie, 96, *96*
Laredo, 312, 340
Laramie, 39, 156
Leadville, 48
Leavenworth, 35
Leavenworth, Pawnee and Western Railroad, 23, 38
Lehigh and Hudson River, 299, 320
Lehigh Valley and Hudson River Railroad, 76, 92, 320
Lehigh Valley and Mahoney Railroad, *265*
Lethbridge Viaduct, 127, *171*
Lewiston, 304
Liberty Bell, 41
Lillington, 291
Lima Locomotive Works, 186
Lincoln, 26, 27, 30, 216, *219*, 220, 240, 344
Litchfield, 303
Little Big Horn, 49
Little Miami Railroad, 17
Little Nugget, The, *236*
Little Rock, 76
Little Rock, and Western Railway, 304
Lockheed Aircraft Corporation, 320
Logansport, 312
Long Beach, *256*, 313
Long Island Railroad, 120, 194
Long Lac, 126
Lookout, 305
Lorton, 229
Los Angeles, 48, 49, 165, 182, 201, 223, 252, 305, 310, 312, 313, 340, 341
Louisa Railroad, 297
Louisiana and Arkansas Railroad, 344
Louisville, 12, 232, 297, 298, 303, 328, 343
Louisville and Nashville Railroad, 90, 293, 310, 329, 331
Lynchburg, 17
Lynchburg and New River Railroad, 17
Lynton and Barnstaple Railway, *266*
Lytton, 157, *247*

Mackinaw City, 305
Macon, 17, 27
Mad River and Lake Erie Railroad, 20
Mad River Railroad, 17
Madison-Lafayette Railroad, 17
Maine, 114
Maine Central Railroad, 114, 304, 340, *342*
Mallet, Anatole, 184
Manhattan Island, 193
Manitoba, 115
Mann, Donald, 114
Manver, 295
Marathon Oil, 344
Markham Yard, 246, *247*
Marinette, Tomahawk and Western Railway, 304
Marriott, J. Willard, 338
Marshall, 48
Martinsburg, 26, *179*
Maryland, 13, 299, 339
Maryland and Delaware Railroad, 305
Maryland and Pennsylvania Railroad (MA and PA), 305
Maryland Central Railroad, 305
Mason, William, *22*, *39*
Massachusetts, 184
Matapedia Valley, 100
Mattawamkeag, 114, 304
McCallum, Daniel C., 27
McCloud River Railroad, 305
McKenzie, William, 114
Medfield Junction, 292
Mellon, Timothy, 339, 343
Memphis, 17, 90, 303, 310, 341
Meridian, 305
Meridian and Bigbee Railroad, 305
Meridian and Bigbee River Railway, 305
Metropolis Bridge, 173
Metropolitan Transportation Authority, 196
Miami, 90, 302, 329, 347
Michigan, 17, 194, 302, 343
Michigan Interstate Railway, 305
Michigan Northern Railway, 305
Middleboro, 292
Miles City, 298
Milwaukee, 182, 298, 313
Milwaukee and Mississippi Railroad, 298

Milwaukee Road (*see* Chicago, Milwaukee, St. Paul and Pacific Railroad)
Minneapolis, 49, 57, *93*, 182, 220, 298, 322, 343, 344
Minneapolis and St. Paul Railroad, 114, 136
Minneapolis, Sault St. Marie and Atlantic Railroad, 136, 153, 343, 344, *344*
Minnesota, 49, 52
Mississippi, 17, 27, 37
Mississippi and Missouri Railroad, 22
Mississippi River, 22, 26, 173, *173*, 302, 329, 332
Missouri, 23, 26, 37, 49
Missouri Compromise (1820), 26
Missouri-Kansas-Texas Railroad (Katy), 305, 325, 340, 344, *346*
Missouri Pacific Railroad, 22, *76*, 93, 181, *205*, *232*, *252*, 288, 305, 312, 325, 340, *340*
Missouri River, 30, 38, 49
Moberly, Walter, 157
Mobile, 17, 27, 303, 323
Modena, 308
Moffat Tunnel, 165
Mohawk and Hudson Railroad, 15, *17*, 20, 213, 305
Mohawk River, 305
Mohawk Valley, 12
Mohrland, 313
Moncton, 100, 115, 136
Monongahela Railway, 305, 344
Monroe, 290
Monroe Railroad, 17
Montana, 57, 136, 170
Montgomery, 27, 323
Monticello, 290
Montreal, 96, *103*, 114, 133, 172, 173, 194, 207, 223
Montreal and Lachine Railroad, 96
Montreal Roundhouse, *144*
Montreal Urban Community Transportation Commission, 299
Moosonee, 308
Morgan, J. Pierpont, 64, 65, *66*, 66, 67, 72
Mormon Trail, 156
Mount Carmel, 309
Mount Clare, 14
Mount Macdonald, 132
Mount Royal Tunnel, 114, 194
Mount Shasta, 305
Mullens, 194
Munger, 312
Muskingum Electric Railroad, 196
Myrtlewood, 305

Nakusp, *113*
Nanty Glo, 295
Nashville, 12, 17, 27
National Grange, 64
National Railroad Passenger Corporation (Amtrak), 92, 196, 198, 205, *207*, 207, *208*, 223, 229, 232, *232*, 290, 294, 300, 307, 316, 321, 336
National Railways of Mexico, 312
National Transcontinental Railway, 115, 120
National Transportation Committee, 81
Nebraska, 26, 251
Needham Junction, 292
Needles, 49
Nevada, 37, 39, 185
Nevada California-Oregon Railroad, *269*
New Albany-Crawfordsville Railway, 17
Newark, 340
New Brunswick, 114, 115
New Brunswick Railway, 114
Newcastle, 36
New England, 12, 23, 26, 65, 96
Newfoundland, 136
Newfoundland Railway, 136, 296
New Haven, *195*, 196
New Jersey, 72, 299
New London, 114, 297, 309
New Mexico, 48, 49, 93
New Orleans, 12, 17, 48, 90, 173, 223, 303, 308, 310, 323, 329, 332, 340, 341, 344
New Orleans Public Belt Railroad, 308
Newport, 309
Newport News, 249, 328, *332*
New York, 12, 13, 20, 23, 41, 46, 60, 72, *78*, *79*, 92, 181, 183, 193, 194, *195*, 196, *207*, 207, *208*, 219, *232*, 299, 307, 308, 319, 321, 337
New York and Erie Railroad, 20
New York and Harlem Railroad, 20
New York and New Haven Railroad, 308
New York Central and Hudson River Railroad, *265*, 276
New York Central Railroad, 20, 46, *48*, 64, 65, 76, *78*, 90, 92, *119*, *181*, 181, *183*, 183, 184, 193, 219, *225*, *284*, 303, 305, 312, 317, 337, 338
New York, Chicago and St. Louis Railway, 65, 308
New York, New Haven and Hartford Railroad, 65, 219, 292, 308
New York, Philadelphia and Norfolk Railroad, 305
New York, Providence and Boston Railroad, 309
Niagara Falls, 96, 114, 172
Niagara River, *101*, 173

Niagara Suspension Bridge, *104*, 172
Nickel Plate Railroad, 76, 251, 332
Norando, 308
Norfolk, 308, 329, 332
Norfolk and Petersburg Railroad, 26, 308
Norfolk and Portsmouth Belt Line Railroad, 308
Norfolk and Western Railroad, 26, 76, *84*, 90, 185, 186, *186*, *189*, 194, 196, 245, 248, 251, *278*, 308, 317, 324, 331
Norfolk Southern Corporation, 331, 332, *334*, 335
Norris, William, 16
North Bay, 126, 308
North Bessemer, 293
North Carolina, 12
North Coast Hiawatha, *93*, 223
North Coast Limited, *66*
Northeast Rail Services Act (1981), 336
Northern Alberta Railways, 148, 296
Northern Cross, 17
Northern Pacific Railway, *49*, 49, 52, *52*, 57, *57*, 64, 65, *66*, 66, 67, 93, *282*, 294, 322
Northern Railway, 96
Northern Securities Corporation, 67
North Louisiana and Gulf Railroad, 308
North Platte, 39, *186*, *341*
Northwestern Pacific Railroad, 310
Northwest Industries, 322
Nova Scotia, 96

Oakdale, 31
Oakland, 340, *341*, *342*
Ocean-to-Ocean Special, *113*
Octoraro Railway, 308
Office of Defense Transportation, 84
Ogden, 37, 39, 40, 57, 184, 300, 310, 312, 340
Ogden, William, B., 37
Ohio, 12, 20
Ohio Canal, 20
Ohio River, 12, 13, 17, 22, 173, 291, 329
Oklahoma and Texas Railroad, 344
Oklahoma City, 305
Olympian Hiawatha, 220, *236*
Olympic Peninsula Route, 310
Omaha, 35, 37, 39, 40, 182, 220, 303, 304, 308, 323, 340, 344
Onantagon, 302
Ontario, 100, 115, 148
Ontario Northland Railway, 148, *308*, 308
Ontario Northland Transportation Commission, 308
Orange and Alexandria Railroad, *157*
Orange Blossom Special, *331*
Oregon, 23, 294, 322
Oregon and California Railroad, 49
Oregon, California and Eastern Railway, 309
Oregon Northwestern Railroad, 309
Oregon Railway and Navigation Company, 49
Oregon Territory, 23
Oriental Limited, *220*
Oshkosh, 313
Othello, 57
Ottawa River, 96, 114

Pacific Great Eastern Railway, *146*, 148, 293
Pacific Railroad Act (1862), 312
Paducah, 173
Palace cars, 216
Palmdale, 162, 165
Panama City, 291
Pasco, *250*
Paskill, *225*
Patapsco River, 13, 193
Pawnee Railroad, 297
Peace River, 126
Pembina, 52
Penn-Central Railroad, 92, 299, 308, 319, 320, 321
Pennsylvania, 12, 13, 299
Pennsylvania Northern, 304
Pennsylvania Railroad, 20, 22, 48, *48*, 60, 65, *69*, 72, 76, *76*, 92, 120, 170, *171*, 177, *181*, 181, 184, 186, 194, *195*, 196, *197*, *203*, 205, 219, *270*, 293, 305, 317, *319*, 319
Pennsylvania Southern, 304
Penobscot Railroad, 304
Pensacola, 294, 322
Peoria, 297
Père Marquette Railroad, 90
Petersburg, 308
Philadelphia, 12, 41, *171*, 194, 214
Philadelphia and Reading Railroads, 65, 177
Philadelphia, Germantown and Norristown Railroad, 16
Pierce City, 49
Piermont, 20
Pine Point, 152
Pine River Pass, 157
Pioneer, 216, *219*
Pioneer Zephyr, *199*

Pittsburgh, 12, 20, 22, 309, 347
Pittsburgh and Shawmut Railroad, 309
Pittsburgh, Clarion and Franklin Railway, 304
Pittsburgh Lake Erie Railroad, 305, 309, 344
Pittsburgh Locomotive Works, 183
Placer County, 35
Placerville, 23
Plymouth, 292
Pockomoke, 305
Pony Express, 23, 254
Portage, 182
Port Alfred, 316
Port Angeles, 310
Port Arthur, *109*, 114, 115, 304, 344
Port Aux Basques, 136
Port Cartier, 141, *152*
Port Colborne, 312
Porter, 302, 307, 347
Port Huron, 96, 194, 302, 343
Portland, 23, 49, 52, 96, 294, 304, 310, *311*, 312, 341
Port Moody, 114
Port Pierce, 302
Port Townsend, 310
Potomac, 13, 310
Powder River, 156, 344
Powhatan Arrow, *84*
Prairie Central Railway, 309
Prescott and Eastern Railroad, *161*
Prince Edward Island, 100
Prince George, 148, *148*, 293
Prince of Wales, *217*
Prince Rupert, 115, 120
Prince Simpson, 115
Promontory, 40, 41, 48, 162, *162*, 172, *313*
Providence, 309
Providence and Worcester Railroad, 309, 347
Provo, 313
Pueblo, 48, 165, 298, 300, 340
Puget Sound, 52, 57, 115
Pullman, 201, 219, *219*, 220, *223*, 223
Pullman Car Company, 216, 217, *217*
Pullman, George, 214, *214*, 216, *217*, 217, 218, *219*

Quebec, 97, 100, 114, 115, 136, 196, *247*, 309
Quebec Bridge, 173
Quebec North Shore and Labrador Railway, 141, 309, *309*
Queen Elizabeth, *124*
Quesnel, 148

Rail Passenger Service Act (1970), 307
Rail Revitalization and Reform Act (1976), 321, 347
Railroad War Board, 72
Rainbow Limited, *76*
Raton Pass, 48
Reading firebox, 181
Reading Railroad, 92, 320
Reagan, President, 336, 338, 347
Red Desert, 39
Red River, 23
Regional Rail Reorganization Act (1973), 321
Regional Transport Authority, 298, 308
Reno, 37, *324*
Republic, 302
Richelieu River, 96
Richmond, 17, 310, 329, 331
Richmond, Fredericksburg and Potomac Railroad, 229, 310, 331, *332*
Rio Grande Industries Inc., 300, 343
Rio Grande Railroad, 49, 223
Rio Grande Zephyr, 223
Rippon, 313
Riviere Du Loup, 96, 100
Roanoke, 76, *189*, 194
Roberts Bank, 152, 245
Roberval and Saguenay Railroad, 310
Rochester, 297
Rock Island Railroad, 22, 37, 93, 170, 304, 319, 322, 341, 343, 344
Rockefeller, William, 57, 67
Rogers, Major A.B., 157
Rogers factory, *179*
Rogers, Ketchum and Grosvenor, 176
Rogers Pass, *123*, 132, *164*, 165, 167
Rogers, Thomas, 176
Rohr, 207
Roma, 152
Rondout, New York, 13
Roomette car, *223*
Roosevelt, 81
Rosebery, *113*
Roseville, 36
Ross Bay Junction, 309
Ross, John, *106*
Rouses Point, 96
Royal Commission (1916), 120
Royal Commission (1931), 132
Royal Gorge, 48, 49
Royal Hudson, 293

Rutland, 303, 313
Rutland Railway, 303, 313

St. Clair River Tunnel, 194
St. Johns, 96, *96*, 100, 114, 136
St. Joe, 288
St. Johnsbury, 304, 313
St. Johnsbury and Lake Champlain Railroad, 304
St. Joseph, 35, 254
St. Lawrence Canal, *97*
St. Lawrence River, 96, 100, *103*, 114, 141, 152, 172, 173, 309
St. Lawrence Seaway, 344
St. Louis, 22, 49, 57, 90, 93, 207, 251, *252*, 288, 294, 298, 303, 305, 308, 310, 322, 325, 329, 332, 340, 341, 344
St. Louis Bridge, 173
St. Louis Southwestern Railroad (Cotton Belt), 288, 310, 312, 341, *344*
St. Maries River Railroad, 310
St. Paul, 52, 182, 220, 294, 298, 322, 343, 344
St. Paul and Pacific Railroad, 52
St. Paul, Minneapolis and Manitoba Railroad, 52, 170
Sacramento, 23, 35, 36, 37, 40, 183
Sacramento River, 35
Sacramento Valley Rail Road, 310
Safe-Pak, *256*
Saginaw, 312
Saginaw Bay, 312
Salt Lake Bridge, 172
Salt Lake City, 165, 223, 300, 312, 313, 340
Salt Lake Trestle, 172
Salt Wells, 39
San Antonio, 305, 344
San Diego, 323, 340
San Diego and Rio Grande Narrow Gauge Railroad, 312
Sandy River and Rangeley Lakes Railroad, *271*
Sandusky, 17, 20
San Francisco, 23, 35, 36, 48, 49, 57, 223, 245, 294, 307, 310, 340, 341
Sandford, 229, 232, 291
San Joaquin Valley, 48, 165
San José, 310
Santa Fe, 48, 49
Santa Fe (railroad) (*see* Atchison, Topeka and Santa Fe Railway Company)
Santa Fe Industries, 322
Santa Fe Southern Pacific Corporation, 290, 342
Santa Fe Trail, 38
Santa Rosa, 341
Sarnia, 96, 194
Sault Ste. Marie, 109, 114, 288
Savannah, 17, 27
Savannah River, 17
Schefferville, 141, 309
Schenectady, 305
Schmidt, Wilhelm, 177
Scott, Thomas A., 48, *48*, 60
Seaboard Air Line Railroad, 96, 310, 329
Seaboard Coast Line, 90, 229, 329
Seaboard System, 308, 310, 329, *330*, 331, 343, 347
Searsport, 292
Seattle, 57, *93*, 165, 182, 223, 294, 312, 339, 340
Seattle and North Coast Railroad, 310
Second World War, *76*, *79*, 136, *143*, 152, 181, 185, 186, 198, 223, 317
Secrettown Trestle, *35*
Selkirk Mountains, 126, 132
Seneca, 309
Sept-Iles, 141, 309
Seward, 288, 339
Seymour, Colonel Silas, 38, 39
Sharon Steel Corporation, 313
Sheldon, 298
Sherman, 27, 38, 157
Sherman Hill, *319*
Shreveport, 304
Sierra Nevada, 23, 48, *161*, 183, 185
Sierra Railroad, 310
Silverton, 57
Silver Tureen, *224*
Sioux City, 35, 323
Sioux Falls, 220
Sitting Bull, 49
Skagway, 152
Skeena River, 115
Skykomish, *164*, *197*
Skytop lounge, *224*, *236*
Slingshot, 251, *252*
Smithsonian Institute, 14
Soo Line (*see* Minneapolis, Sault St. Marie and Atlantic Railroad)
South Bend, 298
South Carolina, 17, 26
South Carolina Canal and Railway Company, 15
South Carolina Railroad, 17
South Central Tennessee Railroad, 310
South Dakota, *240*
Southeastern and Atlantic Railroad, 308
South Eastern Railway, 114

Southern Crescent, 92, 223
Southern Cross, 17
Southern Pacific Railroad, 48, 49, 65, *66*, 93, 156, 162, *162*, 172, 173, 185, 223, *243*, 245, 248, *274*, *277*, 290, 305, 307, 310, *311*, 322, *324*, 329, 331, 340, 341, 342, *342*, 343, *344*
Southern Pacific Transportation Co., 322
Southern Railway, 223, 251, *273*, 293, 308, 317
South Pennsylvania Railroad, 65
South Side Railroad, 26
Sparta, 182
Spokane, 220, 294
Spokane, Portland and Seattle Railroad, 93, 294, 322
Springfield, 17, 49, 216, *219*
Squamish, 148, 293
Staggers, Senator Harley O., 325
Staggers Rail Act (1980), 251, 325
Standard, 310
Standard Oil, 57, 65
Stanford, Leland, 23, 35
Stanford University, *313*
Stanton, 313
Stephen, George, 109
Stephenson link motion, 181
Stephenson, George, 176
Stephenson, Robert, 13, 16, 172
Steubenville, 303
Stevens, A.J., 183
Stevens, Colonel John, 13, 23, 295
Stevens, Robert L., 16, 295
Stoney Creek Bridge, *143*
Strait of Juan de Fuca, 310
Strasburg Railroad, 302
Stratford, 96
Sudbury, 114, 223
Summit Tunnel, 37
Sunset Route, 310
Super Chief, 220, *226*, 290
Super Continental, *133*, 223
Supreme Court, 64, 67, 319, 321, 340
Sutrana coalfield, 288
Swanton, 304
Swastika, 308

Tacoma, 52, 182
Tampa, 329
Taunton Locomotive Company, *39*
Taylors Falls, 52
Taylorville, 297
Temiskaming and Northern Ontario Railway, 148, 308
Tennessee, 17, 26
Ten-Pack, 251, *254*
Terre Haute, 298
Tetonia, *341*
Texas, 23, 48
Texas and Pacific Railroad, 48, *48*, 184
Texas Mexican Railway (Tex-Mex), 312
Thompson, J. Edgar, 60
Thompson River, 106, 157
Thornton, Sir Henry, 120, *140*
Timmins, 308
Toledo, 17, 22, 302, 305, 329, 337
Toledo, Peoria and Warsaw Railroad, 312
Toledo, Peoria and Western Railroad, 312
Topeka, 38, 340, 341, 344
Toronto, 96, 114, 133, 153, 193, 207, 308
Toronto, Buffalo and Lake Huron Railway, *118*
Toronto, Hamilton and Buffalo Railway, *119*, 312
Toronto Union Station, *120*
Total Operations Processing System (TOPS), 245, 248
Trans-Canada Limited, *118*
Transportation Act (1920), 72
Transportation Act (1940), 84
Transway International Corporation, 313
Trinidad, 298
Truro, 96, 100
Tucson, 341
Tucumcari, 341
Tulsa, 305
Tupelo, 27
Tuscola and Saginaw Bay Railway, 312
Twentieth Century Limited, *78*, *79*, 181, 219, *225*
Twin Cities Zephyr, *224*

Ungava, 309
Union Pacific Corporation, 322
Union Pacific Railroad, 30, 35, *36*, 37, *37*, 38, 39, 40, *41*, 41, *42*, 46, *47*, 48, *61*, 65, *66*, *91*, 93, 156, 157, *161*, 162, *179*, 184, 186, *186*, *189*, 201, 204, 205, 217, *219*, 220, 223, *226*, 232, *256*, *272*, 278, *281*, 285, 305, 309, *312*, *313*, *316*, 319, 322, 325, 340, 341, *341*, 342, 344
Union Station, Washington, 307
United Aircraft, 207
United States Army, 23, 152, 156
United States Military Railroads, *26*, 27, *30*, 157, *169*, *177*
United States Railroad Administration, 321
United States Railroad Association, 92
United States Steel Corporation, 344

United States Steel Trust, 65
Utah, 37, 39, 156
Utah Railway, 313
Utica and Schenectady Railroad, 20

Van Buren, 292
Vanceboro, 304
Vancouver, 106, 114, 127, *140*, 223, 245, *292, 293, 316*
Vancouver Island, 157
Vancouver Terminus, *113*
Vanderbilt, Cornelius, 46, *48*, 64, *64*, 65, 72
Van Horne, William, 109
Van Swerigen, 76, 81, 84
Vauclain compound system, 182
Vauclain, Samuel, 177
Vermont, 297
Vermont Railway, 313
VIA-Rail, *143*, 153, *207*, 223, 296, 299
Vicksburg, 17
Victoria, 157
Victoria Bridge, *96, 103*, 114, 172
Villard, Henry, *49*, 49, *52*, 57
Virginia, 12, 26
Virginian Railroad, 90, 185, 194, 251, *271*, 308, 332
Vivian, 194

Wabash Lake, 309
Wabash Railroad, 47, 57, 76, 114, 115, 251, *280*, 308, 309, 332
Wagner Company, 218
Wall Street, 46, 49, 57, 320

Walschaert, Egide, 181
Walschaerts valve gear, 181
War Department, 27
War Production Board, 198
Wasatch, 40
Washington, D.C., 12, 14, 23, 26, 27, 30, 49, 90, 93, 165, 170, 194, *195*, 196, *207*, 207, 223, *232*, 294, 307, 310, 317, 320, 321, 322, 329, 332, 340
Waterford, 312
Waterville, 304
Watuppa, 292
Waukegan, 302, 347
Wausau, 304
Wawa, 308
Weber Canyon, *161*
Western Allegheny Railroad, 293
Western and Atlantic Railroad, *263*
Western Development Company, 48
Western Maryland Railroad, 57, 297, 328
Western Pacific Railroad, 57, 93, 312, 340, 341, 342
Western Railroad of Alabama, 329
Westfield, 216
West Virginia, 185, 245
Westinghouse, 195
Westinghouse airbrake, 67, *69*, 214, 243
West Point Foundry, 13, 15, *17*
West Port, 292
West Shore Railroad, 65
Weyerhauser Company, 309
Wheeling, 12, 20
White Horse, 152
White Pass, 152
Whiteside, 169

Whitney, Asa, 23, 49
Whittier, 288, 339, *339*
Wichita, 49
Willamette River, 49
Williamson, 194
Willimantic, 309
Willits, 295
Wilmington, 308
Wilmington and Western Railroad, 177, 308
Winans, Ross, 177, *179*, 213
Windsor, 96
Winston Engine Company, 196
Windy Point, *247*
Winnipeg, 109, 114, 115, 126, 223
Winona, 302
Wisconsin, 298
Wisconsin and Southern Railroad, 313
Wisconsin Central, 136
Woodruff Company, 219
Wootten firebox, 177, 181
Worcester, 309
Wyoming, 40, 156, 344

Yellowhead Pass, 106, 114, 157
York, 305
Yukon Route, 152
Yukon Territory, 152
Yuma, 48

Zephyr, 92, 196, 197, 220, *223*, 300
Zulu Cars, *217*

Class

800, *91, 271*
2900, *284*
3771 4-8-4, 182
3800 2-10-4, *185*
6500 Series Diesel Electric, *133*
9000, *272*
A, 186
A 2-6-6-4, 186
A 4-4-2, 182, *274*
A-5, *282*
A-6, *274*
AC-4 Cab Forward, *274*
AEM-7, *208*
American Type 4-4-0, 23, *23*, 176, *177, 263*
ASEA Type RC4, *208*
Atlantic Type 4-4-2, 177, *181*, 181, 182, *213*

Big Boy 4-8-8-4, 184, *278*, 313

C-16-60, 265
C30, 204, *314*
C36, 204
Challenger, 184, *281*
Consolidation 2-8-0, 183, *265*

DDA 40X, 204
DDA 40X Centennial, *205*
DRF-30, *288*

E-series, 198, 205
E1, 198
E6, 198, *303*
E6 Atlantic, 181
E6 Electromotive, 198
Electromotive SD 40-2, *203*

F series, 198, 205
F3, 182
F4, 182
F40 PH, 205
F5, 182
F6 4-6-4, 182
F7 4-6-4, *83*, 182
FEF-3, *285*
FT series, 198

General Electric E60, 207

GG-1 locomotive, *195, 197*, 205, 319
GMD SD40-2, *288*
GP, 199
GP5, *332*
GP7, 199
GP9, 199
GP18, *332*
GP20, 204
GP30, *332*
GP38, 204, *342*
GP39-2, *205*
GP40, 204, *327, 328, 329*
GP50, 204
GS-2, *277*

H4, *269*
H8 Allegheny, *278*, 297
Hudson 4-6-4, *78, 125, 127, 146, 181*, 181, *182, 225, 277*

J 4-8-4, *84*, 185, *186, 278*
J1 Hudson, 181
J3a, *276*

K2 Pacific, 181
K4 Pacifics, 76, *181, 270*
K5, 181
K-36, *272*

L2 Hudson, *81*
L3 4-8-2, 182

M1a, 184
M-1000, 201
M-10000T, *219*
Mallet 2-6-6-6, *81*, 185, *185*, 186, 194
Mikado 2-8-2, 184
Mogul 2-6-0, 183

Niagara 4-8-4, *90*, 182, *183*, 183, *284*

P-1, *280*
Pacific 4-6-2, 181
Prairie 2-6-2, 181
President, 14, *84*
Ps-4, *272*

RC4 Type, 207
RTG, 207

S1 4-8-4, 182
Samson type, 96
SD40, 205, *316, 319, 323, 334, 340, 341, 343, 346*
SD45, *334*
SD50, 204, *330, 336, 344*
Selkirk No. 5929 2-10-4, *136*, 184
Shay, 186
SPD40F, 205

Texas type, 184
Triplex Mallet 2-8-8-8-2, 185
Turboliner, *208*

UL-F, *283*

Y 2-8-8-2, 186
Y5, 186
Y6, 186
Y6b, 186, *189*

Locomotives

No. 7, *269*
No. 24, *271*
No. 94, *269*
No. 119, 41, *162*
No. 209 (Atlantic) 4-4-2, *125*
No. 377, *106*
No. 382, *266*
No. 626 4-6-0, *120*
No. 945, *47*
No. 999, *265*
De Witt Clinton, 15, *17*, 213, *213*
Essex, *104*
George Washington, *81*
Lafayette, *260*
Lyn, *266*
John Bull, *259*
John Stevens, *262*
Monster, The, *295*
Jupiter, *162, 179*
Mud Digger, *261*
Old No. 9, *214*
Rocket, 176
Stourbridge Lion, *259*
Thunderbolt, 218